thrill ride

KEYSTONE

A KEYSTONE BOOK

Keystone Books are intended to serve the citizens of Pennsylvania. They are accessible, well-researched explorations into the history, culture, society, and environment of the Keystone State as part of the Middle Atlantic region.

thrill ride

The Transformation of Hersheypark

John R. Haddad

The Pennsylvania State University Press
University Park, Pennsylvania

Library of Congress Cataloging-in-Publication Data

Names: Haddad, John Rogers, Author.
Title: Thrill ride : the transformation of Hersheypark / John R. Haddad.
Description: The Pennsylvania State University Press, University Park, Pennsylvania, [2025] | Includes bibliographical references.
Summary: "Traces the history of Hershey Park from its 1906 founding as a community amusement space to its 1970s transformation into a modern theme park. Explores Milton Hershey's original vision, community ties, local resistance to change, and the park's eventual success as a reimagined attraction"—Provided by publisher.
Identifiers: LCCN 2025022780 | ISBN 9780271099927 (paperback)
Subjects: LCSH: Amusement parks—Pennsylvania—Hershey—History | Hersheypark (Hershey, Pa.)—History.
Classification: LCC GV1853.3.P42 H33 2025 | DDC 791.06874818
LC record available at https://lccn.loc.gov/2025022780

Printed in the United States of America
Published by The Pennsylvania State University Press,
University Park, PA 16802–1003

10 9 8 7 6 5 4 3 2 1

The Pennsylvania State University Press is a member of the Association of University Presses.

It is the policy of The Pennsylvania State University Press to use acid-free paper. Publications on uncoated stock satisfy the minimum requirements of American National Standard for Information Sciences—Permanence of Paper for Printed Library Material, ANSI Z39.48–1992.

contents

illustrations

acknowledgments

The origin of this book lies in a conversation I had over a decade ago with Simon Bronner. Simon and I both taught in the American Studies program at Penn State Harrisburg. (I still do; he has moved on.) During this conversation, I presented Simon with a conundrum relating to research. The topics I had chosen had always necessitated that I go off on two-week junkets to faraway archives. At the time, however, I had small children and was unable to travel for prolonged periods of time. How could I keep publishing? After thinking the question over, Simon came up with a solution. "You teach popular culture and live near Hershey," he said. "Why not write about Hersheypark?"

Simon's solution, though seemingly simple, was couched in his larger philosophy of American Studies. He believed that American Studies professors, regardless of their backgrounds, should study the cultures surrounding the universities where they work. By doing so, they could acquire local knowledge, better relate to their students, and build partnerships with nearby cultural institutions. Simon certainly did his part. Born in Israel to parents who were Holocaust survivors, Simon spent most of his childhood in the urban environments of New York and Chicago. After earning his PhD, he moved to central Pennsylvania to take the Penn State Harrisburg job. In his new home, he studied the folk culture of a rural group that was about as far-removed from his personal experience as one can imagine—the Amish. Inspired by Simon, I decided to "go local" in my own research.

I started by forming a relationship with Hershey Community Archives (HCA). At first, I worked with Pam Whitenack, director of the archive, who was invaluable as a resource. I thank Pam for remaining patient with me during those early visits when my research had not achieved focus. As I cast out fishing lines into different areas of the vast collection, Pam would wheel out box after box for me to inspect. Over the years, I have worked closely with three other superb archivists: Tammy Hamilton, Jennifer Henderson, and Tesa Burns. Jennifer and Tesa, in addition to showing me collections, have also read the entire manuscript, checking every fact, date, and endnote for accuracy. This clearly goes above and beyond an archivist's usual duties, and I am deeply grateful.

Tesa and Jennifer were not the only ones to read the manuscript. I was extremely lucky that Bruce McKinney, who was a manager and decision-maker during the years covered in the book, agreed to sit down for interviews. Bruce, who has a remarkable memory, shared his recollections of the company, town, and theme park in the 1970s. However, it was near the project's end that he really came through. Bruce is the ultimate authority on the story I am telling because he had actually lived it. Knowing this, I asked him if he would read the manuscript to check it for accuracy. Bruce not only agreed; he read it twice! I am forever indebted to Bruce for being so generous with his time and memories.

Many thanks to those at Penn State Harrisburg who have supported this project. I know I can always count on Jeffrey Beck, director of the School of Humanities, and my colleagues in American Studies: Charlie Kupfer, Anthony Buccitelli, Mary Zaborskis, Jeff Tolbert, David Witwer, and Mariah Kupfner. Appreciation also goes to my friends in the library—Glenn McGuigan, Heidi Moyer, Emily Mross, Bernadette Lear, Alan Mays, Fay Youngmark, Sherry Bancroft, and Glenn Rudy. In addition, I acknowledge the undergraduate and graduate students in American Studies, a group of learners whose intellectual curiosity reminds me every day why history matters.

Finally, I am indebted to family members. My parents, Richard and Betsey, offered encouragement every step of the way. So, too, did my brother, Rich; his wife, Sandy; and their three sons, Alex, Tim, and Sam. I am extremely grateful to my wife's family in China—especially my parents-in-law, Wang Qingyi and Yang Xiurong, who epitomize the Chinese tradition of respecting scholars (even those who write on theme parks). As for my wife, Catherine, and children, William and Liz, I am most appreciative of you. You were also kind to humor me when, during family trips to Hersheypark that were supposed to be purely about fun, I subjected you to impromptu history lectures. Don't think I didn't notice when, as I was droning on, you would look over my shoulder longingly at Candymonium!

Introduction

Through the Turnstile

Let's begin by free-associating for a moment. If I say, "Hersheypark," what pops into your mind? Perhaps a rollicking roller coaster where riders scream in ecstatic terror prior to entering a monster loop, spiraling corkscrew, or sudden plunge? Or maybe you imagine a seven-foot chocolate bar who spreads good cheer by posing for photographs with children and smiling incessantly, as frowning is an anatomical impossibility? If your mind conjures up images like these, you are not alone. Hersheypark has earned a reputation for its roller coasters and chocolate-themed fun. At the risk of oversimplifying, one could boil down the park's strategy to a basic mathematical equation: *chocolate theming + thrill rides = success.* Given this formula, the following piece of information may surprise you. Until a very recent renovation (more on that below), the Hersheypark experience did not begin with either strolling product characters or the slightest hint that colossal coasters lay ahead. Instead, visitors encountered something unexpected, curious, and perhaps mildly disappointing.

Fake European architecture. Before guests could reach the rides and attractions they came for, they first had to pass through two unavoidable themed areas built in the early 1970s. Tudor Square presented the architecture of England during the reign of the Tudors (1485–1603), which included Queen Elizabeth's ascendancy to the throne, William Shakespeare's plays, the defeat of the Spanish Armada, and the first English colony in North America. After exiting one Old World area, visitors advanced to a second one. Rhineland recreated traditional German architecture from the 1700s and 1800s, a period that witnessed the heavy migration of Germanic people to Pennsylvania. In this way, Hersheypark's layout resembled an hourglass. The large volume of humanity streaming in from the parking lot was channeled through a narrow passage honoring English and German heritage. Then, as unwanted constriction gave way to welcome expansion, visitors finally reached the fantasia of fiberglass, chocolate, and steel that is twenty-first-century Hersheypark. With their eyes lit up in anticipation, visitors fanned out to revel in the wonderful problem of having too many choices for their amusement.

What did recent visitors to Hersheypark make of Tudor Square and Rhineland? We don't know, but we can make a pretty good guess. If we had accosted parkgoers to inquire, most of them, even those professing a love for history, would probably have judged the two areas to be harmless but out of place in a park that was so obviously themed around candy and famous for its thrill rides. If we had been so persistent as to press guests further, many might have expressed mild surprise not just that Tudor Square and Rhineland existed, but that they enjoyed privileged locations at the entrance. Should a day at Hersheypark really begin with European history? For close to fifty years, it did. From 1973 to 2019, guests experienced Tudor Square and Rhineland first—if, that is, they were paying attention.

Few were. Many visitors blew right past the European twins on their way to their favorite attractions. This behavior did not upset Hersheypark in the slightest. Long ago, it abandoned the vision that had brought these themed areas into existence. In recent decades, the park used the buildings not to showcase history but to sell stuff—souvenirs, T-shirts, candy, and snacks—none of which had anything to do with European heritage (except possibly German Kettle Korn). In short, Tudor Square and Rhineland had become architectural anachronisms.

Hersheypark put them out of their misery in 2019. That year, the park launched a major renovation of its entrance, a massive construction project that converted the plot occupied by Tudor Square into a hard-hat zone. In 2020, Hersheypark unveiled a brand-new themed area in that spot—Chocolatetown. With this addition, Hersheypark was doubling down on its two chief areas of strength: chocolate theming and roller coasters. Now, as guests enter, they are greeted by friendly Hershey product characters and enjoy several options to consume chocolate treats. Chocolatetown is also home to Candymonium, a serpentine steel leviathan that the park promotes as its "tallest, fastest, longest and sweetest coaster." What fate befell the old European attractions? Rhineland was absorbed by nearby Founder's Way, losing in the process what remained of its identity. Tudor Square was demolished.[1]

Yet there was once a time when Hersheypark officials envisioned Tudor Square and Rhineland as exciting new attractions that could lure millions through its gates. In the early 1970s, their European architecture graced the folds of glossy promotional brochures and appeared in television spots across the mid-Atlantic region. Back then, it was the structures belonging to Hershey Park (1906–71) that had to be torn down to make room for Tudor Square and Rhineland, two new themed realms within Hersheypark (1971–present). This book concentrates on that 1970s transformation, explaining how Hershey Park (two words) became Hersheypark (one word).

Behind that simple keyboard maneuver lies a fascinating story. It involves not only the subtraction of old rides and the addition of new ones but something much larger: the evolving relationship between a company and a town. That relationship started back in 1903 when the confectioner Milton S. Hershey, whom many referred to as "M. S." in his time, launched a courageous and mostly successful experiment to reimagine industrial capitalism. Our story focuses on the 1960s and 1970s, a stormy period in that town-company relationship during which a problem forced both sides to make a difficult transition. Upon first glance, this problem does not seem very problematic at all. For six decades, the chocolate company and town adhered to an economic model that worked *too well.*

If that does not sound much like a crisis, just wait. It was. During the industrial revolution of the late 1800s, violence roiled the United States as corporations and organized labor engaged in constant warfare. In the early 1900s, Milton Hershey (hereafter "M. S.") joined other industrialists in seeking an answer, one that would restore peace to society while maintaining productivity at factories. He deployed what was, at the time, a progressive solution to this destructive conflict—paternalistic capitalism. A variety of quid pro quo, M. S.'s paternalism worked something like this. His chocolate company did not merely offer workers a wage-earning job and then leave them to fend for themselves in all other aspects of life. Instead, his company took care of its workforce. In a carefully planned community, workers inhabited nice homes with affordable mortgages, paid minimal fees for subsidized utilities, benefited from free snow removal and garbage collection, partook of easy transportation along company trolley lines, and enrolled their children in quality schools free of charge. For their leisure, they enjoyed multiple recreational and cultural venues such as a zoo, pool, museum, sports arena, library, community center, and theater. Most remarkably, M. S. opened Hershey Park in 1906 for the pleasure of chocolate workers, their families, and the local community.[2] It occupied the core of his vision. M. S. may seem absurdly generous, and perhaps he was. That said, this was a reciprocal relationship, and his employees owed him something in return. They were expected to work hard, exhibit company loyalty, practice clean living, and refrain from the disruptive strikes that had destabilized or destroyed other companies. M. S. was not the only industrialist to attempt this bold experiment. However, most other company towns made critical missteps and failed to survive. Today, we see them only in our history books.

M. S. beat the odds. He proudly referred to Hershey as "an industrial Utopia," a "town that has no poverty, no nuisances, and no evil."[3] Though this statement oozed with hyperbole, there was truth in it. Hershey *was* a nice place to live, work, and raise a family, and most residents *did* feel privileged to settle there. What was the secret to Hershey's success? To put it simply, M. S.'s agreement with his workers was not merely transactional. Both parties not only accepted the reciprocal agreement; they fiercely embraced it as the source of their happiness, stability, and prosperity. Recognizing that the special relationship was what set them apart from other towns, the company and community even based their identities on it. In this way, what had begun as a quid pro quo evolved into something much stronger—a sacred trust that we can call a *compact.*

Hershey Park played a crucial role in the perpetuation of the compact. For decades, residents would arrive at the park with their picnic baskets, send their kids off with a pocketful of dimes to enjoy rides, tap their feet to rousing band music at the Bandshell, cool off in the colossal swimming pool, and close out the day by dancing under the stars in the open-roofed ballroom. The town adored Hershey Park and positively reveled in this summer ritual year after year. For that is what an outing to the park was—a ritual. Indeed, behind what seemed like frivolous fun, something meaningful was taking place. For both the company and the community, Hershey Park symbolized the compact, and, as such, it provided a performative space on which each side could act out its commitment to this vital trust. By staffing, maintaining, and updating the park, the company signaled its compliance with the compact. By patronizing the park, the members of the community reciprocated, performing their acceptance of the compact's conditions. "The park was genuinely for the workers at the chocolate factory" and "the families in town," a Hershey resident recalled. "The love of the place used to tie it together."[4] The operative word here is *tie*. Through Hershey Park, a company and community solidified the bond that enabled them to coexist in a state of peace, prosperity, and contentment that extended beyond the death of M. S. in 1945.

But all good things must come to an end.

In the 1960s, the winds of change blew through Hershey. When they did, they upset a local community that had become too dependent on the company and too inured to the status quo. Much of the change was brought on by external economic forces. In the 1960s, the business climate favored those corporations that understood the massive influence of television and could successfully leverage the power of advertising, marketing, and public relations. While most companies adapted within the shifting environment, Hershey Chocolate chose stasis. Its business practices remained largely unchanged during the two decades following the death of M. S. At a time when many companies were hiring Madison Avenue firms to orchestrate slick marketing campaigns, Hershey did not even advertise its products—that is, until an aggressive rival applied pressure. In response to a fierce challenge posed by Mars, Hershey Chocolate finally woke up in the 1960s. The company hired young MBAs to restructure its business operations, converting the lumbering dinosaur into a modern corporation capable of competing. As a second source of change, Hershey executives supported the construction of a state-of-the-art hospital and medical school—the Milton S. Hershey Medical Center—that attracted outsiders to what had become an insular town. As people of various ethnicities and political orientations moved in, the community howled in protest. The company also—and this was crucial—decided that M. S.'s model of paternalistic capitalism had outlived its usefulness. In a move that shocked residents, the company cut the umbilical cord, so to speak, by discontinuing most free services and amenities. It terminated the compact.

The worst was yet to come. Hershey Park, the centerpiece of M. S.'s vision, had deteriorated over the years. By 1970, it had degenerated into what one executive called "an iron park with a bunch of clanging rides and some picnic space."[5] After intense internal debate, the company elected to subject the park to a complete overhaul. The revamped amusement park would be enclosed in a fence, charge admission for the first time, and cater to regional tourists and those from New York, Philadelphia, Baltimore, and Washington, DC. Except it would not be an *amusement park* any longer. Hershey hired a California-based design firm, Randall Duell and Associates, to transform it into a *theme park* in the mold of Disneyland.

In 1955, Walt Disney unveiled a new and radical form of entertainment. Instead of offering the typical roller coasters and carnival rides of an amusement park, Disneyland invited guests to enter themed realms that used sophisticated Hollywood set designs to place them inside 3D movies. The appeal was powerful and immediate. When it opened, Disneyland probably delivered more smiles, laughs, and screams than any physical space in human history up to that point. It also generated staggering revenues. That said, Walt Disney aspired to more than mere profits. According to cultural historians, Disneyland presented guests with a symbolic landscape, one that served Walt's political agenda during the Cold War. He conceived of, and his "Imagineers" designed, themed realms that could retell legends and myths from America's storied past, honor small-town American values, and shape American dreams for a technological future. "There's an American theme behind the whole park," Walt Disney explained. "I believe in emphasizing the story of what made America great and what will keep it great." By deploying symbols and narratives within these themed realms, Walt Disney hoped to inculcate his patriotic message during the Cold War.[6]

Disneyland's stunning success spawned imitators. Regional theme parks, such as those in the Six Flags franchise, proliferated in the 1960s and 1970s. Modeled off Disneyland but smaller in scope, these parks also entertained visitors by thrusting them into themed environments. Though joining this wave, Hersheypark differed from other theme parks in one critical sense. While those parks were built solely as moneymaking ventures, it is the contention of this book that Hershey executives, along with pursuing profits, were actuated by a social conscience: they wished to help a struggling community adapt to unwanted change. Working collaboratively with Randall Duell and Associates, the Hershey leadership imagined the new park as a symbolic landscape. Like Disneyland, Hersheypark would present visitors not just with a zone of amusement but with a rhetorical space that would engage in an act of persuasion.

Persuade visitors of what? In the wake of the terminated compact, Hershey executives hoped to convince residents who resisted change to make the necessary psychological adjustment. Toward this end, the park placed guests in a sequence of historically themed areas that created the illusion of time travel. No mere passive observers, guests became actor-participants in immersive environments depicting various historical stages. Their journey through time began across the Atlantic with the aforementioned Tudor Square and Rhineland, recreations of two Old World cultures that influenced Pennsylvania. The progression through history carried guests next into themed areas standing for the town of Hershey's past, Pennsylvania's agricultural heritage, and the region's industrial past and present. Hershey's Chocolate World, which opened in 1973 just outside the park, contributed to this story by depicting chocolate production, as did rides themed around coal mining. Finally, guests encountered contemporary attractions, engineering marvels that symbolized the promise of the modern world. The overarching message of Hersheypark was a simple one: change, not stasis, defines civilization. Residents would see "transition in the architecture of the park," explained one Hershey executive, "and be comfortable with change in their world."[7]

Clearly, Hersheypark in the 1970s bore little resemblance to the modern theme parks that readers are familiar with. Today, theme parks attract millions of people by delivering on their promise to submerge guests in wonder worlds inhabited by the wizards, monsters, pirates, costumed heroes, galactic rebels, and the animated characters of their favorite movies. This strategy has been highly successful: in 2024, it contributed to a global theme park industry that exceeded $70 billion in annual revenues.[8] Given the focus on fantasy we see today, many readers will be struck by the design of Hersheypark in the 1970s. It featured history, not fantasy, and was animated by a community-centered vision. No other theme park, past or present, is anything like Hersheypark. It possesses a unique creation story that deserves to be told in a book.

This is a book about a company, community, and park facing challenges during a difficult transition. It differs from other histories of regional theme parks in that it is concerned with more than the rides and attractions inside the park. Make no mistake: those attractions matter. However, they matter because they play a role in a larger story. Indeed, for many of the park's attractions, both new and old, I was able to locate their significance by situating them in this narrative of social, cultural, and economic change in Hershey. To tell that narrative, I read extensively in local newspapers and conducted interviews with key players involved in the redevelopment. I also availed myself of the extensive holdings of Hershey Community Archives, an indispensable resource for any historian studying Hersheypark. During multiple visits, I reviewed company records, internal reports and memos, schematic renderings of planned attractions, fan mail, complaint letters, newspaper clippings, and press releases. Most importantly, I was able to listen to authentic voices from the past. In the 1980s, the Archives launched an oral history project that is still ongoing. Thanks to this remarkable collection, a researcher can access the memories of Hershey executives, company employees, and town residents who lived through this period of change.

The changes of the sixties and seventies transformed Hershey. By the end of this turbulent period, the town and company had found a new equilibrium, and Hersheypark had discovered the lucrative potential of that simple formula: *chocolate theming + thrill rides = success*. However, as we move forward in this book, we simultaneously shoot backward in time. The first sound we hear is not the laughter of children high-fiving a walking Hershey bar. Nor is it the screams of riders on a death-defying looping roller coaster. Instead, we hear the blithe organ melody wafting out of the Carrousel's calliope. This mingles with the rousing trumpets, clashing cymbals, and pounding drums reverberating from the Bandshell, where hundreds have gathered to hear a military band play everyone's favorite Sousa marches. It is summertime in Hershey. As chocolate workers spend their day off at Hershey Park with their families, they revel in the knowledge that life is good. They are unaware that, in the future, when change comes, they will feel intense nostalgia for perfect days like this one.

Chapter 1

Milton Hershey's Sweet Dream

No child wants to see his father get fired. But that is exactly what twelve-year-old Austin Geiling experienced in 1936. Austin's father managed the soda fountain, candy counter, and tobacco section at the Hershey Drugstore, which operated as part of the Hershey Department Store, owned by M. S. Mr. Geiling, therefore, worked for the town's patriarch. One afternoon, a traveling salesman stepped behind the candy counter and became too familiar with a female clerk, wrapping his arm around her waist. Austin's father, busy at his desk, was unaware of the playful flirtation. Though the salesman meant no harm, M. S. strongly disapproved of this sort of behavior. Were he to witness the interaction, trouble would ensue. Of course, the odds that M. S. would walk through the door at precisely this moment were small.[1]

But they weren't that small. That is because M. S. kept a watchful eye on all his properties and assets—the chocolate factory, lumberyard, utilities, and amusement park, to name a few. No detail, regardless of how minor, escaped his attention. "Everybody can see the big things," he once said, "but I look for the little things." When M. S. wished to observe a place, his strategy was to blend in with the crowd. "You wouldn't know that Mr. Hershey was Mr. Hershey unless something happened that he didn't like," remarked one employee, "and then you would find out very quickly."[2] M. S. moved about with stealth, in other words, and one never knew where or when he would appear. Tragically for Mr. Geiling, M. S. chose this moment to materialize. After noting the inappropriate behavior, M. S. took immediate action, informing Geiling that "he was through." Stunned and confused, Mr. Geiling understood neither "what had happened" nor "why he was being let go." Several days later, M. S. visited Geiling at his home to explain his firing. But he did not reverse his decision. "You know how I operate," M. S. said, "and I won't change my mind." Geiling should not take the dismissal personally, M. S. implied, but he was still out of a job.[3]

Though the father experienced the downside of M. S.'s rule, the son would reap the benefits. As Austin grew up, he partook of all the recreational amenities that M. S. provided for residents. He passed countless hours at the community center, swimming in the pool and playing basketball and softball. Of course, Hershey Park played a central role in his youth. The park was a "great place to spend time," he recalled, thinking fondly of the rides, the concerts, and the chance to "chase girls." Hershey also offered steady employment and opportunity for career advancement. After serving in World War II, Austin worked for the Hershey Bears hockey team, oversaw tours of the chocolate factory, and managed the sales representatives for Hershey Chocolate. Both Hershey the town and Hershey the man were good to him.[4]

After his retirement, Austin reflected on his father's termination. Had either he or his father held a grudge against M. S., no one would have blamed them. After all, the patriarch's decision must have seemed hasty, harsh, and unjust. But this is the most curious aspect of this story: neither Austin nor his father ever harbored "bitter feelings" toward M. S. They saw themselves not as unfairly treated but as victims of circumstance. Their surprising acceptance reflects the larger ethos of the Hershey community. The Geilings understood that the moral code of one man governed the town and its institutions. By living and working in Hershey, the family signaled its tacit consent to abide by that moral code—or incur the consequences for violating it. In sum, there was an unspoken agreement in this unusual town between the patriarch and the people. Though Mr. Geiling had done nothing wrong, an improper act had taken place within his zone of oversight, and so he must be held accountable. That was the price of living in Hershey.[5]

For most residents, the benefits of Hershey easily outweighed the drawbacks. They felt passionately about M. S.'s chocolate factory, his town, the way of life he fostered, and the man himself. The purpose of this chapter is to explain where these strong emotions came from and how they connected to Hershey Park. The chapter begins by recounting how M. S. entered the chocolate business, studied models of paternalistic capitalism, and launched his planned community. It explains how M. S. and his workers entered what we may call a compact. In brief, M. S. offered employees not just jobs but a rich array of services and amenities. Those employees reciprocated by working hard, exhibiting loyalty, and following M. S.'s code. This chapter discusses Hershey's Italian Americans, a group that started out as outsiders but gradually became loyal stakeholders in the compact. It also covers the 1937 strike, a disruptive episode that saw workers challenge the compact and inject turbulence into the town's otherwise placid history. Finally, the chapter explores Hershey Park, both its role as a symbol of the compact and its massive presence in the memories and identities of residents.

The Birth of an Idea

M. S. was born in 1857 in Derry Township to a family within the Pennsylvania German community, a group commonly referred to as the Pennsylvania Dutch.[6] His childhood years were steeped in the traditional Mennonite values of honesty, hard work, and frugality.[7] An aspiring entrepreneur in the confection industry, M. S. endured a decade of struggles, setbacks, and failure in Philadelphia, Chicago, and New York before launching his first successful business, the Lancaster Caramel Company, in 1886.[8] In 1893, he made the sudden decision to switch to milk chocolate during a eureka moment in Chicago at the World's Columbian Exposition. With his cousin Frank Snavely at his side, M. S. stood spellbound as he beheld an exhibit of German chocolate-making machinery. As the moving machine parts converted cocoa beans, sugar, and cocoa butter into rich chocolate, M. S. realized the vast potential of both the machine and its delectable product. Dismissing caramels as a mere "fad," he declared his new direction: "I'm going to make chocolate!"[9] In the years that followed, M. S. lived up to his pledge, converting a spontaneous idea into a full-fledged vision. The pioneering nature of that vision becomes apparent when we realize that, back then, milk chocolate was not the ubiquitous commodity it is today. In the 1890s, milk chocolate was an expensive confection enjoyed mostly by affluent Europeans; few Americans had tasted it, and many had never heard of it. M. S. would transform this luxury for European elites into a pleasure for the American people. He would democratize chocolate (fig. 1).[10]

Fig. 1 Milton S. Hershey. Courtesy of Hershey Community Archives (hereafter HCA).

To democratize anything, one needed to avail oneself of mass-production techniques. These, however, were fraught with peril. While they did succeed in lowering costs by efficiently producing goods in high volume, they inevitably placed poorly paid wage laborers in grueling factory settings. For long hours, workers performed repetitive tasks, often in hazardous working conditions. To improve their situations, laborers increasingly banded together into unions that used strikes to force corporations to accede to their demands for higher pay, reduced hours, and safer working conditions. Since corporations took measures to resist organized labor's efforts, perpetual warfare defined the era, and many conflicts exploded in violence. As strife dominated newspaper headlines, some industrialists imagined a better way—or at least tried to.[11]

In the 1880s, George Pullman, a Chicago-based manufacturer of railroad sleeping cars, tried to end the war by presenting a new industrial model—paternalism. Quite ambitiously, he erected a company town south of the city, where the company's workers, managers, and executives would live harmoniously in a bucolic setting. That, anyway, was the hope. Before explaining how the grand scheme fell apart, we should note that Pullman's workers did experience a substantial improvement in living conditions. Instead of dwelling in shabby urban tenements, they resided in a meticulously planned community, complete with clean water, verdant parks, and tree-lined streets. Though workers could not own homes, Pullman did offer, at affordable rents, comfortable cottages equipped with indoor plumbing and electricity. The working class, in short, occupied the sort of home typically associated with the middle class. Workers could partake of other amenities as well, such as libraries, theaters, stores, and recreational facilities. In creating his "capitalist utopia," Pullman was partly driven to solve the great problem of his age. That being said, a clear profit motive also radiated at the core of his vision. By improving his workers' quality of life, he hoped to increase their productivity in his factory.[12]

Pullman's experiment failed. One problem was cultural: he asserted too much control over his workers' behavior. Wishing to inculcate morality, he banned bars and taverns, prohibited tenants from congregating on their front porches, insisted on proper attire, and assigned monitors to surveil residents. He even selected the library books that his workers were allowed to read. Not surprisingly, many workers chafed at Pullman's attempt to regulate their behavior, resenting not just the restrictions he imposed on their freedoms but also the implication that their own cultures were inferior.[13] A second, related problem was economic. During the Panic of 1893, orders for sleeper cars plummeted. In response to diminished demand, Pullman laid off one-third of his workforce and cut the wages of remaining laborers by 30 percent. Since he did not also reduce rents—a critical misstep—families found themselves unable to make ends meet. For many workers, the wage cuts struck at the heart of their manhood. Before 1893, the workingman had tolerated Pullman's emasculating paternalism because, inside his own home, he could still fulfill the traditional male role as the provider to his wife and children. But as his family struggled to pay rent and buy food, he could no longer claim to be a breadwinner. In this way, the economic problem of reduced wages exacerbated the already festering cultural problem.[14]

Early in 1894, the workers called a strike after negotiations with Pullman failed. One month later, the American Railway Union, led by Eugene Debs, voted to support the strikers by launching a national boycott of Pullman cars. Mayhem ensued as cargoes of goods failed to move along clogged rail lines, and saboteurs destroyed tracks and set fire to train cars.[15] In July, President Grover Cleveland ordered federal troops into Chicago, a move that sparked a riot. A mob ten thousand strong wreaked havoc in the rail yards and set fires all over the city.[16] A conflagration at the world's fair destroyed many of the buildings and exhibits that had inspired M. S. the previous year.[17] Twelve people lost their lives; many more were imprisoned. Finally, in August, an injunction from the federal government led to the arrest of the strike's leaders. The upheaval was over.[18]

Though the strikers lost, George Pullman perhaps suffered the most. Most obviously, his dream of solving the great problem of the industrial age went up in smoke. In addition, the federal government convened a commission that November to investigate the origins of the calamity. Its findings poured more salt into Pullman's open wounds. The report, which largely faulted Pullman, viewed as highly problematic his insistence on being "both landlord and employer." As a major cause of the strike, it cited the unwillingness of Pullman *the landlord* to reduce rents at a time when Pullman *the employer* was cutting wages. In 1898, Pullman started the sad process of closing down his model town. His dream lay in ruins.[19] After all, how could anyone reasonably point to his model as worthy of imitation?

One might expect Pullman's downfall to have quashed any remaining enthusiasm for planned communities. Surprisingly, this was not the case. In the strike's aftermath, a group of urban reformers treated Pullman's experiment as an instructive case study; instead of consigning the concept to the scrap heap, they concluded that Pullman's model, though flawed, had also innovated in ways worth preserving. In other words, there was still hope for the planned community. Entrepreneurs, taking their cue from these experts, resurrected the idea for the twentieth century. However, in doing so, they took pains to preserve the advantages of Pullman's model while avoiding its disastrous mistakes. In 1905, there were only fifteen planned industrial communities in the United States, all founded before the Pullman debacle. However, by 1939, over seventy populated the American landscape. This group included U.S. Steel, which founded a company town in Alabama; Goodyear Tire and Rubber, which established a community in Ohio; and the Norton Company, a manufacturer of commercial abrasives, which opened its model town in Massachusetts.[20] And in Pennsylvania, M. S. eyed possible locations for his factory and planned community.

Before building, M. S. sought models from which to borrow. Though no one knows for sure, he may have visited Pullman's planned community in 1893.[21] If so, he surely recognized after the strike that his key concepts would have to come from elsewhere. Most likely, M. S. found more inspiration across the Atlantic, where his wife, Kitty, liked to visit. During a trip to England, M. S. probably toured George Cadbury's planned community.[22] To protect his workers from the "unwholesomeness of city life," Cadbury made the bold move in 1895 to relocate his chocolate-making operation to a rural site outside of Birmingham called Bournville. Convinced of the beneficial effects of country life, he encouraged employees to engage in wholesome activities, such as physical exercise and gardening, in the fresh air and greenery of their bucolic setting.[23] By engendering a new way of life, Cadbury claimed to be "alleviating the evils which arise from the insanitary . . . housing accommodation" in the cities and providing the "working classes" instead with "the advantages of outdoor village life." If Pullman offered workers amenities, Cadbury delivered far more. Bournville residents enjoyed a school, library, lecture hall, gymnasium, bath, swimming pool, playground, village green, and wooded areas.[24] Bournville was, as the company called itself, a "factory in the garden."[25]

There was one last difference between Cadbury and Pullman, and it was surely one that caught M. S.'s eye. Whereas Pullman insisted on maintaining control over his properties, Cadbury encouraged homeownership for employees and provided each unit with a garden.[26] The perceptive M. S. almost certainly observed Cadbury's stunning achievement. The visionary industrialist had created not just an impressive physical space but something intangible of even greater valuable—a reciprocal relationship between the industrialist and his labor force. After Cadbury gave workers Bournville, the workers owed him something in return. "The *quid pro quo*," writes historian John Bradley, "was employee commitment and loyalty."[27]

M. S. now had everything he needed. Back in Pennsylvania, he moved quickly to consummate his plan. In 1900, he sold his caramel company for $1 million. He used that money to invest in his chocolate-making business, which generated profits almost immediately. He then quietly bought up property in an obscure place called Derry Church, eventually acquiring around one thousand acres. What exactly was Derry Church? Though consisting of woodsy areas, green pastures, and small farms, Derry Church was, above all else, a blank space awaiting the action of some external agent. It was the kind of place where one could project a vision.[28]

Out of Nothing . . .

For anyone who was paying attention, M. S. did drop a clue that he was planning something big. Early in 1903, he dispatched surveyors to Derry Church to collect measurements regarding the features and contours of the land.[29] Since they performed their work inconspicuously, most residents neglected to read much into their presence or even notice them at all. Residents first learned of Hershey's grand plan when the *Harrisburg Independent* broke the news in February 1903: "A new town . . . will be built midway between Derry Church and Swatara . . . by M. S. Hershey, the Lancaster chocolate manufacturer. . . . The town will be laid out along plans of modern manufacturing communities which are now springing up, all over this country, patterned after those in England. It will contain grass plots for pleasure parks in which there will be fountains and stone walks."[30] Though the article did not mention Bournville by name, it did intimate that M. S. planned to borrow Cadbury's model. The new town would be "patterned after those in England" and feature manicured nature ("grass plots for pleasure parks"). But that was only the beginning.

True to the Bournville model, M. S. proceeded to build a state-of-the-art chocolate factory and surround it with civilization. His titanic factory consisted of sixteen buildings that, exceeding two football fields in combined length, handled all phases of chocolate making. The facility enabled "stream-lined production," an executive explained years later. "Our materials are received at one end of the plant and naturally flow through the plant from one end to the other."[31] Though workers had strenuous jobs, the quality of life justified their effort. Over the next four decades, M. S. built the facilities and infrastructure that made life pleasant, convenient, and productive: roads, utilities, a water main, a sewer system, community buildings, recreational facilities, parks, trolley lines, garbage and snow removal systems, a library, and a swimming pool.[32] He also provided workers with retirement plans and insurance benefits covering accidents, sickness, and death.[33] To educate residents, he built schools and opened the Hershey Junior College, where residents could earn degrees without paying tuition.[34] In sum, M. S. generously offered many services and amenities, and residents took full advantage. "I was enjoying the benefits of Milton Hershey's philanthropy," wrote one resident, "and the whole system the way it was operated."[35] "We didn't know what it was like to live in a real small town," said another, because "we had everything they had in the big city—maybe more."[36]

Most importantly, M. S. built modern homes. At a time when many Americans burned kerosene for illumination and relieved themselves in outhouses, the families of chocolate workers lived in comfortable houses equipped with central heating, electricity, and indoor plumbing. M. S. also avoided Pullman's largest misstep by encouraging workers to own rather than rent these units.[37] If workers owned their homes, M. S. reasoned, they would take care of their properties and become stakeholders in the community. "It was our first modern home," recalled one man who moved to Hershey in 1911 as a boy. Instead of "outhouses," "dirt roads," and "one-room schoolhouses," the family enjoyed "electricity," "telephones," and "cobblestone" streets. "Moving to Hershey," he said, "was like moving to paradise."[38]

Of course, all this construction cost money. However, M. S. did not view investment in the community as lost revenue. He understood, as his biographer, Michael D'Antonio explains, that the money had a way of cycling back into his pocket. The Hershey economic ecosystem worked something like this. M. S. paid workers with earnings from chocolate sales. Since the town was fairly isolated, employees typically spent their money at businesses owned by M. S.: they shopped at his stores, rode his trolley, paid bills to his utility companies, and passed their leisure hours at his recreational facilities. In this way, the money M. S. paid out in wages tended to circulate through the local economy before returning to M. S. himself, perhaps for reinvestment. To illustrate this "perpetual motion machine," D'Antonio shares an anecdote that M. S. was fond of repeating. One day, M. S. encountered a man who wished to ride the trolley but lacks fare. After

M. S. fished a nickel out of his pocket, the man dropped it in the trolley's fare box, and off he went. Did M. S. just lose five cents? Since he owned and operated the trolley, he knew that nickel would soon find its way back to him.[39]

The experimental planned community proved to be a success. In 1924, Edward Woolley, an editor at *McClure's* magazine, visited Hershey after hearing about the remarkable company town that had managed to achieve harmony without sacrificing productivity. As a publication, *McClure's* had a reputation for hard-hitting investigative journalism; indeed, it was *McClure's* that, in 1902, published Ida Tarbell's exposé of the strong-arm tactics and corporate abuses of John D. Rockefeller's Standard Oil. However, Woolley, after interviewing M. S. and touring the town, penned a glowing piece that declared the rumors to be true. "I found numerous families of plain factory workmen," he wrote, "living in trim little houses," while in other industrial cities, such people typically inhabited "disreputable tenements . . . surrounded by hideous litter and filth." Woolley also noted approvingly Hershey's other amenities—the trolley system, modern schools, the swimming pool, and Hershey Park.[40] James Young of the *New York Times*, after visiting Hershey in 1923, remarked that "it would be hard to find an industrial community that excels it." Whereas other industrial towns consisted primarily of "concrete and iron," Young noted the "pleasant vistas" of Hershey. When the worker gazed out the window, he saw trees, flower beds, and bridges arching over a brook, not "soul-chilling" sights like "ash piles" and "rubbish." Young wrote that Hershey is "the town of smiles."[41]

Workers were not the only beneficiaries of M. S.'s largesse. When Young interviewed M. S., he learned about the Hershey Industrial School, the centerpiece of a philanthropic vision formed by M. S. and his wife. In 1905, M. S. created the Hershey Trust Company as the legal entity through which he and Kitty would express that vision. In 1909, the couple signed a deed transferring to the trust nearly five hundred acres of farmland as well as a fortune in company stock. Unable to have children of their own, M. S. and Kitty had decided to build a school for orphan boys.[42] There was a logic behind the decision to take in only boys. "The orphan boy," he explained to Young, "has a harder time than anybody else." Whereas relatives would readily adopt orphan girls because they were "useful in the home," society viewed boys as a "nuisance" and cast them aside. M. S. also stressed the importance of the father in the proper development of a boy. "When a boy doesn't happen to have any sort of dad," M. S. continued, "he is a special mark for destiny." Often, that destiny was not a happy one. Since prisons were filled with boys who "never had a chance," M. S. had resolved to intervene: "I am going to give some of them a chance, in my way."[43] Gene Sajeski, who endured a challenging childhood in Pennsylvania coal country, was one of many boys who was happy to have this chance. "Coming into Hershey," he said, "was like leaving Hell and entering Heaven."[44]

His way combined the expected classroom instruction with something unconventional—farmwork. As historian James McMahon explains, M. S. insisted that students grow fruits and vegetables and care for animals. Along with inculcating the value of hard work, agricultural experience would teach a boy to care for something other than himself. Students would also benefit from seeing produce from the school's farm—literally the fruits of their labor—on the dinner table. In 1918, three years after Kitty's death, M. S. gifted the trust most of his remaining fortune, a sum totaling $60 million, to aid the continued expansion of the school.[45]

M. S.'s civilization-building depended on an influx of money from the outside world. After all, the steady stream of profits from chocolate sales fueled his construction projects and philanthropic endeavors. In other words, sales had to be robust for his planned community to flourish. Fortunately, they were.

The Product

The Hershey bar was a marvelous product, and M. S.'s state-of-the-art factory churned them out on a scale the world had never seen. By employing mass-production techniques, M. S. lowered the cost of the milk chocolate bar to a price nearly everyone could afford—five cents. A luxurious treat costing only a nickel, the Hershey bar was ubiquitous; one could find it at grocery stores, train stations, newsstands, and drugstores all over the country. As a brand, the Hershey bar was iconic and had few rivals. Though Cadbury sold a similar product, it did so on a different continent, leaving Hershey to command the American market. Sales reached $1.3 million in 1906 before soaring to $5 million in 1911. Though Frank Mars entered the candy business at this time, his company remained small for years, and his products, at least at first, did not compete directly with the Hershey bar. Inexpensive, universally loved, and without rivals, the Hershey bar was a magical commodity.[46]

It even sold well without advertising. In the early 1900s, most food companies with aspirations to reach a national market launched aggressive publicity campaigns. They did so by hiring agencies and placing slick advertisements in popular magazines with high circulation rates. In this way, they achieved nationwide brand recognition and convinced consumers to trust the quality of their products.[47] An outlier, M. S. shunned advertising. He did so because he believed a quality product achieved results on its own. "The best advertising is the right kind of goods," he said in 1923. "People will learn about them and buy all that you can make."[48] M. S. also viewed each Hershey bar as a kind of advertisement. "His name was printed large in silver letters on his wrappers," wrote author Roy Bongartz, "so that wherever they might fall, they became an effective ad in themselves."[49] Even litter worked to M. S.'s advantage. In 1923, faculty members at New York University conducted a study to determine the most recognizable brands in each category. The results substantiated M. S.'s position: Wrigley led in gum, Del Monte in canned fruit, Gorton's in fish, Welch's in grape juice, and Coca-Cola in soft drinks. In chocolate, consumers were most familiar with Hershey.[50]

A strategy that did not include advertising still evinced plenty of marketing savvy. That is because M. S. understood that his factory's pastoral setting could enhance the appeal of the product, if consumers could be reminded of it. Starting in 1909, he shrewdly had picture cards inserted inside every Hershey bar. These "bar cards" depicted pleasing Hershey scenes, such as the contented cows of a dairy farm that contributed milk to chocolate making.[51] As consumers munched on their chocolate bars, they contemplated the wholesome environment that produced one of chocolate's key ingredients (fig. 2). M. S. accomplished the same goal in another way by distributing a booklet that conveyed the health benefits of Hershey's chocolate and cocoa. Targeting mothers, this giveaway also included lyrics scripted to fit a popular song that reinforced the message of the bar cards:

A beautiful town in a valley lay,
Where a lot of people night and day

Fig. 2 Hershey bar card. Courtesy of HCA.

Make Hershey's Chocolate and Cocoa
As clean and pure as the falling snow.
And the green grass grew all around, all around.
And the green grass grew all around . . .
A little child said to her mother dear,
"Cocoa and Chocolate are healthful, I hear."
"Yes," said her mother, "if they're pure and fresh."
Said the child, "Well, that means Hershey's I guess."
For the green grass grew all around, all around.
For the green grass grew all around.[52]

With these shrewdly crafted stanzas, M. S. unlocked the power of association. Indeed, the lyrics encouraged potential customers, at the mere mention of Hershey, to imagine a town ensconced in the gentle hills, green pastures, and friendly farms of rural Pennsylvania. They also helped make his brand synonymous with food purity and childhood innocence. Cleverly constructed, these pictures and poems undermined any claim that M. S. was either passive or naive when it came to product promotion.

Such pastoral Pennsylvania imagery belied the global nature of chocolate making. Though milk really did come from local dairy farms, chocolate's two other main ingredients, cocoa and sugar, did not. In procuring them, the company was susceptible to price fluctuations and shortages in the global commodity markets. M. S. recognized that a spike in commodity prices could force him to raise the price of the Hershey bar, something he was loath to do. For years, M. S. had been vexed by two firms that combined to monopolize the markets for granulated sugar made from beets and sugarcane. When World War I precipitated a sugar shortage, M. S. took bold action to guarantee an undisrupted supply. In 1916, he bought land in Cuba and proceeded to build "Central Hershey." Over the years, this complex would expand to cover sixty thousand acres and include vast sugar plantations, multiple mills, a refinery, a power plant, an electric railroad, and a company town, complete with recreational facilities and a school for orphans. M. S. was obviously endeavoring to transplant in Cuba much of the same paternalistic model that had worked in Hershey. In 1920, Hershey's operation harvested about 150 million tons of cane, which it converted into nearly thirty-two million pounds of sugar. M. S. never tried anything comparable with cocoa beans, which are grown in West Africa and South America; however, he did endeavor to influence the market to secure advantageous prices for his enormous orders.[53]

As the company expanded in the 1920s, M. S. realized that its various sectors had little overlap with one another. In 1927, he decided to break it into three separate entities: the "Hershey Corporation" handled sugar production in Cuba, the "Hershey Chocolate Corporation" (renamed Hershey Foods in 1968) oversaw the making and selling of chocolate, and "Hershey Estates" (renamed HERCO in 1976) encompassed the offices and facilities relating to the planned community. More specifically, it managed Hershey's real estate holdings, services and utilities, the trolley, and all retail outlets. As perhaps its largest responsibility, Hershey Estates staffed, maintained, and operated the town's crown jewel—Hershey Park.[54]

A Park for the People

The term *amusement park* today conjures up images of bright lights, thrill rides, hot dogs, and cotton candy. Hershey Park was not like that, at least not at first. In 1906, when the 150-acre park first opened, the idea of an amusement park was still relatively new. In 1893, the World's Columbian Exposition in Chicago had included the Midway Plaisance, a zone designed solely for pleasure, which M. S. probably visited. The carnival atmosphere of the Midway contrasted sharply with the more solemn mood and reverential tone that prevailed in the fair's stately exhibition halls. By entertaining fairgoers with sideshows and attractions (including the first Ferris wheel), the Midway existed to make money.[55] While the Midway did turn a profit, its legacy transcends finances. It provided the inspiration for an entirely new cultural form—the amusement park. Just two years later, entrepreneurs who had visited the Midway carried the idea to a coastal site in Brooklyn, and Coney Island was born. For decades, Coney Island would entertain visitors with thrill rides, human performances, beaches, carnival games, and dancing.[56]

Years would pass before Hershey Park would resemble Coney Island. In fact, Hershey Park was, in the beginning, only that—a park. In the model of Bournville, it provided town residents with a pleasing experience in a manicured natural environment. "One would be surprised to find such a sylvan spot on the outskirts of a large city," said M. S.'s nephew, Joseph Snavely, "but to find it in a little manufacturing town, was most incredible."[57] During the park's first year, one could take a stroll, enjoy a leisurely boat ride, hold a family picnic, and watch a baseball game. In its third year (1908), M. S. added a carousel and commenced hosting vaudeville acts in the pavilion. The park received substantial development in 1910. Guests could now ride on the Miniature Railway; sway, swing, and twirl in the dancehall; consume soda, popcorn balls, and saltwater taffy; and enjoy a rousing concert at the new Bandshell. To cool off on a summer day, they could climb stairs to a platform elevated forty feet above the ground and then shoot down a hundred-foot toboggan slide on a wooden board into a colossal pool. They could also visit the zoo. With squirrels, raccoons, ducks, deer, and bears, the zoo at first exhibited mostly the same animals one might see in one's backyard (it would add exotic animals in the ensuing years). Though built primarily for local residents, Hershey Park also attracted out-of-towners who packed their picnic baskets and used either the local trolley system or the Philadelphia and Reading Railroad to visit. As evidence of the park's growing regional reputation, it drew ten thousand people on July 4 in 1912.[58] "The transformation of the park," Snavely observed, "was one of the most remarkable developments of the town."[59]

Though Hershey Park possessed intrinsic value, M. S. did not overlook the strategic advantage of its *image*. In the 1910s, bar cards started

Fig. 3 Hershey bar card. Courtesy of HCA.

depicting fun scenes of visitors riding the Miniature Railway or frolicking in the giant pool (fig. 3).[60] Though seemingly simple, these cards played a critical role in attracting people to Hershey. In the region, they amounted to advertisements for Hershey Park; children would enjoy a chocolate bar, study the card, and beg their parents to take them to the park. By presenting the town as an ideal place to raise a family, the cards also helped draw workers to the chocolate factory. In sum, M. S. deployed these images to create a synergy between his park and his chocolate: each one enhanced the value of the other.

In the 1920s, Hershey Park grew as the stock market boomed. At the center of the expansion lay the park's first roller coaster, the Wild Cat, built by the Philadelphia Toboggan Company. Almost a mile in length, the wooden coaster thrilled riders with its elevated peaks and terrifying drops.[61] Other new attractions included bumper cars, various kiddie rides, and a shoot-the-chutes. With the latter, riders careened down a tall slide in a small boat, splashed into the pool, and then scudded over the water's surface. In 1929, Hershey Park closed the original pool and replaced it with a larger swimming complex. The "Seashore at Your Door," as it was called, included a bathhouse and veranda so that spectators could comfortably watch the bathers while shielded from the sun. In the space previously occupied by the old pool, the park installed a water-themed attraction, the Mill Chute. Riders floated along in a water channel, sometimes entering enclosed spaces, before surging down a steep slope into a pool of water. As a highlight of the decade, John Philip Sousa performed before thousands on July 4, 1925. Two years later, M. S. instituted free tours of the chocolate factory (though groups had been informally touring the facility since 1910).[62] No other park in the region offered as many attractions as Hershey Park.

During the Great Depression, the park enjoyed a surprisingly robust decade. It managed to flourish even during a time of extreme economic hardship. By this time, M. S. had come to attribute the park's success to his strategy of regular "changes." "We endeavor to make some improvements each year," he explained. "That is what makes our park so popular. People like a change, you know." In the 1930s, M. S. added a fun house complete with slides, a human roulette wheel, and a revolving barrel. In the new Custer Car Ride, guests drove gasoline-powered cars around a controlled track.[63] In the Pretzel Dark Ride, riders in automated cars entered a dark building where ghosts, snakes, and hideous faces confronted them as they moved along a tortuous course.[64] The park's ballroom also upgraded its weekend dances by hosting top performers from the big band era: Duke Ellington, Benny Goodman, Tommy Dorsey, Glenn Miller, Artie Shaw, and Guy Lombardo.[65] In this way, Hershey Park offered guests an affordable way to laugh, splash, scream, and twirl during the Great Depression.

The Compact

An amusement park can sometimes be more than just a profit center and entertainment zone—and that is the case here. Hershey Park contributed to the strong relationship bonding the company to its workers and the larger community. For more than three decades following its inception, the town enjoyed peace and prosperity. An island of tranquility, it remained immune from the civil unrest and work stoppages that bedeviled other industrial towns. What was the source of Hershey's gyroscopic stability? As with Cadbury's Bournville, an underlying quid pro quo between labor and ownership harmonized life and work in Hershey. However, the term *quid pro quo*—which implies a purely transactional partnership—does not fully capture the dynamic in Hershey, where the two sides embraced a larger vision. A better term is *compact*.

The compact in Hershey had two major components. First and most fundamentally, it was an agreement between two parties—in this case, a company and its workers—involving a set of reciprocal obligations and benefits. Each side promised something valuable to the other, and each side trusted it would receive something substantial in return. In specific terms, the Hershey arrangement looked something like this. The company did not merely offer laborers a wage-earning job and then leave them to fend for themselves in other aspects of life. It took care of its workforce in all the ways described above (affordable homes, utilities, municipal services, transportation, free education, and recreational facilities). In return for this largesse, laborers worked hard at their jobs, practiced clean living, exhibited loyalty to the company, and refrained from engaging in the labor agitation that destabilized other companies.

The compact's second component, which was aspirational in nature, appealed to humanity's innate yearning for a better world. It was this element that allowed the relationship to transcend the merely transactional quid pro quo. Simply put, the two sides shared a common vision. They believed that if they worked together, a higher form of society would emerge. Jobs would be plentiful. Labor unrest would be nonexistent. The economy would remain perpetually strong. Streets would be clean and orderly. Childhood would be safe, healthy, wholesome, and happy. Charitable organizations would flourish. Leisure time would be fun and relaxing. In short, a high quality of life would be enjoyed by all—not only by the rich. Just as the Hershey bar had democratized a confection previously enjoyed by European elites, so, too, did the town of Hershey give ordinary working-class people access to the good life. It was this mutually held belief in societal betterment that allowed Hershey to rise above the typical company town and become truly special—at least, in the opinion of M. S. and many of his employees.

Since the compact was tacitly understood rather than formally codified in a legal document, there is no text one can cite to prove its existence. That said, one can discern its presence in the reflections of M. S., his employees, and town residents. M. S. glowingly described Hershey as the next, and perhaps final, evolutionary stage in social organization. It was "an industrial Utopia," he claimed, "where the things of modern progress all center in a town that has no poverty, no nuisances, and no evil."[66] M. S.'s biographer Michael D'Antonio saw him as truly motivated by his utopian vision.

"He believed that . . . he would preside over an industrial and agricultural utopia," D'Antonio writes, "a company town . . . where farmers and factory workers and their bosses and their families could live in happy comfort." Elevated above the ordinary company town, Hershey would shine as a "beacon of humane and moral capitalism" and "the perfect American place."[67] Gideon Kreider, who owned a local newspaper, saw M. S. as sincere in trying to uphold his end of the compact. M. S. "never was interested in money for the sake of money," Kreider observed. He pursued wealth "to build and to improve" society, not to acquire "power" or "be considered a rich man."[68] Gil Nurick, a lawyer who provided various Hershey entities with legal counsel, believed that the compact gave the people something quasi-sacred in which to believe and bonded them to its creator. "People who have tasted of his philanthropy," Nurick explained, "maintain a loyalty and devotion which are almost unique." Their admiration of M. S. approached the level of veneration: "It's almost religion."[69]

Adoration for M. S. and the compact did sometimes resemble a religion. Those who revered M. S. passionately defended both the man and his town from critics. Richard Bacastow grew up in Hershey and served in World War II before enrolling at the University of Pennsylvania's Wharton School of Economics (he later worked for Hershey Chocolate). One morning, he was sitting in an auditorium as the professor lectured on the day's topic—the company town. The professor described an actual town where "paternalism was rampant." Leaving the town unnamed, he asserted that the patriarch lived "on a big hill" and ran his community "as an autocracy." When the professor disclosed the town's identity, Bacastow recoiled in shock. It was Hershey. After gathering himself, Bacastow formed his rebuttal. And why not? The "company town" that the professor denigrated had infused his youth with joy and dependably employed his father for decades. Though his father's positions did not generate great wealth, the family always had food, drove an automobile, and owned rather than rented their house. In attaining economic stability, Bacastow's family was not rare: "The people of Hershey never knew what unemployment was." Having lined up his arguments, Bacastow prepared to refute the professor's portrayal. "You're all wrong," he blurted out. He then proceeded to debunk the whole notion that Hershey was "a typical company town." That, he insisted, was pure "academic myth."

We do not know exactly what Bacastow said in his rebuttal. However, later in life, he identified the special quality that, in his view, allowed Hershey to transcend mere "company town" status. He did not use the word *compact*, but he did come up with a different term to capture the company's symbiotic relationship with its workers—*synergism*. Bacastow believed that the two sides, by sharing a vision, accomplished a result neither could have achieved alone. On the ownership side, he credited M. S. for redirecting profits into social uplift rather than hoarding them. "He was very careful to do things for . . . the community," Bacastow explained, as well as for one unfortunate group—the orphans. As for employees, they showed "dedication and loyalty" to this vision because they enjoyed participating in something larger than themselves. Working for the company, Bacastow explained, was about "contributing to society" rather than "the dirty bottom line."[70]

Edwin Zechman, who managed Hershey's drugstore, contested the mere suggestion that Hershey was a company town: "It was not a company town, damn it!" In Zechman's opinion, a company town runs on coercion: an autocratic factory owner forces powerless workers to play by his rules. Life in Hershey, he insisted, looked nothing like this. M. S. did not make anybody patronize his stores and institutions, Zechman made emphatically clear. "Nobody had to. Nobody was forced to. Nobody was compelled to at all, ever." People *chose* to live and work in Hershey, Zechman asserted. In defending the founder and his vision, Zechman clarified that he was not trying to "make a god out of Mr. Hershey." Rather, he felt strongly that M. S. was "a fine man" who had "built something"; therefore, it was "damned important that we remember him" rather than "denigrate him."[71] In this way, Zechman exhibited fierce loyalty to M. S. and the compact.

Other residents also pushed back (though less vociferously) against negative portrayals of M. S. Howard Kishpaugh, an Episcopal minister, did not see Hershey as a community dominated by a patriarch. "You can call it paternalism," he said, "but I don't see it as that." The reason, Kishpaugh explained, was that M. S. used his power to help rather than exploit people. "I think the people of Hershey have benefited," he elaborated, "from the investment of the industry into the life at Hershey." While appreciating M. S.'s many gifts to the community, Kishpaugh agreed with Zechman's point about coercion: residents were *not* beholden to the company. "We didn't owe Hershey anything," he explained. "We were just a part of the community who enjoyed the life here."[72] John Shuey, a lifelong resident, also saw something special about Hershey but struggled to articulate his thought in words. "I think Hershey is a wonderful place," he declared. But "exactly what it is, I'm not sure." Though he could not pin down Hershey's special quality, he knew that something set it apart: "You can look at any of the communities around here, and I think you won't find anything that matches Hershey."[73] "Mr. Hershey was a kind and generous person who always thought of what good he could do in this world," said Aimee Rex, who grew up in Hershey. "I don't think there's another place like it, and it's all due to Mr. Hershey."[74] Peter Kurie, who conducted an ethnography of Hershey, found that this sentiment was commonplace. "In the view of insiders, as well as outsiders looking in," he discovered, "Hershey remains a community of exception: an isle of prosperity and security in a precarious sea, buoyed by the founder's entrepreneurial and philanthropic legacies."[75]

Hershey's Outsiders

An Italian American man recalled the impetus behind his family's move to Hershey. As a boy, he lived in a small town in western Pennsylvania where his father owned a general store that stocked Hershey products. One day, as his father was managing his inventory, his eyes happened upon a picture on a box of chocolate bars. It was, in the son's remembrance, "a beautiful illustration"—the kind printed on bar cards. The father stopped what he was doing and studied the card. Clean, wholesome, and industrious, Hershey appeared to be the ideal place for the family to settle down. Acting on impulse, the father "decided to take a trip to Hershey," the son recalled, "to see if he could find employment." He did, and the family relocated.[76]

This was an unusual case. In the early twentieth century, Italian families did flock to Hershey, but few did so after falling under the spell of a picture. It was far more common for an Italian immigrant, after disembarking at Ellis Island, to learn about a job in the quarries outside of Hershey where his stone-working skills were in demand—at least for a while. The quarries ceased providing reliable employment around the time of World War I. Released from these jobs, Italian men turned to the nearby chocolate factory. It absorbed not just them but their wives, who were hired to work in the wrapping room.[77] After this first wave of immigrants put down roots in Hershey, they were joined by more Italians attracted by the promise of steady work and a growing Italian community where one could converse in one's native tongue, maintain Old World traditions, and practice Catholicism.[78]

Life was not easy for Italian workers and their families. During the decades before World War II, they experienced no small amount of bigotry. In an area heavily populated by Pennsylvania Germans, the residents of Hershey's "Little Italy" felt like outsiders. The mainstream Germans derogatorily referred to them as "wops" and "dagos" (the Italians responded in kind by calling their antagonists "Dunkards").[79] Old religious hatreds also fueled the town's ethnic divide, as the Protestant Germans distrusted the Catholic Italians. One Pennsylvania German, looking back at his youth, recalled his father's prejudice as having a religious basis. His father "didn't hate Italians," but he would have "had a fit" if he had caught his son dating an Italian girl. "He sure didn't want an Italian daughter-in-law."[80] Another non-Italian agreed that "the division between a Protestant and a Catholic was very strong." "If you were even dating a Catholic," he recalled, "it didn't go down too well with the families."[81] "I had to break up with a lot of boys because I was Catholic," recalled Nita Deaner, who said that "a lot of families were prejudiced." She did add that her family was "accepted" in the mixed neighborhood in which they lived.[82] Unfortunately, her experience was not shared by all Italian families. Non-Italian Hershey residents took measures to prevent Italians from joining their neighborhoods. Should an Italian family attempt to move out of Little Italy and into a new neighborhood, the residents there might circulate a petition to keep them out.[83]

In addition to discrimination, Italian families faced other challenges. Raised in Italian-speaking homes, the children struggled when they matriculated at Hershey's English-speaking schools. One recalled the "traumatic" first day when "my mother had to drag me to school, crying."[84] Samuel Tancredi, whose father started in the quarry before being hired by Hershey, also had a rough first day. When the teacher called on him, he turned to a fellow Italian and asked, "Che dice?" (What is she saying?). Misjudging Samuel as flippant, the teacher seized him "by the scruff of the neck" and dragged him out to the hall. When the principal noticed the boy standing there, he escorted him to his office, seized his paddle, and unleashed "a hell of a good whaling." "I learned English pretty fast after that," Tancredi recalled.[85]

Challenges notwithstanding, the Italians established themselves in Hershey. Most saw M. S. as a force for good. Some even revered a man whom they fondly referred to as Il Padrone—the master.[86] Nita Deaner described many Italians as "grateful" to the "benefactor" who "brought them here and gave them jobs." Others adopted a more critical eye while still offering a mostly favorable assessment. "I'm sure you've heard stories about Mr. Hershey" that portray him alternately as a "saint" and a "devil," offered Tancredi. The truth, he said, was somewhere in between. If M. S. noticed an idle employee who should have been working, he fired him on the spot. That said, Tancredi pointed to an aura of saintliness that surrounded M. S.'s larger project. "There aren't many people who have been able to make a real big success of their lives," Tancredi elaborated, "and then use those monies in such a beautiful way to benefit so many people."[87] Many Italians felt grateful to M. S. for helping them unify splintered families. In the early 1900s, Italian men often voyaged alone to America to find work, leaving their wives and children in Italy. By saving wages from the chocolate factory, these men were able to reunite their families in Hershey. Italians also expressed gratitude to M. S. for supporting the local Catholic church, Saint Joan of Arc. When informed that M. S. donated funds to all places of worship without favoring any, many Italians nevertheless insisted that he reserved a special place in his heart for them.[88] On holidays, Italian families happily served the turkey M. S. gave them, though from their culinary perspective, the ungainly bird seemed like a strange thing to eat.[89] Millie Pichini Landis, who described Thanksgiving as "kind of a mystery" to Italians, recalled wondering, "Why do I have to eat turkey today?"[90]

Peter Foschetti, who interviewed members of the Italian community in the 1970s, saw M. S. as the primary reason for the "strong bond" that tied Italians to the town and factory. One Italian woman described how children would go to work for the company in their youth and retire fifty years later. "Every one of them started as kids," she elaborated, "and they've never known what it is not to work" for Hershey. They have "chocolate syrup in their veins," she jested.[91] Jean Ranerio came from this kind of family. Both of her parents worked for Hershey for decades (her mother wrapped Kisses). When Ranerio was old enough to work, she was hired to be a "knock-out girl"—she used a hammer to knock finished chocolate bars out of their metal moldings. Though the work was tedious, Ranerio had no regrets. "If I had to do it all over again, I would start at Hershey again," she said after her retirement. "I think anybody that works in there should be grateful."[92]

Italians professed general contentment with their treatment by the company. Like other Hershey workers, they understood and embraced the compact. But there was one breach in their fidelity, and it happened during the Great Depression. Though M. S. adopted bold strategies to cope with the economic crisis, many workers, Italians included, grew frustrated and disgruntled with him and his company. The 1930s would test the strength of the compact by delivering the most severe incident of labor strife in the town's history.

The Great Depression and Strike

After the stock market crash of 1929, the country entered the worst economic crisis in its history. Throughout the decade, national unemployment fluctuated, sometimes approaching a staggering 25 percent. An astounding one in four people could not find work.[93] As bleak as the national scene was, one community mostly succeeded in keeping out the scourge of joblessness—Hershey. "The town of Hershey suffered no hardships due to the Depression," said Monroe Stover, who lived in Hershey at this time.[94] "There was no Depression in Hershey," recalled June Herr, another resident. "Everyone that would have been laid off in the factory got a job in construction."[95]

Herr and Stover were referring to the proactive measures M. S. took to shield the town from misery while his company rode out the economic storm. In this effort, he was aided by two positive factors. First, the continued profits generated by the Hershey Corporation in Cuba bolstered finances in the town. Second, many Americans continued to plunk down a hard-earned nickel for a Hershey bar, though they did so less often. As a result, chocolate sales dipped substantially but did not crash: profits fell from $7.4 million in 1929 to $4.2 million in 1933.[96] This weakened demand meant that M. S. could produce chocolate, but not at peak capacity. Instead of laying off workers, he reduced the maximum number of hours an employee could work from sixty to forty. No one was thrown out of work, but a family would have to survive on less income. Of course, not everyone worked for the chocolate factory. To take care of local residents who lost their jobs, M. S. initiated a series of construction projects that mirrored Franklin Roosevelt's Works Project Administration, though on a smaller scale. The town got a new school, office building, luxury hotel, garden, golf courses, sports arena, and community building complete with a gymnasium, swimming pool, library, and theater. Collectively, these projects created jobs and pumped $10 million into the local economy.[97] "I gave them employment in the construction of these buildings," M. S. told the *New York Times* in 1937. "I made work for them during the depression. There was no depression in Hershey."[98] Samuel Hinkle, an employee who would later ascend to be president of the company, credited M. S.'s "vision and courage" in launching a jobs program that kept at bay the "dire ills" afflicting the rest of America.[99]

Town residents—Italians especially—also approved of M. S.'s leadership during the crisis. "My recollection is that Mr. Hershey extended himself," said Richard Bacastow, citing the construction projects. In contrast with neighboring towns, where "we could see people . . . picking coal along the railroad" or "selling apples," in Hershey "we never really knew poverty."[100] "The wages at Hershey were low," recalled Samuel Tancredi, "but the work was steady and you could depend on some pay. For me, keeping a family of four on what I was earning, it was pretty wonderful to have a job."[101] "Hershey made sure that people had some income," echoed Jean Ranerio in the 1990s, and "I hear older people still talking about that."[102] Peter Foschetti agreed that the Italian community genuinely appreciated M. S.'s "efforts to keep everyone employed."[103] Though Hershey fared better than most places in the 1930s, it did not escape the decade unscathed. In 1937, a labor strike roiled Hershey's usually calm economic waters.

The strike raises the question: if Hershey's crisis management was so adroit, why was the company vulnerable to labor agitation? The answer is that some of the company's actions did generate discontent. First, it severely curtailed worker hours. Though nobody got laid off, workers brought home far less income in the 1930s than they did in the 1920s. As a consequence, people who had previously enjoyed stability now had to scrape by. Second, some employees resented the company's attempt to manage their personal lives outside of work. An employee would receive a stern warning, for instance, if he consumed too much alcohol. "How do they know what we do outside the factory?" an irritated worker asked before answering his own question: "They've got spies, dirty stool-pigeons, who run to the company every time they learn something." *Forbes* magazine, which spoke to workers in 1937, described them as no longer wanting "to be treated as children of a kindly father."[104]

Third, workers felt insecure in a precarious environment where a small violation could cost them their jobs at any moment. Though the company's habit of firing people for minor infractions had always provoked angst, the Great Depression amplified this stress. Life was "very, very hard" on workers with "family responsibilities," remarked Tancredi, because a dismissal amounted to a "death sentence."[105] Ignazio Romanucci summed up the nervous situation this way: workers were gripped by a "fear psychology."[106] Fourth, factory workers resented the Hershey Industrial School. Tancredi recalled the outrage when workers learned that the school spent $3,000 annually per orphan, a figure that dwarfed the yearly pay of a chocolate worker. "We're expected to keep our families on meager pay," workers complained, "while they brag about it costing $3,000 to keep one boy."[107] William Dearden, who became CEO of Hershey Foods but was then a student at the school, corroborated Tancredi's account. "Part of the genesis of that strike," he indicated, was that workers believed that "Mr. Hershey was giving too much to the kids . . . and that [workers] should be getting more."[108] In sum, conditions were ripe for a strike despite M. S.'s preventative efforts.

Outside agitation provided the spark that lit the kindling. Early in 1937, the Committee for Industrial Organization (CIO) arrived in Hershey after a prolific year of organizing. In 1936, the CIO had orchestrated more than four hundred sit-down strikes. Most notably, the CIO had helped the United Automobile Workers score a major victory at the General Motors plant in Flint, Michigan.[109] After that triumph, the CIO set its sights on Hershey. "As the nation's largest chocolate maker," writes Robert Weir, who studied the strike, "Hershey was the confectionary equivalent of General Motors and the logical target." In nearby Palmyra, the CIO met with discontented chocolate workers to help them organize a local chapter of the United Chocolate Workers union (UCW). At first, these unionizing efforts looked promising. Many workers were receptive to the UCW, which was able to secure

80 percent of the factory's labor force. As more workers joined the union, M. S. attempted to stem the tide by raising wages 20 percent. His efforts were not enough. On April 2, the UCW launched its sit-down strike.[110]

The specific event that triggered the strike was the company's abrupt decision to lay off more than one hundred workers. William Murrie, the company's president and M. S.'s right-hand man, cited the seasonal nature of the chocolate business as the rationale for the layoffs. "The chocolate and cocoa business," he explained, had entered the "dull season" when fewer workers were needed. Despite Murrie's characterization of the layoffs as routine, the company likely acted out of fear that the new union would demand a "closed shop"—a labor arrangement in which a company agrees to hire union members only. Viewing a closed shop as intolerable, M. S. and Murrie may have used the pretext of seasonal layoffs to justify removing key unionists from their positions.[111] On April 1, the union leaders, claiming that the layoffs violated seniority rules, called a meeting to formulate a response. At the meeting, leaders cautioned against calling a strike, recommending instead patience and additional organization. They argued that the union should increase its membership rolls first and then, with greater leverage, contest the layoffs. Unfortunately, outraged union members, described by one observer as "riled up," rejected this prudent approach and demanded an immediate strike. They got their wish. The next day at 11:00 a.m., the union president waved a red handkerchief on the factory floor, signaling to workers that the strike was on. The strikers had every reason to believe that a strategy that had worked in Flint would also succeed in Hershey.[112]

It didn't. Weir argues that union leaders made key errors that undermined their effort. When they hoisted the CIO banner on the company flagpole, it was positioned higher than the Stars and Stripes. This provocative but foolhardy act only emboldened the CIO's harshest critics, who accused it of being anti-American and procommunist. It was a public relations disaster. As perhaps their most grievous error, strike leaders failed to contemplate the effect their forced work stoppage would have on local dairy farmers, who daily delivered 240,000 quarts of milk to the plant. Since the plant was shut down, there was no outlet for the milk that cows kept producing. One frustrated farmer told a local newspaper that he had dumped 1,200 pounds of product. Outraged by the loss of sales, dairy farmers joined townspeople and other Hershey employees in forming an angry opposition to the strikers. Finally, organizers failed to grasp that Hershey was fundamentally different from Flint. The town was ensconced in an agricultural region known for its conservative politics. Not surprisingly, the "proletarian ethos," Weir points out, was far weaker in Hershey than it was in industrial Michigan. Labor agitation here would not garner the same level of public support.[113] Further augmenting the local pro-Hershey sentiment was the compact. M. S. enjoyed a special relationship with many employees, area farmers, and local residents. Since he remained for them a beloved figure—a patriarch who provided for his people—they remained steadfastly loyal. During the strike, loyalists held rallies that attracted as many as ten thousand people.[114]

On April 8, after several days of failed negotiations, emotions overheated. A procompany mob, several thousand strong, stormed the chocolate factory armed with clubs, sticks, and iron pipes. Their purpose: to solve the festering problem with violence.[115] In addition to the loss of milk sales, this group was "aroused," the *New York Times* reported, by the "whole idea . . . of a sit-down strike in this intensely patriotic community." Overwhelmed by the siege, the strikers exited the factory, "holding their hands high above their heads in surrender." Some strikers had been subjected to physical abuse at the hands of loyalists. "There were many bloody faces," the *Times* reported, and "twenty or so were really hurt."[116] "I can see clubs and I can see broken heads and I can see the blood," said one Italian witness (fig. 4).[117] In the end, the workers did get a union, but it was not the one organized by the CIO. The more moderate American Federation of Labor stepped in to organize a Local 464 of the Bakery and Confectionery Workers. Though this union did negotiate a contract with the company, the result was far less than what labor organizers had originally imagined. "In Hershey," Weir summed up succinctly, "Goliath won."[118]

What does the strike tell us about the compact? Most obviously, it exposed hidden fractures in the compact previously masked by economic prosperity. However, in subtle ways, the strike also demonstrated the compact's enduring strength. We can discern M. S.'s emotional investment in the compact in his reaction to the strike. M. S. publicly dismissed the strike as the work of a few "radicals." "Four or five of them simply misled a small minority of the chocolate plant employees into this strike," he told the *New*

Fig. 4 Strikers forced out of the chocolate factory with violence. Courtesy of HCA.

York Times.[119] Privately, however, M. S. knew that a large number of employees had not only joined the strike but had done so of their own volition. This fact shook him at his core. The strike brought "terrific strain" on M. S., said the company's personnel director. "He could not understand . . . that people whom he was caring for would turn on him." "He was deeply hurt," recalled an executive's son, "and felt that all he had done for the town had been forgotten."[120] He "couldn't understand why they were moving against him . . . after he had provided all these facilities," recalled Sam Hinkle. The strike "cut him to the quick."[121] M. S. found the strike disturbing because he believed deeply in the compact and had assumed that among the workers the feeling was mutual.

He was not far off. The behavior of striking workers suggests that they also embraced the compact, even though they differed with M. S. in their interpretation of it. At other factories with labor unrest, strikers would routinely denounce ownership and destroy property and equipment. In contrast, Hershey's chocolate workers showed little malice toward M. S.

Remarkably, they even chose to maintain the machinery while occupying the plant. This respectful behavior tells us that, according to their understanding, a peaceful sit-down strike was allowable within the parameters of the compact. Michael D'Antonio puts it this way: "For them the strike was more like a family squabble than an angry revolution."[122]

The compact's strength manifested itself in other ways. We see it in the fiery passions of townspeople, farmers, and nonstriking Hershey employees. These groups clearly felt that the strikers had violated a sacred trust. Finally, the compact's strength is implied in the fact that it had taken extraordinary circumstances for the strike to happen at all. That it had required an aggressive effort by the CIO during the Great Depression, the worst economic calamity in U.S. history, to disrupt production in the factory suggests that an invisible force had been holding Hershey together all along. That invisible force was the compact.

From Italians to Americans

For the Italian community, the unionizing effort and subsequent strike held both positive and negative consequences. On the issue of union membership, Italian workers did not behave as a bloc—some joined while others demurred. Though the union did attract a higher percentage of Italian workers than non-Italian workers, that was mostly because Italians tended to hold the most physically taxing factory jobs. They were more eager than non-Italians to support any movement promising to improve conditions.[123] Unfortunately, the Italian workers' higher union membership made them convenient targets in the strike's aftermath. Some Hershey residents inaccurately accused them of starting the conflict.[124] That the Italians "got the blame," Tancredi recalled, left behind "scars," "sores, bad feeling, suspicion and doubt."[125] As for the strike's positive effect, Peter Foschetti found that it jump-started the integration of Italians in mainstream Hershey society. Italian workers, by joining the union, worked side by side with non-Italians toward a common cause. "It was after [the strike], that we all got along," recalled one Italian worker. "They stopped calling us bad names." The two sides learned to trust each other, thus lifting the cloud of suspicion that had previously divided the town along ethnic lines.[126]

World War II accelerated this integration. According to Foschetti, second-generation Italians agreed that "if bad feeling between Italians and non-Italians had not died out" before the war, it "vanished" during the war. As young Italian men went off to fight, their families and the larger Italian community vigorously supported the war cause back home. "Everyone worked hard for the victory," remembered one Italian woman. "We didn't have time to fight [with each other]."[127] In short, the war delivered a unifying event that swept away any remaining ethnic division.

In the end, the assimilation of Italians in Hershey is a story that spans three generations. In the early 1900s, Italian immigrants (the first generation) lived in an ethnic enclave, spoke little English, and followed Old World traditions. Their children (the second generation) faced prejudice at school and felt caught between two worlds. "At home I was an Italian," one second-generation Italian recalled, "and the minute I left home, I had to pretend I was an American."[128] The third generation, thanks to the war, grew up with a luxury denied to both their parents and grandparents: they lacked even an awareness that discrimination had existed. "My kids play football and hockey," one second-generation mother shared, describing her children as "Americans with Italian names." "We were Italian-Americans," a second-generation mother stated succinctly. "The kids are all Americans."[129]

Besides the end of ethnic strife, it was good to live in Hershey after the war for other reasons. Though M. S. died two months after V-J Day, the town nevertheless enjoyed prosperity during the postwar years. Residents who recalled Hershey from the late 1940s to the early 1960s refer to this period as a "golden age."[130] It was a time when one could enjoy all those Hershey entertainments—the theater, dance hall, factory tours, swimming pool, sports facilities, and band concerts. Those who were children during this time look back wistfully on their youth. Of all the recreational venues, none generated more fond memories than Hershey Park.

Hershey Park in Community Memory

Hershey Park surged in popularity in the golden age. During these decades of economic prosperity, the park frequently added exciting new attractions. In 1946, the Comet Roller Coaster replaced the Wild Cat. Thrilling riders by hurtling them at high speeds through deep drops, the Comet drew massive crowds. "We had a ball!" longtime resident Mary Hubler remembered. "There was a line up there all the time." In 1944, the park replaced the old carousel with a new one that dwarfed its predecessor. Its four concentric rows of horses could accommodate sixty-six people at once. Most riders saddled up on a "jumper," a horse that would rise and fall as the Carrousel revolved. Featuring 1,788 light bulbs, the incandescent attraction illuminated summer nights.[131] One aspect of the Carrousel required skill. When it reached top speed, daring riders would reach out and try to snatch grabbable rings from dispensers as they passed by. Though most rings were made of iron, the rider who seized the lone brass ring won a free ride. Richard Seiverling remembered watching the "fanatics" go for the brass ring.[132] This challenge aside, young people also congregated at the Carrousel hoping to meet romantic partners. Henry Stump first spoke to the young woman who would become his wife here because, in his words, "this was the way it was done."[133]

In the 1940s and 1950s, the ballroom continued to book the best bands touring the country. When Tommy Dorsey passed through Hershey, he liked to arrive several hours early so that his band could squeeze in nine innings of softball before the evening performance. Sometimes, more people showed up than the ballroom could reasonably accommodate. As the band played its hits, dancers would jostle against one another on the congested dance floor (fig. 5). One August night in 1947, Hershey had to suspend ticket sales after nearly seven thousand people packed the venue to hear Vaughn Monroe. In the 1950s, Hershey Estates renovated the ballroom by removing part of the roof, allowing guests on clear nights to dance under the stars. The remodeled facility was appropriately renamed the Starlight Ballroom. Edwin Zechman's "very happy memories" included Saturday dances in the ballroom. "You used to get all dolled up" in "white suits, linen or cotton," and "get the girl and go." "It was a happy time."[134]

It *was* a happy time. Later in their lives, many residents volunteered to share memories of their idyllic early years in Hershey. As one reads their oral histories, one cannot help but make four observations. First, when community members reminisced, they almost always funneled to the same place—Hershey Park. They wished to talk about the old park and its meaningful connection to their lives. Second, one cannot miss the uniformly

Fig. 5 A crush of couples trying to dance on the ballroom's crowded dance floor. Courtesy of HCA.

positive nature of their recollections. Their memories of the park are usually pristine, blemished not even by a speck of negativity. In describing the park, they adopted the same tone that an elderly Adam and Eve might have employed when questioned about their youths in Eden. "When we went to the Park," one resident recalled, "we thought we were going into a happy paradise."[135] "It was like a little utopia for kids," said another.[136] One elderly woman said that her "old memories" were "like a dream."[137] The joy that residents felt in the park echoes through their oral histories as nostalgia.

Third, community members ascribed significance to the fact that Hershey Park was not enclosed in fencing and did not charge admission. It "was all open," recalled George Lafferty, and "everything was free." "You could go where you wanted," "spend what you wanted," and "if you wanted to ride you bought tickets."[138] "It was a family park then," remembered another resident, who stressed that there were "no fences."[139] Residents viewed the free and open nature of Hershey Park as highly meaningful; they understood the park as a special place that existed *for them*. This feeling of entitlement is what Mary Shenk, a local teacher, was expressing when she referred to it as "our *people's* Park."[140]

Fourth, you observe the underlying sameness of their park memories. With some variation, a day at the park followed a clear pattern. After a family arrived with its picnic basket, the group enjoyed a midday meal at the Picnic Pavilion, which gave way to an afternoon of rides, arcade games, swimming, baseball, and ice-cream cones. Later in the day, the family congregated at the Bandshell to take in a rousing concert. After the show, families with small children trooped back to their cars (or to the trolley), while teenagers and adults headed to the Starlight Ballroom for an evening of big band music and dance. Save for minor differences, everyone seemed to be describing the same day—what we might call the *Perfect Hershey Day*—which they enjoyed repeatedly during their youth.

Robert Rath recalled a day at the park as a great family event. "It was a big day out for families," he recalled. "There were picnic tables all over the place . . . and you could pick and choose what you wanted to ride." Rath loved the penny arcade, the ballroom's bands, the Comet (which he once rode fourteen times in a row), and the Fun House, where he was such a "regular" that the operator admitted him at no charge. When he was older, he sold refreshments near the Carrousel.[141] Cy Little remembered taking the trolley to Hershey Park during the Great Depression. A typical day included a picnic, Bandshell concert, and rides. With a few dimes jangling in his pocket, he enjoyed the Fun House, Mill Chute, Wild Cat, and Carrousel, where "you grabbed the brass ring and would get a free ride." He harbored genuine affection for the Starlight Ballroom, where "people could dance under the stars."[142] Helen Jane Whiteman described outings to the park with her great uncle, who loved band music. When young, she would ride the Carrousel and the Miniature Railway before attending a concert. As she got older, she would spend the day at the pool and then spread out a blanket and "listen to the big bands" like Guy Lombardo or Rudy Vallée outside the Starlight. As an adult, she would cap off her Perfect Hershey Day with an evening of dancing.[143]

Others, too, shared their experiences in the park. "I have very happy memories of my life in Hershey," remarked June Herr, who remembered

Sunday picnics, the Wild Cat, the Carrousel, the Miniature Railway, Bandshell concerts, and dancing in the ballroom. "That was a great time for me."[144] James Stover reminisced about picnics, band concerts, arcade games, and his favorite rides. He especially liked the Mill Chute because "you could put your arm around your girlfriend" in the ride's dark tunnel. Stover appreciated that everyone, regardless of income level, could afford the park. "You didn't need a lot of money in your pocket," he commented, "because the rides only cost a nickel, and of course there were a lot of free things," such as band concerts.[145] "Now we came over to the park, and that was wonderful," recalled Ruth Troutman, whose family always brought a picnic. Over the course of the day, she would visit the Fun House, ride the roller coaster, and dance in the ballroom.[146] Carol Lucas, who frequented the park in the 1950s, recalled the Comet, Carrousel, Funhouse, pool, and the big bands at the Starlight. "Those are some fond memories I have of the way Hershey used to be."[147] Harvey Deitrich reminisced about the free band concerts, dancing, swimming pool, milkshakes, nickel-and-dime rides, and the quest for the Carrousel's brass ring. "Boy, I tell you," he commented in 1998, "there is nothing like good old Hershey. . . . I miss it."[148] He was not alone. That everyone possessed a nearly identical set of memories suggests the prevalence of the Perfect Hershey Day. And that everyone cherished those memories, clinging to them as the years rolled by, is indicative of the Perfect Day's emotional power.

Indeed, beneath Hershey Park's appearance of carefree fun and frivolity, something meaningful was taking place. When families spent the day at the park, their members grew closer to one another and their beloved town. Hershey Park also reminded the company and community of the special relationship that bonded them. In this way, the park emerged as a contact zone, a place where the community and company met. Thus, the park provided each side with a space to *perform* its commitment to the compact. By maintaining, staffing, and updating Hersheypark, the company signaled its continued compliance with the terms. By patronizing the park, members of the community reciprocated, performing their continued acceptance of the compact's conditions. "The park was genuinely for the workers at the chocolate factory, the families in town, and for people around the region," a Hershey resident recalled of this era. "The love of the place used to tie it together."[149]

Conclusion

On October 13, 1945, M. S. passed away shortly after celebrating his eighty-eighth birthday. He died a poor man, at least on paper, having transferred nearly all his assets to the Hershey Industrial School trust fund.[150] He left behind a thriving town that had enjoyed prosperity and stability for four decades. Both the company and town credited the compact for much of this success. Today we tend to look with disapproval upon any society organized around paternalism. Though this critical view is justified, we should also acknowledge that M. S. delivered a quality of life that far that surpassed what most workers and their families would have experienced had they settled elsewhere.

As Hershey moved into the post–M. S. era, both the company and town remained committed to the compact. At the company, M. S. continued to cast a shadow over operations in the 1950s. The leaders who followed in his wake, conservative by nature, tried to adhere to his vision rather than innovating. They saw no reason to question the compact. Town residents, who loved living and working in Hershey, also continued to embrace the compact in the 1950s. Though fully aware that true paradise does not exist in this world, many nevertheless believed that Hershey came awfully close with its benevolent employer, free services and amenities, and beloved amusement park. They were loath to see their way of life change.

But change was coming . . .

Chapter 2

Chocolatetown Meltdown

At Milton Hershey's funeral, several thousand people showed up to pay their respects. In delivering the eulogy, the Reverend John Treder tried to convey the significance of M. S.'s life. He did so with the full understanding that, with the passing of the patriarch, the community was drifting into uncharted waters and would need a guiding principle. Drawing from scripture, he likened M. S. to Moses and the town to the promised land—the "land that floweth with milk and honey." He went on to predict that, when posterity reflects on the achievements of M. S., it "will marvel at the amazing success of this great industrial enterprise" and "at the beauty of this community." However, the most important part of M. S.'s legacy, Treder insisted, was intangible: "a vision . . . of a better life for other men." It was a vision that, in Treder's opinion, must survive the death of the visionary. To help effect that outcome, Treder urged everyone to "pledge" to "go forward in the spirit in which [Hershey] was founded and with the same vision." Treder, in so many words, called for the continuation of the compact. After the service, a procession of cars a mile long snaked its way to the cemetery, located on a tranquil hilltop overlooking the town. With eight alumni of the Hershey Industrial School serving as pallbearers, M. S. was laid to rest.[1]

Three years later, a journalist visited Hershey. Though his purpose was to write about the company's continued refusal to advertise, he found himself intrigued by the community. Sensing that there was something different about these people, he adopted the tone of an anthropologist studying tribal life. He described them as a "somewhat insulated race" who refer to visitors from Virginia or Ohio as "foreigners." They adore their quality of life, he reported, much of which they owe to the generosity of the founder. "They have accepted from Milton Hershey," he observed, "a lot of creature comforts, entertainment facilities and scenery embellishments" and "are proud of them." Content with their world, the people exuded a "deep-rooted stability" that was "almost uncanny." He concluded that Hershey is not so much a "town" as a "state of mind."[2] His portrayal, though ostensibly complimentary, had an ominous tone. The happiness and stability of Hershey, though real, depended on both free services and continued shielding from the vicissitudes of the outside world. In this way, the article implicitly begged a question: how would residents who had grown accustomed to Hershey's unusual way of life react if it were taken away?

It was taken away. "There was an infusion of change," one former executive said of the 1960s. "Change came quickly, it was dramatic, and it wasn't subtle."[3] Change, as this chapter explains, assumed three forms. First, the Hershey Chocolate Corporation, in response to competition from Mars, initiated a wave of long-overdue modernizations. Comprehensive in scope, these reforms touched nearly every aspect of the business. Second, Hershey constructed a state-of-the-art medical center that attracted a new and, at least at first, unwelcome kind of person to town. Third, Hershey Estates initiated a plan to discontinue or sell off the services and amenities that had been given freely to the community for generations. From the perspective of local residents, the number and magnitude of the changes were jarring. Though no one referred to Treder's "pledge" from 1945, the changes convinced many that the Hershey corporate entities had abrogated their responsibilities to the compact. Conditioned over the decades to view Hershey as an island of stability, residents now saw their world as thrown out of order.

Hershey's Mars Problem

Before the 1960s, Hershey executives never lost sleep worrying about Mars. Not only did the chocolate colossus dwarf Frank Mars's company in size, but it also sold a different kind of confection. Whereas Hershey produced solid chocolate (think of Hershey bars and Kisses), Mars specialized in "enrobed products"—milk chocolate poured over a candy core consisting of ingredients such as nuts, caramel, or nougat.[4] Where did that chocolate coating come from? In what was a true symbiosis, Hershey supplied Mars with chocolate.[5] Given this partnership, Hershey executives enjoyed the luxury of not having to fret about Mars. After all, Mars was a customer, not a rival. Unfortunately, the relationship changed when Forrest Mars, the founder's son, seized control of the company in 1964.

Born in 1904, Forrest Mars became estranged from his father, Frank Mars, at the age of six when his parents divorced. A chance meeting in 1923 initiated the start of a hot and cold father-son relationship. The two sometimes worked brilliantly together. In fact, it was Forrest who urged his father to make enrobed bars in the Chicago factory and leave solid chocolate to Hershey. Enrobed bars were not only easier to mass-produce, but they also cost less since the ingredients were cheaper than cocoa beans. Convinced, Frank Mars partnered with Hershey to obtain the chocolate coating. The Milky Way, which epitomized this variety of candy bar, debuted in 1924, and Snickers and 3 Musketeers followed in the early thirties. It was shortly after these product launches that the father and son had a major falling out. "This company isn't big enough for both of us," Frank Mars reportedly declared as he cast his son out. "Go to some other country and start your own business." Forrest did exactly that, traveling first to Switzerland to work for the Tobler and Nestlé companies, and then to England to observe Cadbury's operation.[6] Returning from exile after his father's death in 1934, Forrest prepared to unveil his own product—small chocolate pellets with a delicate candy shell. To obtain the chocolate for the pellets, Forrest traveled to Pennsylvania to strike a deal with M. S. As part of the agreement, Forrest agreed to hire Bruce Murrie, the son of William Murrie, M. S.'s right-hand man. Indeed, as Joël Glenn Brenner has revealed, Murrie was the source for the second "M" of this product's dual-letter name—Mars and Murrie or "M&M."[7] During World War II, Hershey engineers even designed and installed the machinery that Forrest needed to make M&M's. Hershey "sent all that technology and equipment to Mars," recalled Richard Bacastow, which "exploited the opportunity."[8]

Forrest Mars sought much more than a successful candy brand. He harbored a secret ambition to topple Hershey as the nation's top chocolate manufacturer. However, as driven as he was to end Hershey's reign, he did not apply pressure on his rival until the mid-1960s. Before then, his aggressive plans were held in check by family members who owned part of the company. Forrest finally achieved total control in 1964 when his half sister Pattie, dying from cancer, sold him her shares.[9] Now in full command, Forrest took deliberate measures to dethrone Hershey. He began by ordering his engineers to make Hershey-quality chocolate within six months. In 1965, he stunned Hershey by canceling their long-standing partnership. Mars would produce its own chocolate from now on. Since chocolate coating constituted 30 percent of Hershey's total sales and Mars had been the largest customer, the loss in revenue gashed Hershey's balance sheet. It was an opening salvo.[10]

Moving swiftly, Forrest took measures to enhance both operational efficiency and product quality. He renovated the Chicago plant by adopting the latest machinery and mechanizing all aspects of production. So that workers could handle the new equipment, he held mandatory retraining sessions at night and on weekends. The result was a factory that, every minute, churned out 2,500 Snickers bars, fully packaged and ready for sale after passing through his new self-loading wrapping machines. These Snickers bars contained more peanuts and caramel than ever before thanks to an executive order from Forrest, who also increased the size of 3 Musketeers.[11] Forrest did not expand his candy bars out of generosity to consumers. Visually, the voluminous Mars products now enjoyed an advantage when placed alongside the thin rectangle that was the Hershey bar. "People walked up to the candy counter and they'd see this flat little Hershey bar for a nickel and right next to it, a giant Milky Way," a boastful Forrest Mars supposedly said before asking rhetorically, "Guess which one they'd pick?" The comparison was not entirely fair because the air in whipped nougat contributes to a Milky Way's bulk. Even so, Mars's comment points to a truth: he was determined to exploit any edge he held over his rival.[12]

In advertising, Mars wielded a massive advantage. In the postwar period, food companies pumped large sums into marketing, seeing it as the key to greater profits.[13] Mars jumped on the trend. Hershey did not. In 1948, Percy Staples, who succeeded M. S. at the helm, articulated a position on advertising that defined the company well into the 1960s. "We're no closer . . . to becoming an advertiser," Staples stated, because "we've simply never felt the need for it." "The Hershey spirit" and "Hershey products," an executive echoed, "are the company's best advertisements."[14] In stark contrast, Forrest Mars believed that his best advertisements were actual ads, and he budgeted accordingly—$30 million each year.[15] If Hershey executives were paying attention, they noticed that Mars advertisements adopted a familiar strategy. In one television commercial from the 1960s, a farm boy in a bucolic cow pasture munches on a Milky Way as the voice-over emphasizes the product's wholesome attributes: "A Milky Way is loaded with farm fresh milk and the whipped-up whites of country eggs. . . . And that's why we call Milky Way the good food candy bar."[16] Mars was blitzing the country with commercials that deployed the same strategy as M. S.'s bar cards: they encouraged consumers to associate a Milky Way with wholesome dairy farms.

Forrest Mars had revolutionized his father's company. But did his measures work? In his free time, Forrest would haunt retail establishments, examining shelf displays and purchasing his own products to confirm their quality. If anything were wrong, even something minuscule, employees would experience the wrath of the perfectionist owner. One night, after buying a bag of M&M's, he detected that part of the letter *M* had not printed properly on the candy shells. Apoplectic, Forrest telephoned an unfortunate plant manager at 3:00 a.m. to issue an ultimatum: either hustle to the factory to initiate an immediate product recall or accept termination.[17]

Employees at Mars came to expect this sort of behavior from their boss. Larry Johns, who worked in sales, described Forrest as a "unique person" who expected employees "to perform" and "insisted on the highest quality in all of his company's products." Though admiring his boss, Johns allowed that "Mars had quite a temper."[18] Bill Suhring in marketing was equally respectful of Forrest's gifts but less diplomatic when it came to that fierce demeanor. He described Mars as a "volcanic man" and "dictator" who gave his employees "gray hairs and ulcers." "He'd rush into the plant," Suhring recalled, "screaming at the top of his voice to the production workers that they produced crap." By acting this way, Mars lent the "impression he was unstable," Suhring explained, when in fact the opposite was true: "He was a very stable man." Though the workplace caused stress, Suhring conceded that Forrest—irascible but rational—"ran one heck of a company." That said, Suhring suspected that the man had no friends.[19]

But making friends had never been Forrest's driving purpose. Defeating Hershey was. By relentlessly pursuing this single objective, he achieved it. In 1966, Hershey enjoyed a substantial lead over Mars, selling annually

$150 million to Mars's $90 million. But Mars closed the gap with stunning rapidity. After just three years, Mars drew even.[20] Though Mars was clearly winning the competition, Forrest was acutely aware that his greatest advantage lay in the fact that his opponent—astoundingly—showed little awareness that a contest even existed. A lack of a competitive spirit seemed ingrained in Hershey's corporate culture. "Mr. Hershey never thought competitively," explained J. J. Gallagher, the general sales manager, in 1948. "He never wanted to get all the business, and we don't want to get it all today. We don't drive our men."[21] What if Hershey were to find ambition? After pondering this exact question, Forrest directed Bill Suhring to conduct a hypothetical study every year. The purpose: to figure out what would happen to Mars's market share if Hershey were to wake up and start advertising. "We were concerned," Suhring recalled, "that if the sleeping giant . . . ever flexed its muscle, it could cause chaos."[22]

The Sleeping Giant

At M. S.'s funeral in 1945, the patriarch's top brass processed behind the casket in order of seniority. Leading the way was Percy Staples, a loyal executive with an engineering background who had earned M. S.'s trust. As Staples assumed leadership of the company, he had big shoes to fill. That was because the "dynamic personality" of the man he was replacing had, in the words of Samuel Hinkle, "influenced almost every major decision made from 1903 to 1945." M. S.'s "insatiable drive," Hinkle elaborated, "sent his chocolate company into unchallenged first position, and his community to the status of America's Model Town."[23] Unfortunately, Staples's personality was anything but dynamic. Hinkle described him as an "introvert" whose "natural desires tended towards isolation" and who was reluctant even to attend local events and functions, such as company Christmas parties. Rather than relate to actual people, Staples hid himself away and obsessed over the global price of cocoa beans.[24] Gil Nurick said Staples had a "tortured mind" and treated employees only slightly better than "serfs." When Staples died in 1956, he was replaced by Samuel Hinkle, who, according to Nurick, was able to "humanize" the company's leadership. An approachable man with a hands-on style, Hinkle contrasted favorably with his aloof predecessor.[25]

Hinkle brought major change to some aspects of the operation while leaving others unaltered. In the early 1960s, he decided to build chocolate plants outside Hershey for the first time in the company's history. What prompted the bold move? The answer was simple economics. Though the cost of shipping products to the West Coast was both substantial and rising, those Hershey bars, when they reached store shelves, sold for the same five cents. Thus, transportation costs were eating into profits. "We knew we'd have to go to California someday," Hinkle recalled, because of the "shipping costs of our merchandise to the West Coast." Interestingly, the company built its first new plant not in California, but in Canada—Smiths Falls, Ontario. Hinkle explained the logic behind this decision. "Before we invested" in California, "we had to know whether we could make Hershey's chocolate out there." Hinkle characterized the factory in Canada as "an experiment" to determine whether duplicating the chocolate outside Hershey was possible. At first, tasters noticed a subtle difference in the flavor of chocolate produced in Canada. The issue was resolved, however, and Hershey opened a large plant in Oakdale, California, in 1965. Moving production out of Hershey was not the only change to take place under Hinkle. Two years earlier, he oversaw the acquisition of the H. B. Reese Candy Company, maker of the peanut butter cup.[26] After these two moves, a company long known for being a "one-product, one-plant firm" had transformed itself into a "multi-product, multi-plant corporate organization."[27]

These were important additions, to be sure. That said, Hershey still lagged behind in the business world. Using a computer analogy, one could characterize the company's problem as being one of software, not hardware. Hershey wielded plenty of industrial capacity with its multiple factories (that was the hardware). However, in the dynamic business climate of the 1960s, being able to mass-produce was no longer sufficient. The focus was shifting away from production and toward public relations, sales, marketing, and advertising (the software). Anyone who turned on a television, opened a magazine, or walked into a store could identify this trend. In 1960, the *Wall Street Journal* asked Hinkle why his company remained an outlier by refusing to advertise. "Our minds are not closed," Hinkle responded, but "we haven't convinced ourselves the time has come."[28] In reality, the time had long since passed. Something was holding Hinkle back. Richard Zimmerman, who worked under Hinkle, theorized that his boss had been shaped by the priorities of an earlier economy. Hinkle's formative experiences had occurred during the war, when the emphasis was squarely on production—how much can your factories produce? Since "one didn't worry about sales and marketing" back then, Zimmerman explained, Hinkle "never understood modern marketing." He had a producer's mentality. With this mindset, he invested heavily in new factories but did not even think to build a marketing department.[29]

Richard Zimmerman recalled an anecdote that epitomized the archaic nature of Hershey's business practices. In the early 1960s, Hershey did not bother to collect market information. As long as Hershey sold the candy it produced, why bother to track the competition? However, one employee, acting on his own initiative, decided to compile some industry data. His findings told a disturbing story: Hershey was steadily losing market share to Mars. When Zimmerman showed the numbers to Hinkle, the latter dismissed them as untrustworthy. "Well, nobody can believe those industry figures anyway," he said, brushing aside alarming data that would have pushed other executives into a panic. Zimmerman knew better. "I'm not sure [Hinkle] ever really did understand," he later reflected, "that the market was moving away from us."[30]

Zimmerman cited a second example, one involving the acquisition of Reese's, that also revealed how woefully behind the times Hershey had become. Though that acquisition stood as one of Hershey's successes, for Zimmerman it also exposed Hershey's backward business culture. After the deal was finalized, Zimmerman found himself telephoning the *Wall Street Journal* to give them the story. Though the call itself was not surprising, the strange part was that Zimmerman was the one making it. He was not in public relations. He was only contacting the press because *Hershey had no public relations office.* For Zimmerman, the anecdote crystallized Hershey's predicament: while other companies were hurtling into the future, Hershey remained stuck in the past.[31]

Dynamism was clearly lacking and stasis prevailing in a company unwilling to emerge from its founder's shadow. Executives based their decisions on what they guessed M. S. would do, not on what was best for the company. "A quarter century after his death," Hinkle wrote in the 1960s, "top level decisions are still weighed with deliberations as to how Mr. Hershey might have felt about them."[32] Though Hinkle wrote these words with pride, they were actually symptomatic of a major problem: Hershey had become too conservative. Having conducted business in the same way for decades, only a crisis could jolt the company out of complacency. That crisis had a name: Forrest Mars. As Mars rapidly gained, Hershey steadily lost. Between 1966 and 1968, Hershey's after-tax profits fell by over 20 percent, from $25 million to under $20 million. "Those were very difficult years for Hershey," said Jack Dowd, Hershey's sales promotion manager. "The company was not waking up to the fact that in Forrest Mars they had a huge new competitor."[33]

The Giant Awakens

The company did, at long last, wake up. Though Hinkle could not modernize the company, he hired two forward-looking people who could: Harold Mohler and Bill Dearden. Mohler brought rich life experience to Hershey. During World War II, he had been a navigator for a B-17 bomber (nicknamed the "Flying Fortress") and a prisoner of war in Germany. Trained as an engineer, Mohler served as Hinkle's assistant, impressing him with his business acumen. He played an instrumental role in the acquisition of the H. B. Reese Candy Company. When Hinkle retired, Mohler took the helm.[34] In Zimmerman's view, Mohler understood the gravity of the crisis and possessed the traits to lead Hershey into the "modern age." He called Mohler a "man of action" and a "people person" who grounded decisions in "common sense." Crucially, he was "deft at ascertaining trends."[35] Observing that the company was mostly white, Mohler worked hard to hire minorities. Mohler "was trying to be a little ahead of the game," one executive recalled, "so he was starting to work on diversity issues." Aware that women were entering the workforce in large numbers, Mohler tried to make it easier for a female employee to have a baby, take time away, and return to a job that had been held for her.[36]

Mohler also kept abreast of nationwide trends in sales, marketing, and public relations, and recognized that Hershey had fallen behind. To address the problem, he recruited young people with fresh perspectives and relevant skills. Unlike past hires, many of the new employees were not from Hershey and arrived highly credentialed with MBA degrees. It was Mohler who hired Jack Dowd. Raised in New England and educated at Harvard Business

School, Dowd epitomized Mohler's preferred outsider. Confident but not cocky, Dowd told superiors what he thought, even if his view challenged established practice. During the job interview, Mohler informed Dowd of the company's long-standing refusal to advertise. "I'm vividly aware of that," Dowd responded before uttering a bold prediction: "You're going to be advertising." Dowd, who had read up on Hershey, proceeded to lay out, point by point, the factors that would force Hershey's hand: it was losing market share, its new products were not selling well enough, and children were not buying their products as much as adults, an ominous fact that carried grim consequences for the future. After hearing Dowd's argument, Mohler did not commit to advertising, but he did offer Dowd the job.[37]

In hiring young people, Mohler worked closely with Bill Dearden. Dearden first came to Hershey in 1935 at the age of thirteen, when the premature death of his mother pushed his family into crisis. Unemployed and responsible for raising three children, Dearden's father made the hard decision to enroll his oldest child at the Hershey Industrial School, an institution that Dearden later credited with teaching him "self-reliance." As a boy, he spent part of each day milking cows, mopping floors, and washing dishes—and was grateful. "We thought Mr. Hershey was ten feet tall," he said reverentially, adding that, "because of him, we never thought of ourselves as poor orphans." Dearden described his graduation in 1940 as "one of the best days of my life" because M. S. himself, "always my hero," shook his hand. Dearden went on to serve in two wars and earn his MBA from Harvard before joining Hershey in 1957. Mohler and Hinkle recruited Dearden even though, the latter confessed, he did not "know anything about chocolate except that it was great to eat." Though Mohler and Dearden could not literally see eye to eye on anything (the 6'5" Dearden towered over his colleagues), the two made the same diagnosis of the company's ills and offered the same prescription. Hershey had lost market share, in Dearden's view, because "Mars was out-advertising us" and "out-hustling us." He and Mohler agreed that the solution was to "start a real marketing department" and "hire a lot of younger men in the sales force." Specifically, Dearden sought applicants "who were aggressive and wanted my job."[38]

Dearden's first recruit was John Rawley, a Harvard MBA and veteran of the Korean War, who arrived in 1964 with corporate experience at the Scott Paper Company. When Rawley set foot in Hershey, he felt as if he had entered a time machine. "My first perceptions" he recalled, "were that the business was largely being run as Mr. Hershey had left it." Though selling candy in "a changing economy" in a "changing world," Hershey had remained "stagnant." Modern practices that had been adopted everywhere else "were just not present." When Rawley tried to set clear objectives for the sales force, he learned to his astonishment that the company had sent the same letter out to sales agents for eleven straight years. But the problem was not just the stale letter; it was the absence of data. Without statistics capturing the present distribution of Hershey brands, it was impossible to ask agents to set goals for the future. How can you know where to go if you don't know where you are? To obtain data, Rawley pitched an idea to Dearden. What "we need very badly," he insisted, "is accurate information" on the nationwide "availability of your products at the retail level." Dearden agreed, and Hershey commissioned the A. C. Nielsen Company to perform market research.[39] Hershey was finally acquiring data. That was the good news.

The bad news was the data itself. After Nielsen submitted its report, Jack Dowd attended the meeting where the key findings were revealed. Given Mars's recent surge, everyone present had psychologically prepared themselves for disappointing numbers. However, what they heard that day was not just disappointing—it was shocking. Nielsen found that, nationwide, 30 percent of retail outlets that carried Hershey products were out of stock. For some time, Hershey executives had known that consumers were starting to choose Mars. What they now discovered was that their own products were often not even on shelves. "I'm going down with the *Titanic*," Dowd thought to himself. Anecdotal evidence corroborated Nielsen's findings. Dearden observed that at grocery stores in town, which should be Hershey's home turf, prominent displays of M&M's, 3 Musketeers, and Snickers eclipsed those of Hershey products. Larry Johns, hired in 1968, reported a similar issue at an A&P grocery store. At checkout, he observed handsome displays of Mars products. Where were the Hershey bars? After searching the aisles, he found them in the back of the store next to the kitty litter—old, broken, and covered with dust.[40]

But Johns remained optimistic. That was because, in his opinion, Hershey now had the right leadership to address the crisis. Still, Hershey had work to do if it were to keep pace with Mars. Johns knew Mars well, having worked in sales there for three years. "When I was with Mars," he remembered, "we didn't consider Hershey, in a sales sense, to be competition." Now at Hershey, Johns isolated the problem—the people.[41] There was a "dearth of talent," agreed Zimmerman, who described the sales team as "old tobacco salesmen" who perhaps "knew the territory" but were "burned out."[42] Austin Geiling, who had provided support for sales agents before Johns arrived, understood his job as "to keep the salesmen happy" and "functioning," but nothing more ambitious than that.[43] Johns aspired to greater things. He endeavored to overhaul the department by hiring energetic new people, phasing out unmotivated agents, and retraining those willing to learn. As part of that retraining, he emphasized modern sales techniques. "They didn't know a thing about market share" or "what it meant to actually be a salesman." They did not even grasp commonsense things, such as that Hershey bars should be placed at the eye level of a ten-year-old. By revamping the sales team, Johns hoped to guarantee that stores would have Hershey products in stock and properly displayed when the company finally started to advertise. "The fastest way to kill a product," Johns explained, "is to advertise it and have consumers out there looking for it and not finding it." But Johns was in sales. If Hershey were to venture into advertising, his colleague in marketing, Bill Suhring, would have to take the lead.[44]

Like Johns, Suhring had fled Forrest Mars's dictatorship. "Most all of us knew we didn't want to remain there," he said of Mars. Suhring worked under Dearden, whom he characterized as an "action-oriented philosopher." In his view, Dearden had formulated a bold vision to remake the sales department and open a marketing department. What is more, he possessed the "guts" to execute that vision in the face of resistance.[45] Astoundingly, many Hershey employees did not even know what marketing was. According to Jack Dowd, the salespeople that he and Johns tried to retrain thought marketing was "what their wives did . . . with a shopping cart." They also failed to comprehend the difference between marketing and sales. To enlighten them, Dowd explained using the simplest of terms: the purpose of sales "was to push" product into the store; the point of marketing "was to suck it out."[46] Though businesses employed a variety of marketing strategies, all understood advertising as indispensable to their success—all except the outlier in central Pennsylvania.

That changed on September 11, 1968. On this watershed date in Hershey history, the company finally decided to advertise.[47] After Dearden authorized Suhring to lay the groundwork, the latter compiled a "brand plan" for each product. That meant figuring out exactly who could be expected to purchase the product so that advertisements could target the right demographic. One had to know, in other words, whether to place an ad on "kids' shows" or in "senior citizens magazines." With respect to Reese's, Suhring discovered that a large percentage of Americans had never heard of the brand. "What an opportunity to tell them about it," he recalled thinking, "and stimulate sales." He knew that advertising could unleash the untapped consumer demand for the peanut butter cup.[48] To handle its initial foray into advertising, Hershey hired Ogilvy and Mather, a firm that had recently lost the Mars contract and was thrilled to pitch candy again.[49]

At first, Ogilvy generated advertising for four products, including the peanut butter cup. The earliest Reese's television commercials used slapstick comedy to educate viewers about the candy's two major ingredients—chocolate and peanut butter. One spot featured a silly man with a bow tie, absurdly eating peanut butter straight out of a jar with his fingers while walking through an urban construction site. Musing to himself about his love for peanut butter, he fails to notice an open manhole and falls in, crashing into a worker wearing a hardhat and holding a chocolate bar. "You got peanut butter on my chocolate!" accuses the construction worker. "You got chocolate in my peanut butter," counters the pedestrian. Though each man expresses annoyance, this turns out to be a happy accident. After sampling the novel combination, the two instantly recognize the synergy of chocolate and peanut butter. Of course, the combination is not novel at all. When a second construction worker materializes holding a package of Reese's cups, his self-satisfied expression conveys the ad's message: one can find the delectable treat in any store (fig. 6).[50]

It was clever, but was it effective? To measure the impact, Hershey ran this and similar commercials for six months in seven test cities. The rest of America, exposed to no ads, served as the control group. "As soon as we started advertising, the sales of Reese's took off," Dowd recalled. The ads "galvanized" people who "started buying the product."[51] When the sales figures rolled in, they vastly exceeded expectations. "There must be something wrong with that particular set of statistics," some Hershey people asserted,

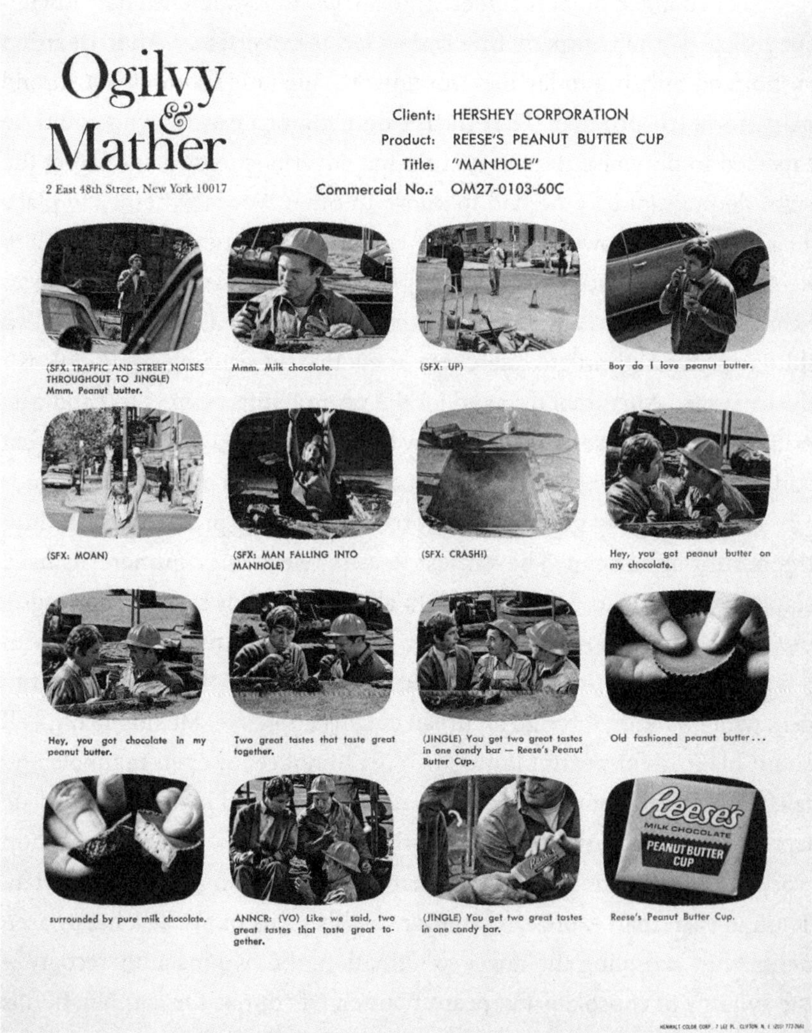

Fig. 6 Still frames from a 1969 Reese's television advertisement. Courtesy of HCA.

because "we've never seen anything that good."[52] Suhring, who reviewed the numbers with Dearden, described the latter as "scared that our tests were working so well." In the seven cities, Reese's sales surged 40 percent. The implications for a national campaign were obvious. "You replicate that nationwide," Suhring said, "and you've got quite an increase in everything. And by golly, it happened."[53] At long last, Hershey had leveraged the power of advertising.

The company modernized in other ways. In 1970, it hired Ken Bowers to handle public relations. Growing up nearby, Bowers had frequented Hershey Park as a child. Though holding a good position at AT&T, he was attracted by the "wholesomeness" of the chocolate company and the "wonderful community." He also was "impressed" that the company "was ready to make some changes in my very discipline." That said, change would not be easy. When he first arrived, he was told bluntly that "our policy is we really don't respond to the media." Bowers recalled that Hershey was not a "talkative company." But Hershey people did become extremely verbal when complaining about the media. They would often grouse about factual inaccuracies in stories in *Forbes* or *Business Week*. "It's just another example," they would gripe, "of why it doesn't pay . . . to be cooperative with these people." Though Hershey blamed the media, Bowers knew better: the company's nonexistent relationship with the press was at fault. Fortunately, this was a problem that Bowers was trained to fix. He set about doing exactly that by "pounding away" at his colleagues' resistance with a fresh idea. The more we "cooperate" with the press, he explained repeatedly, "the better our odds are of getting a more accurate . . . story." In this way, Bowers nudged Hershey out of its "low-profile" stance with the media.[54]

Finally, Hershey also invested heavily in computers. Samuel Tancredi, the son of Italian immigrants, started working for Hershey at the age of eight, picking up litter in Hershey Park. Showing initiative, Tancredi ascended through the ranks, eventually reaching the sales and records department, where he worked with early computer systems. When Hershey purchased an IBM System / 360 mainframe computer in 1966, Tancredi was the one who figured out how to operate it. Tancredi's mastery of the new technology allowed Hershey to hire the consulting firm Arthur Andersen to develop its first management information system (MIS). Working within the new MIS, Tancredi developed Hershey's first sales forecast, the importance of which could not be overstated. Tancredi explained that the sales forecast would allow Hershey to anticipate the demand for its products. Once demand was known, the company could determine how many finished goods to manufacture. With that figure, the company knew exactly how much it would need to procure in terms of commodities and packaging materials, how much warehouse space it would require, and how many workers it would have to hire. In this way, MIS allowed for a data-driven approach that could transform every aspect of the chocolate business.[55] Tancredi, Richard Bacastow recalled, "laid the groundwork for what is now an excellent information system."[56]

A "Traumatic Time for the Community"

Before the 1960s, Hershey executives seldom deviated from the status quo. Coming from the area and revering M. S., they lacked the will, desire, and training to challenge established practice within the company. In contrast, the new hires of the 1960s often hailed from somewhere else. As transplants, they had no memories of M. S., were not beholden to his vision, and lacked sentimental ties to the town. Even the new hires who had grown up in Hershey brought a fresh perspective because they had received their MBA degrees from institutions like Harvard or the Wharton School at Penn. "We were the first generation of people that had never worked for Milton Hershey," said one new executive, who described the transitional moment as a "baton-passing time."[57] Though the new hires respected M. S.'s legacy, they obeyed a different authority—their modern business educations. An observant resident who moved to Hershey in 1964 described the shift: whereas M. S. had been a "benevolent patriarch," the "people who are running the Hershey businesses now are businessmen, interested in business."[58] In making decisions, the new hires were not preoccupied with asking, "What would Milton Hershey do?" They knew that this question paralyzed the company by blocking innovation. As we have seen, this new generation shook up the company by embracing sales, marketing, advertising, public relations, and technology. They also—to the chagrin of the community—looked to discard archaic practices that were holding the company back.

In the 1960s, Hershey executives started to question the viability of the compact. For decades, Hershey Estates had either subsidized or offered freely snow removal, garbage collection, leaf pickup, utilities (telephone, water, and electricity), and a community center. Residents also enjoyed free tuition at Hershey Junior College thanks to the generosity of the M. S. Hershey Foundation. In the company's accounting records, many of these services and amenities appeared under the mundane title "Community Expense." In truth, they were not mundane at all. They held immense significance for town residents because, taken collectively, they constituted the company's obligation with respect to the compact. In other words, they set Hershey apart from all other towns. But should the company provide them in perpetuity?

That was the question that executives contemplated. In 1967, they asked Ken Wolfe to explore the issue from an accounting perspective. Wolfe epitomized the new kind of Hershey hire. From nearby Lebanon, Wolfe had spent many Sundays as a boy at Hershey Park. "We'd drive to Hershey," where "I'd get some ice cream," "go to the Fun House," and take in "a free band concert" under the "big shade trees." In short, Wolfe understood well the magic of the Perfect Hershey Day. Though his parents had blue-collar jobs (his father was a frequently laid-off mechanic for Bethlehem Steel), Wolfe attended Yale, where he paid his way by taking campus jobs. A football player, he was a member of the historic 1960 team—the last to win every game. After graduation, Wolfe served in the navy and studied at Wharton before returning to the area as a married man with two children—and no job. On the suggestion of his wife, he dropped by Hershey without an appointment. During this cold call, he found himself whisked away into interviews with Hershey's top brass—Mohler, Dearden, and Zimmerman. "What is this place?" he wondered. It turned out that Wolfe had walked through the door at precisely the right time—just after an accountant had retired. From Mohler's perspective, Wolfe possessed the right profile to help Hershey modernize. Since the company had grown too "inward-looking," Wolfe recalled, Mohler endeavored to hire "people from the outside with different perspectives." With his newly minted Wharton degree, Wolfe had gotten very lucky.[59]

For his first assignment, the company tasked Wolfe with investigating Community Expense. "I'm not sure anyone really knew precisely how big it was," Wolfe remembered, because the costs were spread out across multiple Hershey entities. To gather data, Wolfe had to visit numerous offices, which he did. After crunching the numbers, he shared with superiors his incontrovertible conclusion—Community Expense was costing Hershey a fortune. Leadership now knew the extent of the financial drain, but would it act? Wolfe was unsure. On the one hand, Hershey possessed an intensely conservative culture that Wolfe witnessed every day ("You did not take off your suit jacket all year long"). On the other hand, he understood the transitional nature of the present moment, a time when the "traditional ways of doing things" were "being challenged."[60] Richard Zimmerman, who scrutinized Wolfe's findings, acknowledged that "there were a lot of dollars . . . going into Community Expense." Zimmerman saw Community Expense as problematic for two reasons. First, he worried that outside shareholders would object to so many expenditures that did not enhance profitability. Second, he pointed to a demographic shift: whereas half of all residents had worked for the company when M. S. was alive, that number had dropped to one-third and was continuing to fall. "As fewer and fewer residents were employees," he explained, leaders started to question the free or subsidized services. Unable to justify the financial obligation, Hershey took the "major step" of jettisoning much of Community Expense.[61]

The job of divesting the company of these assets fell partly to Ned Book. From Cleveland, Ohio, Book arrived in 1968 with a background in hotel management. "I was this young whippersnapper," Book recalled, "from the outside world who came in here with these new ideas." As an outsider, Book observed that an "inbred laissez-faire, lackadaisical attitude" was preventing the company from competing. He found Community Expense especially alarming. "I couldn't fathom," he recalled, "that a company was so philanthropic that it supplied all these municipal services to the town." What appalled him most, however, was the town's privileged "attitude." Book encountered "old timers" who demanded special treatment because, as they were fond of saying, "my father had worked for Mr. Hershey." Perhaps the father did, but the son did not, and that was the problem. Residents behaved as if they were "entitled" to free services and happily invoked M. S. to defend their position, proudly asserting, "That's the way Mr. Hershey meant it to be." Book thought otherwise. Contesting their monopoly over a deceased man's unknowable plans, he argued that M. S.'s "intention" had never been "to supply free services to people who weren't working for his company." That was bad policy because it consumed capital that could be used to grow the business. The "die" having been "cast," Hershey moved to end its role as "the keeper of the community." It was this decisive action that effectively terminated the compact. For town residents, the decision delivered a painful blow. "It was a very traumatic time for the community," Book recalled, "when they were weaned off of all these municipal services."[62]

Weaning is exactly what Book tried to do. The company took measures to spare the community the jarring experience of losing the services all at once. Quoting Porky Pig, Harrisburg's *Patriot-News* explained that Hershey Estates was not abruptly cutting services and saying, "That's all folks." "They are moving slowly, trying to detach themselves gracefully from an untenable situation." Nevertheless, the newspaper understood the significance of the moment. "For many families in this unique community," the paper reported, "a benevolent era—dating back to the days of Milton. S. Hershey—is about to end."[63] In 1972, a correspondent for New York's *Newsday* focused on the diminished strength of the company's bond with the community. "As this process goes on," he wrote, "the company's grip on the town weakens, and the relations between the two gradually become dependent [only] on goodwill."[64] If the loss of the compact were not enough, the community was also contending with another major change that threatened to alter its identity.

Strangers from the Outside

Starting in the 1960s, the challenge posed by Mars forced Hershey to hire a new kind of employee—an outsider bearing an advanced degree. At roughly the same time, a second event accelerated the shifting demographics of the town: the establishment of the Milton S. Hershey Medical Center (HMC). The plan to erect a world-class medical facility in the fields outside a town famous for chocolate sprang from the mind of one man. "Unquestionably," recalled Gil Nurick, "the idea originated with Sam Hinkle."[65] The idea was "a pet of Sam Hinkle's," echoed Richard Zimmerman, who called Hinkle "a potent force behind its concept and execution." For years, Hinkle had harbored a fascination with medicine, one that intensified when he suffered a heart attack in the early 1960s. After this health event, he stepped back from day-to-day affairs at Hershey Chocolate and shifted his attention to the establishment of the HMC.[66]

Though the HMC was a colossal undertaking, Hinkle knew that money was not an obstacle. This was because the Hershey Trust had a rather enviable problem. After covering all expenses associated with the Milton Hershey School (the name of the school for orphans since 1951), the trust still produced a surplus year after year. To solve the "problem" of too much money accumulating, Hinkle posed to himself a variant of the town's most famous question: "What would Mr. Hershey have done had he seen that

Fig. 7 Milton S. Hershey Medical Center in 1967. Courtesy of HCA.

[money] mounting up?" The answer surprised no one. "My conclusion," Hinkle said, "was that he was so interested in relieving human suffering . . . that he would certainly approve . . . a fine medical school and teaching hospital." And just like that, the deceased patriarch had endorsed the idea.[67]

To oversee and manage the new facility, Hinkle chose Penn State, the only major university in the state that did not already operate a medical school. In April 1963, Hinkle broached the plan to Eric Walker, Penn State's president. In Hinkle's retelling, the skeptical Walker at first scoffed at an idea he deemed impossible. Yet when Hinkle dangled $50 million in start-up money before Walker, the latter's "eyes popped" and his tone changed. "That would be different," he said.[68] Almost immediately, wheels began to turn. In August, the *Patriot-News* announced the project. In November, Walker approved the site, a 120-acre plot of bucolic farmland. After a groundbreaking ceremony in 1966, the multiphase construction got underway. A few years later, a visiting Nobel laureate comically remarked that never before, when delivering a lecture, had he been able "to look out the window and see cows grazing in the pasture."[69] In truth, the location was peculiar: the HMC did not fit in with its pastoral surroundings (fig. 7).

The HMC's personnel seemed equally out of place, at least at first. As a giant magnet for the professional class, the HMC attracted a new kind of resident to Hershey: physicians, scientists, laboratory technicians, academic administrators, and nurses. In three ways, the newcomers altered the demographic complexion of Hershey. First, the HMC complicated the ethnic makeup of a town previously defined by a simple binary—Italians and Pennsylvania Germans. Dr. Eugene Jacques, the superintendent of schools, saw the diversity reflected in his student population. There were "people coming in from all over the world," he noticed, mixing with the "Pennsylvania Dutch and Italians."[70] According to ethnographer Peter Kurie, the HMC "recosmopolitanized the population" by bringing in "nonwhite and non-Christian citizens," including Jewish residents.[71] Second, the HMC precipitated an infusion of liberals into what had been a bastion of conservative politics. Bruce McKinney, a young manager at Hershey Foods whose wife was a Democrat, liked to joke that, before the HMC, there were just three Democrats in Hershey, and "she was one of them." Third, the HMC brought about a sudden infusion of white-collar employees into a town with a blue-collar identity. "All these people with professional backgrounds," McKinney recalled, moved in what the local population saw as "strange and mysterious ways."[72]

C. Max Lang did not consider his movements to be either strange or mysterious. That said, the HMC's first faculty member understood that newcomers like himself were upsetting the status quo. Hershey, he remarked, had always been a "very stable town where people were born, lived, and died." Along with staying put, they had come to depend on the company's free services. "The town's people felt that Hershey should provide everything," a local resident told Lang. Curiously, many residents—while demanding services—opposed the HMC, even though its hospital promised to offer first-class health care. Though that kind of thinking defied logic, Harold Mohler advised Lang not to expect logic. "There is nothing more difficult than explaining something to someone who isn't interested in understanding," Mohler said, adding that "it's much easier for the average person to be critical than to be logical." Lang figured out that the local opposition was directed less at the HMC itself and more at the people it attracted—outsiders like him. George Harrell, the first dean of the medical school, warned Lang that the community felt "considerable angst" about "outsiders" joining "their" community. Lang himself saw the community as an "extremely conservative," "tight knit social group" that was accustomed to "a town run their way." They worried that people with "new faces and ideas" would "transform their town."[73]

Lang hit the nail on the head. Town residents fretted that presumptuous outsiders would try to change the culture of Hershey. Howard Phillippy, an engineer at the factory, recalled hearing an "awful lot of criticism about Hershey not being the place it was with the advent of the Medical Center."[74] Robert Raffensberger, the fire chief, recalled townspeople moaning, "There goes the end of Hershey." The HMC, they felt sure, would "bring in a lot of people, and pretty soon they're going to be running the place."[75] Such fears were not entirely unfounded. In an effort to be proactive, George Harrell and his wife met with local clergy to help them prepare their congregations for the major changes. Having established medical complexes before, the Harrells understood the impact that the HMC would have. At the event, Mrs. Harrell confessed that she held "mixed feelings" as to what the HMC would do to "small-town Hershey." "There are going to be big changes here once the Medical Center comes," she warned, because "that small-town point of view" will have to give way to "an entirely different approach."[76]

Her admonition proved to be prophetic. The new residents showed neither reverence for Hershey's unique history nor deference to its established ways. There was an "influx of new people," recalled Dr. Jacques, and they did bring a "different approach" to community affairs that caused friction with the "old-line people" who were "content to let things continue as they had been."[77] "Obviously the Medical Center changed the demographics dramatically," agreed Zimmerman, "in terms of people's social conscience," their "demand for the arts," and their calls for "a better school system."[78] The new people wanted Advanced Placement classes in the schools, complained factory worker Philomena Castelli, and "started building fancy houses up in the hills."[79] According to Bruce McKinney, locals derisively referred to one construction site as "pill hill."[80] "There was really a division," McKinney remarked, "between these new people . . . wanting all these things" and the old residents who maintained that the newcomers "didn't have the right to demand . . . changes."[81] Robert Payne, who would later work for Hersheypark, saw the opening of the HMC as a pivotal and, sadly, divisive moment in Hershey's history. Whereas "everybody knew everybody" previously, "the whole town changed when the Med Center went in." The physicians and administrators, he elaborated, did not "have their heart in Hershey like" those who were "born and raised here." These self-asserting individuals forced change on the town before moving away "to chase their careers," leaving the community "stuck with their ideas." Payne clarified that he did not believe "everything should've stayed the way it was." That said, he did not approve of "certain things."[82]

The new residents refused to apologize for making demands and for insisting on improvements. In their view, an infusion of new thinking was exactly what was needed to jolt the community out of its complacency and dependency on the company. "I think that M. S. Hershey spoiled his people," one new resident opined. "You can see it now, the way they don't know how to take care of their own affairs." As newcomers clashed with established residents, it became clear that the most immediate effect of the HMC was to cleave the town in two: "Old Hershey" and "New Hershey."[83]

Hershey Boils Over

For decades, Hershey had enjoyed mostly peace and contentment. Starting in the 1960s, a community not accustomed to change was forced to accept an extra-large dose of it: Hershey Chocolate modernized its business practices, the HMC attracted new residents to town, and Hershey Estates terminated the compact. The collective effect of these changes was to spark outrage in the community. When Hershey Estates announced its decision to stop paying for streetlights, a crowd of "irate citizens" stormed a public meeting.[84] After the closing of Hershey Junior College, which had provided residents with a free education, anger boiled over. "They were up in arms," Dr. Jacques remembered, and public meetings were "jammed" with angry people.[85] Margaret Clark, a longtime Hershey resident who accepted the college's closing, recalled that others did not. People "were very upset about the Junior College," she said, to the point of becoming "unkind."[86]

Kindness was in short supply. Bruce McKinney noticed the upwelling of anger, which, he said, expressed itself through different channels.

Though Hershey did not have a newspaper at the time, people verbalized their outrage in nearby news outlets. "They were writing letters" to newspapers, McKinney recalled, referring to the *Patriot-News* and *Hummelstown Sun*. People not wishing to put pen to paper voiced their ire at community venues. They "would go to an organizational meeting of some sort," McKinney said—such as the Friends of the Library, the school board, or the Rotary Club—to protest, demand answers, or simply "vent." "Why are we doing this? Why are we doing that?" they would ask, when "we used to do it this way."[87] Though McKinney favored the new developments, he understood the community's reaction. "Anytime that you change what was passed down to you," he explained, "especially if you feel the change brought adverse effects, people struggle to adjust." Not only were local residents adjusting to new circumstances, but they also held negative perceptions of the changes being forced on them.[88]

The developments were so dramatic that they altered the town's identity. Ethnographer Peter Kurie interviewed a man named Brian who grew up in Hershey. After attending college out of state in the sixties, he chose to move back in the early 1970s because Hershey was "special": "I remembered what a wonderful place it was." Though he had been away for only a short period, these had been critical years of change. The Hershey he returned to was a different town. Though it remained pleasant, it had lost what had made it distinctive. "Hershey did not stay as special as when I grew up," he reflected, adding that his children saw the town as adequate, but "no more special than any other place."[89] Edward Tancredi also witnessed this transformation. Born in 1914, he worked in the chocolate factory for decades (his brother operated the IBM mainframes). "The town has changed tremendously," he said, "from when I was a youngster." How exactly? Using the analogy of a family, he said the community had always had a "daddy . . . taking care of everything." However, in the absence of that father figure, Hershey no longer behaved like a family. It had "lost its closeness."[90]

Conclusion

"Everybody really liked [Hershey] the way it was," Ned Book said of this tumultuous period in town history, "but it really couldn't stay that way."[91] What Book meant was that, in the 1960s, the combined pressure of multiple economic forces (most notably, that exerted by Mars) rendered change unavoidable. Though inescapable, all this change did profoundly alter life in Hershey, just as residents feared it would. It brought in strange new faces and voices, and it left the compact in tatters. But the biggest domino had yet to fall. In December 1971, Hershey Estates dropped a stunning announcement on a community already reeling: massive changes were in store for Hershey Park.

Chapter 3

The Disney Treatment

Throughout the summer of 1970, the Starlight Ballroom held Saturday-night dances that harked back to an earlier era. At these nostalgia-saturated events, parkgoers—most of whom were getting up in years—donned white linen suits and swing skirts and twirled under the stars while the music played. It was Hershey in the fifties all over again. On Labor Day, the Starlight held its final dance, after which the band stopped playing, the curtain dropped, and the dancers drove home.[1] At around this same time over at the Carrousel, the oscillating horses slowed to a halt and the calliope music faded to silence. Summer at Hershey Park was over. This year, however, it was not just the summer season that was drawing to a close. This was the end of Hershey Park as M. S. had conceived it.

The community received hints that change was afoot. A series of personnel moves suggested that Hershey Estates was preparing for something big. In 1971, the company asked Bruce McKinney to move over from Hershey Foods to help with the park. McKinney had no experience with amusement parks except that he liked to visit them.[2] He joined John O. Hershey (no relation to M. S.), who had been brought over from the Milton Hershey School, where he served as head. That same year, Estates hired an outsider, John Hart, to manage operations at the park. The addition of Hart aroused the community's suspicions. A popular theory held that the park's management was heading in a new direction and desired a fresh face.[3] That theory became more credible when, quite ominously, Hershey Estates erected fencing around the park's perimeter.[4] Large-scale change was coming.

Fig. 8 Bruce McKinney (*left*), Lou Santangelo (*center*), and John O. Hershey (*right*) describing the coming renovation at an informational event that followed the initial press conference. Courtesy of HCA.

On December 13, 1971, Hershey Estates made a major announcement at a press conference held at the Hershey Country Club. To say that the news jolted the community would be an understatement. In a room packed with journalists, John O. Hershey, Bruce McKinney, and John Hart stood before a banner that read, "Preview of the New: Destination Hershey" (fig. 8). Using pointers, the speakers directed the audience's attention to dozens of drawings and maps that helped the gathering visualize the substantial change that was to come. Hershey Estates intended to overhaul Hershey Park, converting the old amusement park into a "major cultural, entertainment and leisure-time complex." Specifically, it planned to sell off old rides or demolish them, install state-of-the-art attractions, fortify the fence encircling park grounds, charge admission, and lure tourists from Philadelphia, Washington, and New York. The redevelopment would consist of six phases spread out over five years. Hershey Park, the *amusement park*, was officially dead.[5]

Hersheypark, the *theme park,* was about to be born. Later that day, the *Harrisburg Evening News* reported that Hershey Estates intended to construct a theme park, "second only to Disneyland and Disney World."[6] A relatively new form of amusement, the theme park burst onto the American scene with Disneyland's sensational opening in 1955. With its elaborate theming, Disneyland would serve as the model not just for Hersheypark but for the many regional theme parks that followed in its wake. Of course, Hersheypark's new themed attractions would require plenty of space. To make room, Hershey Estates scheduled demolitions for structures that rested on land needed for the redevelopment. The list of casualties, the *Evening News* reported, included a beloved venue from the park's golden age: "Plans call for the historic Starlight Ballroom to be razed." Though the structure was not demolished until 1977, that last dance on Labor Day symbolized the end of an era.[7]

What to Do with Hershey Park?

In the 1960s, Hershey executives agreed that the park's best days lay in the past. Ned Book described the facility as "an iron park with a bunch of clanging rides and some picnic space." In Book's opinion, the very attribute the community cherished most—that the park was free and open—contributed to its poor condition. "If you don't put the fence around it" and "charge admission," Book explained, "you never generate the revenue to maintain" the park, and it predictably suffers. He also bemoaned the fact that "hordes of people" routinely descend on the park, "don't pay anything," and leave behind "trash."[8] The park's openness also prompted safety concerns. Since people could enter from multiple points and at any time, including at night, park security never knew who was inside the park and what they were doing. Vandals could easily destroy property and abscond without getting caught. In fact, that happened. In 1964, the park received negative publicity after a group of teenagers damaged several rides. Though the park hired more security officers and issued them walkie-talkies, acts of vandalism succeeded in damaging the park's reputation. Some families stopped visiting because they no longer viewed the park as a safe and wholesome environment. As the sixties drew to a close, the halcyon days of Hershey Park appeared to be over.[9]

"You reach that Y in the road," summed up Ned Book, when you ask yourself, "What do you want to be?"[10] It was the right question to ask, but not an easy one to answer. Behind closed doors, Hershey leaders debated three pathways forward. "The alternatives" for the park, Bruce McKinney remembered, were to "close" it, allow it to "deteriorate," or "invest" in it.[11] Facing a difficult choice, Arthur Whiteman, the head of Hershey Estates, decided to put someone he trusted in charge of the situation. He summoned Dr. John O. Hershey and asked him to investigate the park because he was receiving "complaints" about "how dirty" it was. Hershey had played a substantial role in establishing the HMC. As head of the Milton Hershey School, he had also worked with Gil Nurick to change the institution's deed of trust to allow Black orphaned boys to attend. Though able to handle big jobs, Hershey did not claim any expertise in this area: "What do I know about a park?" The dutiful Hershey nevertheless accepted his assignment. After surveying the grounds, he realized that he could not make an informed decision without comparing Hershey Park to other venues. "I'd like to go look at some of the other parks," he told Whiteman, "and see how things are done there." Hershey flew to popular tourist destinations, asked "all kinds of questions" to the "top people of different parks," and dictated his observations into his pocket recorder. After returning home, he advanced a fourth alternative. "What we ought to do," he suggested, "was to get a consulting firm . . . to do a feasibility study." A feasibility study for what exactly? To determine whether Hershey should not just upgrade the park, but also invest "many millions of dollars to *redo* the park."[12]

Following Dr. Hershey's advice, Hershey Estates commissioned a feasibility study. It hired Economic Research Associates (ERA), a firm founded by Harrison "Buzz" Price, which Dr. Hershey had learned about during his travels. Buzz Price had played a seminal role in the emergence of the theme park industry. After graduating from Stanford Business School, Price stayed on campus to work in the economics division of the university's consulting firm, Stanford Research Institute (SRI). In a stroke of luck, SRI assigned Price to handle Walt Disney's new project in 1953. Walt had requested a feasibility study for a new kind of entertainment complex that he hoped to build in Southern California. After the success of Disneyland, Walt wished to have Price at his disposal for future projects. In 1958, he helped Price found ERA, with the understanding that he could retain Price's consulting services as needed. According to Price, the "endorsement" from Walt Disney "was the ultimate seal of approval." As other entrepreneurs sought out Price's services, ERA attracted all the business it could handle. In just eight years, a company that had started with just two employees expanded to seventy-five. By the time Dr. Hershey came calling, ERA had established itself as the industry leader in theme park feasibility studies.[13]

In March 1971, ERA delivered its report. To say that it was eye-opening would be an understatement. ERA set the total cost of the renovation at a hefty $21.7 million. Though clearly a daunting figure, this investment would, ERA claimed, "provide for a park with higher capacity and quality than existing comparable theme parks for approximately the same cost." In short, Hershey would own a major asset: a theme park superior to what anyone else had (excluding Walt Disney). ERA next situated this hypothetical park in Hershey's geographic region—and that was when the magic happened. It placed Hershey at the center of four concentric circles: its primary market (people living 0–50 miles away), secondary market (50–100 miles), tertiary market (100–150 miles), and tourist market (150–200 miles). ERA then compared the populations from which Hershey would draw with those of existing theme parks, such as Cedar Point (near Cleveland) and Six Flags Over Georgia (Atlanta). Though the Ohio and Georgia parks edged out Hershey in the primary-market category, Hershey enjoyed massive advantages in the secondary, tertiary, and tourist markets due to its proximity to major cities: Baltimore, Philadelphia, Washington, and New York. Thanks to these "untapped northeastern markets," Hershey theoretically enjoyed access to fifty-four million people, far more than either Cedar Point (twenty-five million) or Six Flags Over Georgia (thirteen million). Given Hershey's advantageous geography, ERA estimated that Hersheypark would attract 1.3 million visitors in 1973, 2.2 million in 1977, and 2.6 million by 1982. In terms of total revenue, Hershey would reap $7.4 million in 1973, $15.4 million in 1977, and $20.6 million by 1982. Though operating expenses would consume roughly half these earnings, the numbers were still jaw-dropping. According to projections, Hershey would break even after only six years. Through statistics, ERA painted a pleasing portrait of promise, profits, and possibility.

If Hershey executives needed any more incentive, they received it when they read ERA's ominous warning regarding the consequences of nonaction.

The amusement park landscape, ERA explained, had recently undergone a seismic shift. By effecting a "quantum jump in quality expectations" among parkgoers, Disney had created a hostile environment for old-style amusement parks. Out west, Disney had spawned imitators, theme parks that followed the Disney model but on a smaller scale. In just a few years, these had driven traditional amusement parks into bankruptcy. The same story was unfolding in the East. "This phenomenon is apparently emerging in the East coast," too, ERA stated ominously, with Disney World in Florida and the planned openings of theme parks in Pennsylvania and Virginia. Before long, ERA predicted, eastern amusement parks, "as they now exist, will suffer." Given these trends, ERA concluded that "Hershey Park is almost forced to upgrade its facilities." If it did, the forecast looked bright: "Hershey Park could easily become one of the dominant recreational parks in its region." If it did not, the park faced a bleak future.[14]

John O. Hershey hoped to forestall this "bleak future." Though he surely found ERA's data-driven recommendation persuasive, he also factored in the perspective of local residents who had formed strong emotional bonds to Hershey Park over decades. Dr. Hershey understood, Bruce McKinney remembered, that the park "had a rich heritage" and "to let it go would be to put a stamp of negative feeling within the community." He preferred to "close it" than to keep it open as a "deteriorating hard-iron amusement park."[15] Of all the alternatives, closing the park presented the easiest and least expensive option. For this reason, some executives made the case for closure. "If it's going to take too much money," they advised, "then let's just . . . fold it up."[16] McKinney opposed closure on the grounds that the park was the heart of the town. "We can't let Hershey Park just go," he said, because "the economic heartbeat would fail."[17] In the end, Dr. Hershey favored renovation, even though this move would come with a "pretty high price tag."[18]

Hershey executives understandably worried about the cost—over $21 million. "I don't know how this thing is going to be financed," one of them fretted. Surprisingly, Hershey Estates came up with the capital for the renovation because the sale of Hershey's utilities—part of the larger dismantling of M. S.'s paternalism—was generating revenue. "The park needed this infusion of cash," McKinney recalled, and "a lot of it was . . . coming from the sale of the utilities." In short, Hershey Estates was experiencing a onetime financial windfall thanks to the termination of the compact, "and the park was the beneficiary."[19] In the end, Hershey Estates decided to take the plunge into the theme park business.

The Prototype

Richard Zimmerman once half-jokingly argued that Hershey Park should aspire to "out-Disney Disney."[20] Though that was an unrealistic goal, Hershey did attempt to hew to Disneyland's model while also producing something distinct. What exactly was Disneyland, and how was it different from an amusement park? Buzz Price pondered these very questions during that fateful 1953 meeting with Walt Disney in which the latter tried to put his ineffable vision into words. "Walt described what he had in mind," Price recalled. "It sounded strange, unlike anything you would expect in an amusement park."[21] That's because it wasn't an *amusement park*. It was a *theme park*. However, Disney could not simply say "theme park" because the term did not exist (it first appeared in 1958).[22] America had amusement parks—many of them, in fact—but nothing else. As Walt explained the mysterious place, Price struggled to comprehend the concept. From what he could gather, it seemed to be a "park based on an unnamed new approach."[23]

That new approach would revolutionize the amusement industry. Before an incredulous Buzz Price, Disney proceeded to sketch the hypothetical park's layout. Walt imagined a 160-acre complex, sequestered from the outside world by a high dirt berm and encircled by an old-fashioned railroad. Visitors would enter through a single location, a themed area resembling a turn-of-the-century Main Street. From there, they would venture out into "four thematic activity areas" that Walt named the "World of Tomorrow, Fantasyland, Frontierland and Adventureland." In these themed zones, guests would not find any of the standard amusement park rides, like a Ferris wheel or a tunnel of love. Walt did not even want a rollercoaster or, for that matter, any thrill rides at all. He was "committed," Price learned, "to creating a storytelling environment." Given this vision, all rides and attractions would have to be "customized" to fit their respective stories. Walt's park had other novel features. Unlike many amusement parks, it would be completely safe, immaculately clean, and beautifully landscaped. Guests would stay for about eight hours, far longer than the typical outing to an amusement park, and they would spend triple the money. What Walt had imagined was a prototype for a new kind of entertainment.[24]

Once Price grasped the vision, he faced an immediate challenge. How could he generate a feasibility study for a tourist destination that had no precedent? To gather data, Price studied zoos and amusement parks, the closest things to comparable venues he could think of. He also traveled to Chicago to attend the annual convention of amusement park owners. His plan: to solicit the opinion of industry leaders. Using caviar as bait, he lured four prominent park owners to his hotel room, where he delivered a two-hour "dog and pony show" on Walt's new concept. After he finished, the four men rendered a unanimous verdict: "It would not work." When asked to provide reasons, the owners followed with constructive criticism. First, they wondered why, if the goal was to make money, Disney omitted "proven moneymakers" like amusement park rides, hot dog carts, beer stands, and carnival games. Visitors would surely "leave with money left in their pockets" when the goal was to fleece them. Second, the group questioned the logic of installing unique rides, each one customized at tremendous cost, when "off-the-shelf rides are cheap" and "the public doesn't know the difference." Third, they noted that the Main Street was "loaded with things" that require upkeep but "don't produce revenue," like the town hall, fire station, and horse-pulled carriages. Main Street was also problematic because, as the park's sole entrance, it was sure to cause a "terrible bottleneck." Fourth, the group lambasted "Walt's screwy ideas about cleanliness" and "landscape maintenance." His obsession with these expensive priorities that "customers never really notice" was tantamount to "economic suicide." In sum, Disney was breaking every rule in the book. He was sure to "lose his shirt." It was, in Price's words, a "chilling evaluation." Devastating though the feedback was, it did not deter Disney, who quickly "brushed it off" and forged ahead. As for Price, he harbored serious doubts about the project. "I failed to grasp," he recalled, "that a revolution . . . was underway."[25]

It would take more than courage and creativity to launch this revolution. Walt would require capital—and lots of it. In a brilliant move, he reached an agreement with ABC to put Disney content on television. It was a mutually beneficial deal that dramatically improved the fortunes of both companies.

In the early 1950s, ABC lagged behind rival networks CBS and NBC. The Disney partnership gave ABC programming from the most creative force in children's entertainment. In exchange, Walt Disney received the money to complete the construction of Disneyland. Finances aside, Walt benefited in one other way. Since the first television show would air ten months before Disneyland was scheduled to open, Walt could use television to promote his creation.[26] "I saw that if I was ever going to have my park," Walt said, "here, at last, was a way to tell millions of people about it—with TV."[27]

Thanks to this partnership, Americans first encountered Disneyland not as a physical space, but as a TV show. This fact was significant because it meant that Disneyland—before it assumed its physical form in concrete, steel, wood, and fiberglass—would exist in children's imaginations as an intangible realm of myth, folklore, and fantasy. Disneyland became, in Michael Sorkin's phrasing, an "anti-geographical space."[28] In the first episode of *Walt Disney's Disneyland*, which aired in October 1954, Walt explained the park's duality to young viewers. "You'll find that Disneyland the place and Disneyland the TV show are all part of the same," he said. As an "amusement park, an exhibition, a city from the *Arabian Nights*, a metropolis of the future," and "a place of hopes and dreams, facts and fancy," Disneyland "will be unlike anything else on this earth."[29] In the ten months that followed, Walt shrewdly used his television presence to build anticipatory excitement for Disneyland.

During those months, construction at Disneyland proceeded on a tight schedule. Overseeing the project as general manager was Buzz Price's former boss at SRI—a mercurial man named C. V. Wood. Price described Wood as a mathematical wizard. He could "estimate space, time, velocity, volume, revenue, cost and frequency and other physical variables," Price claimed, "with a mental arithmetic that was quick as a flash."[30] Wood somehow completed the park on time and under budget.[31] On July 17, 1955, the ten-month buildup reached a crescendo with the long-awaited opening. In this nationally televised live event, Walt unveiled the finished product. Ninety million Americans, just over half the population, tuned in to watch the spectacle.[32] In the months and years that followed, Disneyland would exert a powerful magnetism, pulling to Southern California millions of vacationers who were eager to experience the wonderland they had seen on television.

The Disneyland Model

Walt Disney had created a new model for entertainment. Since the designers of Hersheypark would borrow heavily from this model, we need to both define it and ascertain the secret of its immense power and appeal. Some conceive of Disneyland as the next progression in the evolution of the amusement park. In other words, it offered a bigger and better version of what one could experience at Coney Island or Hershey Park. But this line of thinking overlooks one crucial fact—Walt Disney disliked amusement parks. When he visited Coney Island, the filth, tough-looking carnies, and "tawdry rides" repulsed him. According to historians Gary Cross and John Walton, the amusement park provided the unattractive "other" against which "Disneyland could be defined by contrast." The amusement park was not the precursor to Disneyland but rather its "photographic negative."[33]

It is far more fruitful to conceive of Disneyland as the most advanced phase in the continuing evolution of the story. For millennia, human beings have been telling stories, often in the form of myths or legends, to entertain themselves and understand their world. According to David Younger, who studies themed environments, the advent of the book meant that humankind no longer needed to tell stories orally; they could now be transmitted "through words on a page." In the twentieth century, the cinema carried the story into a new medium, "moving images on a screen." This progression culminated with the theme park, which "tells stories with created environments" that one can physically enter.[34] In sum, the best way to comprehend Disneyland is to see the motion picture—and not the amusement park—as its most immediate antecedent.

In the 1950s, Walt Disney was ready to take the bold leap into an entirely new medium. Though he excelled at telling stories for the big screen, he had become bored with making movies.[35] John Hench, a Disneyland designer, claimed that Walt had seen "the limits of motion pictures." "As you sit in a darkened [theater]," Hench elaborated, "you have a kind of vicarious experience" that, while entertaining, is "not the same as if you actually walked down the street yourself." Seeking a more immersive experience, Walt envisioned Disneyland as a "three-dimensional film," where the guest could step inside a fantasy and become the main character. To create this novel "kind of reality," Disneyland would require a new category of artist-technician. Buzz Price coined the name "Imagineer" by fusing *imagination* with *engineer*—and the nomenclature stuck. Nearly all of Disneyland's Imagineers moved from the movie studio, where they had previously worked as set designers, architects, special effects experts, and art directors. "All of us came from motion pictures," Hench recalled. "That's the reason the park is what it is, like stage design." Indeed, Walt and his Imagineers conceived of Disneyland as a "series of stories" where guests would move through a "logical flow" of storyboarded "scenes."[36] In its daily operations, Disneyland even adopted film and theater terminology to help all parties involved understand their roles: "stage managers" referred to a "script" when directing "cast members" (costumed employees), who were either "onstage" (visible to guests) or "backstage" (in a restricted area).[37]

In 1955, Disneyland had the unique ability to place visitors in a convincing cinematic environment. More than anything else, this storytelling capability is what distinguishes it—a theme park—from the amusement park, which depends heavily on rides. "Theme parks are cultural mind maps," note Margaret King and J. G. O'Boyle, "symbolic landscapes built as storyboards of psychological narratives." As a result of this focus on stories, "a theme park without rides is still a theme park," but "an amusement park without rides is a parking lot with popcorn."[38] At great cost, Walt Disney had constructed elaborate symbolic landscapes. But to what purpose? One possibility is simple escapism: Disney captivated guests by transporting them from their everyday lives into a realm of fantasy. But Disney's own Imagineers rejected this theory. "Entertainment is usually thought of as an escape from problems," observed Hench, but "what we are selling is not escapism but reassurance." Disneyland, Hench and others contended, helped people feel reassured about themselves, their values and beliefs, and American ideals and traditions.[39]

That the park offered reassurance acquires special meaning when we remember its historical context—the Cold War. In the 1950s, both Democrats and Republicans reached a consensus that prevailing over the Soviet Union eclipsed all other national priorities. The Cold War would be fought on many different fronts. Most obviously, the high-stakes contest would require the United States to invest heavily in arms production and space exploration. However, there was also a social and cultural front. The Soviet Union's emphasis on using propaganda to promote the superior way of life under communism pressured the United States to respond with its own messaging, highlighting the advantages of capitalism. To compete, the United States needed to present to both its own citizens and the world a convincingly attractive image of the national character and American way of life. "Americans felt compelled to mount a countervailing crusade to identify a distinct vision of the good society," writes historian Steven Watts, and showcase a positive version of "American history, the American character," and the nation's "bedrock values." It was in this "process of national self-definition" that Walt Disney contributed to the Cold War agenda.[40]

Though Disney trumpeted American values in movies and television shows, his theme park surpassed all other cultural forms in terms of its rhetorical power. Steeped in patriotism, Disneyland sought to persuade visitors to embrace Walt's ardent belief in America. "As visitors moved through Disneyland," Watts writes, they "encountered a series of populist political emblems that . . . reinforced an American way of life" and "promoted an unproblematic celebration of the American people and their experience."[41] There was nothing subtle about it. Indeed, Walt Disney himself pointed to Disneyland's pro-Americanism. "There's an American theme behind the whole park," he explained. "I believe in emphasizing the story of what made America great and what will keep it great."[42] In Disney's opinion, America's past made it great. Disney emphatically stated that he wished not merely to "entertain kids" but to help them "learn something about their heritage."[43] He accomplished this goal with two themed realms—Main Street, USA, and Frontierland—both of which depicted the past in an uncritical light. He based the former on Marceline, Missouri, the small town where he had spent several formative years as a child. "Many of us fondly remember our small hometown and its friendly way of life at the turn of the century," Disney remarked. "To me, this era represents an important part of our nation's heritage."[44] With Frontierland, he brought to life the mythic West, a colorful realm of pioneers, cowboys, Indians, trading posts, forts, and log cabins from the past.

But the past was not truly past. What was paradoxical about Disney's reconstructions of history was that, unlike a museum exhibit, they were *not* retrospective—they were forward-looking. That was because the two themed areas inculcated what Disney had identified as traditional American values. Main Street promoted hard work, thrift, family, and community; Frontierland celebrated freedom, rugged individualism, and the pioneering spirit. These values took on politically charged meanings in their Cold War context. Though formed in the past, the values enjoyed renewed relevance in the present. They distinguished Americans from Russians, Disney believed, and would help the United States win the Cold War. In terms of their political purpose, Main Street and Frontierland dovetailed with Tomorrowland, where Disney projected confidence in the nation's technological future. Through attractions such as Rocket to the Moon and Autopia, Disney sought to inspire young people to embrace science, an educational priority that took on added significance given the exigencies of the Cold War. The rising generation of scientists, technicians, and engineers would play a critical role in helping the United States outpace the Soviet Union.[45]

Though children encountered pro-American content in many places in the 1950s, it was more likely to sink in at Disneyland. The park had a powerful effect on people, children in particular, rendering them more receptive to ideological messaging. The experience left guests feeling as if they had been transported to another time and place, such as the Old West. In his dedication to Frontierland, Disney boldly promised that the "adventures" will "give you the feeling of having lived . . . during our country's pioneer days." As a result, "all of us, whether 10th generation or naturalized Americans, have cause to be proud of our country's history." Frontierland, Disney believed, could instill national pride in guests, even those whose families were new to the country. Was this true? Cross and Walton argue that the immersive nature of Disneyland intensified the absorptive power of its pro-American message. For children, a trip to Disneyland did not merely "teach a patriotic and moral lesson" in the same vein as "social studies classes," through which children were known to snooze. Operating at a deeper psychological level, Disneyland accomplished something profound: it engendered in youth a "socially binding emotion." Young people exited the park differently from how they had entered it, changed by their experiences. They were more optimistic, patriotic, and invested in the nation's Cold War mission.[46]

For adults, Disney's historically themed areas evoked nostalgia, but even this emotion had a present-day purpose. For instance, the point of Main Street was not simply to tempt older visitors to yearn for yesteryear. Main Street was themed to resemble Victorian America, explained John Hench, "which is probably one of the great optimistic periods . . . where we thought progress was great and we all knew where we were going." However, when one visited Main Street, one did not feel nostalgia for turn-of-the-century towns because, as Hench pointed out, "there was never a Main Street like this one."[47] Unlike a real Victorian town, Main Street was clean, perfect, and built on a reduced scale. "We had every brick and shingle and gas lamp made five-eighths true size," Walt explained. "This cost more, but made the street a toy, and the imagination can play more freely with a toy."[48] So what were people feeling nostalgia for? Hench knew the answer. Main Street, he contended, "reminds you of some things about *yourself* that you've forgotten." Guests remembered a time when they had been young, hopeful, and optimistic about their nation's future. By having this effect, Main Street reassured people about themselves and the promise of America.[49]

Americans of all ages loved Disneyland, with many hailing it as "one of the wonders of the modern world."[50] In the years that followed the opening, Disneyland exceeded SRI's expectations in all quantifiable categories. After just six months, the park celebrated its millionth visitor, well ahead of schedule. By 1960, the annual number of guests topped five million; that number reached ten million a decade later.[51] To keep the millions of visitors happy, Disneyland added close to five thousand employees between 1955 and 1970. According to a survey that Disney conducted, these guests were actually happy inside Disneyland. In 1959, 98.6 percent of visitors expressed satisfaction with their experience, and 83 percent stated their intention to return.[52] No amusement park could elicit an overwhelmingly positive response like this.

These contented parkgoers were likely to consume other Disney products. That is because the stories and characters that children adored at Disneyland could be enjoyed again in other formats—all of them purchasable. Thanks to the company's interlocking nature, Disney enjoyed a true synergy: each sector enhanced the profitability of the others. For example, a child who visited Sleeping Beauty's castle at Disneyland could watch the movie *Sleeping Beauty* (1959), play with a Sleeping Beauty doll, read the Sleeping Beauty storybook, and listen to the Sleeping Beauty phonograph record. "Integration is the key word," Roy Disney told the *Wall Street Journal.* "We don't do anything in one line without giving a thought to its likely profitability in our other lines."[53] These synergies led to rapidly escalating profits. In

1954, the company's gross income stood at $11.6 million. In 1955, the year Disneyland opened, that number more than doubled. In 1959, gross income surged to a staggering $58.4 million. In Steven Watts's words, Disneyland was the "command center linking together . . . the studio's myriad projects in television, movies, music, and merchandising." Its seductive power persuaded millions of families to make an expensive pilgrimage to Anaheim.[54] The centerpiece of a moneymaking empire, Disneyland inspired entrepreneurs elsewhere to dream about replicating its success.

Parks Proliferate

In 1956, Roy Disney fired C. V. Wood, jettisoning one of the key individuals responsible for bringing Disneyland into existence. Since the Walt Disney Company seldom invokes the name C. V. Wood today, the rationale behind his dismissal remains cloaked in mystery. One possibility is that, after Disneyland opened, Wood ruffled Walt's feathers by claiming too much credit for the park's success.[55] "Two egos don't easily co-exist," speculates Barry Hill, a theme park historian, "and Walt couldn't take it anymore."[56] As another possibility, the Disney brothers may have viewed Wood as too slick for their family-oriented brand. Although Buzz Price admired Wood's abilities, he conceded that there was a touch of the con artist in him. "He was one of the strangest, damnedest, boldest, smartest, most shameless and colorful characters ever to careen through this business," Price observed. "He walked in the worn footpath of P. T. Barnum." Wood liked to share tips to help others impress business associates. When delivering a presentation, for example, one should always "bring a big stack of books." "It can be the Mexican Mining Laws of 1924 but bring a big stack." "Always walk fast," Wood also advised, so that "they'll think you are doin' something."[57] Whatever the reason, Disney parted ways with the man the Associated Press dubbed "space-age Barnum."[58]

Wood did not walk away empty-handed. After all, his résumé included the most magical phrase in the entertainment business: "master planner and builder of Disneyland."[59] Wood shrewdly leveraged his Disneyland credential, using it as a springboard to new business opportunities. In 1956, he founded his own company, Marco Engineering, hung out a shingle, and waited for clients. He did not have to wait for long. In the wake of

Disneyland's triumph, entrepreneurs dreamed about transplanting Walt's model in their region.[60] Wood won clients because he was the only person on the planet, other than Walt himself, who could claim expertise in theme park development. According to Buzz Price, Walt Disney may have "revolutionized" the theme park industry, but it was C. V. Wood who carried the vision into the "backcountry," where it could be "sold to the unsuspecting like snake oil." In the late 1950s, Marco secured contracts to build the first three regional theme parks: Magic Mountain (Colorado), Pleasure Island (Massachusetts), and Freedomland (New York). All three eventually filed for bankruptcy, though the latter two managed to hold on for several years before closing. Though each park had unique problems, their failures followed a common pattern: the parks promised an experience rivaling Disneyland but lacked the resources to deliver it. In short, they were overpromoted and undercapitalized. The early theme park industry, Price stated bluntly, was defined by "a harsh learning curve."[61]

Fortunately, theme park development improved after early misfires. Randall Duell, one of Marco's first hires, used each project to hone his craft. Duell's early childhood mirrored that of Walt Disney himself. Born in 1901, Disney enjoyed five idyllic years in Marceline, Missouri, a small agricultural town, before the family moved to Kansas City in 1910.[62] Similarly, Randall Duell was born in 1903 on a farm in rural Kansas, where the family lived for nine years before moving to California in 1912.[63] Thanks to their parallel childhoods, Duell and Disney understood small-town America and the difficult adjustment anyone faced when moving to the city. Their experience aligned with a larger demographic shift in America that saw millions transition from the farm to the city. Indeed, the 1920 census revealed that, for the first time, more Americans lived in urban areas than in rural ones.[64] In 1925, Duell graduated from the University of Southern California with a degree in architecture. When the Great Depression wiped out most construction projects, Duell turned to Hollywood, where he found work as an art designer for MGM. For more than two decades, he designed sets for movies, compiling a résumé that included *Singin' in the Rain* (1952) and *Blackboard Jungle* (1955).[65] With Disneyland's success in 1955, the prescient Duell predicted that there would be growing demand for creative people with his skills in the embryonic theming industry. In 1956, he joined Marco Engineering and, in the ensuing years, worked at both Pleasure Island and Freedomland. Though neither park survived, no one blamed Duell.[66]

At Pleasure Island, Duell designed multiple themed environments, some of which borrowed from Disneyland's example. For instance, there was a Main Street and a Western City, where one could ride the Old Smokey Railroad or the Old Chisolm Trail, a dark ride that featured a gunfight and hanging. Though Pleasure Island imitated Disneyland in some respects, Duell also created unique theming that drew from New England's regional culture—specifically, its maritime history and literary heritage. He designed Clipper Cove, where one could slurp a bowl of clam chowder, to resemble a New England fishing village. The Moby Dick Hunt, a ride inspired by Herman Melville's classic novel, climaxed with a terrifying encounter with the white whale, which rose majestically out of the water. The Wreck of the Hesperus, a dark ride based on Henry Wadsworth Longfellow's famous poem, carried guests out to sea, where a violent storm sent them to the watery depths, a fantastic realm ruled by Neptune. At the park's center, Duell placed a towering structure, Hawkes Point Lighthouse, which gave Pleasure Island its eye-catching symbol, much like Sleeping Beauty's castle in Disneyland. Pleasure Island remained open from 1959 to 1969.[67]

That was five years longer than Freedomland, located in the Bronx (the northernmost borough of New York City). Though Freedomland included one area themed to resemble New York, the park aspired to reflect all of America. After entering, a guest passed through Little Old New York, a central hub resembling Disney's Main Street, before heading out to one of the historical realms: Chicago (during the Great Fire of 1871), the Great Plains, San Francisco (during the earthquake of 1906), the Old Southwest, and New Orleans (during Mardi Gras). Like Disneyland, Freedomland presented a vision of the future, Satellite City, which celebrated technology and offered space-age rides.[68] Also like Disneyland, Freedomland claimed to place the guest in a three-dimensional movie. "You see, hear, and *live* the true history of our land," boasted a guidebook. "*You* help fight the Chicago fire, *you* are 'attacked' by hostile Indians, *you* participate in the dramatic action stories that highlight our American heritage." After opening in 1960, Freedomland was plagued by financial turmoil from which it never escaped, leading to its closure in 1964.[69]

Though his first two ventures failed to achieve long-term viability, Duell used these experiences to master his trade. His breakthrough came with Six Flags Over Texas, which opened in 1961 in Arlington. The genesis moment for this theme park occurred when developer Angus Wynne and Tommy Vandergriff, the mayor of Arlington, visited Disneyland. Inspired by what they saw, they wondered if Texas might host the country's second Disneyland. When Walt declined, they turned to the only other company in the industry—Marco Engineering. After securing the contract, Wood tapped Duell to handle the theming for Six Flags. With design motifs taken from state history, the park allowed visitors to explore six themed areas, one for each flag that had flown over Texas: Mexico, Spain, France, the Confederacy, Texas, and the United States.[70]

For the purposes of this book, Six Flags Over Texas proved to be pivotal for two reasons. First, it became the first non-Disney theme park to survive. In fact, it did more than survive: it flourished. Its success demonstrated that a theme park lacking the Disney brand could become a permanent fixture in its region. Had Six Flags followed the others into the graveyard of failed regional parks, it is doubtful that Hersheypark would ever have come into existence. Second, the Six Flags venture marked the end of Randall Duell's tenure with Marco. Partway through construction, Angus Wynne fired Wood but retained Duell. At this juncture, Randall Duell and his wife, Rachel, formed their own company based in Santa Monica, California—R. Duell and Associates (RDA). The new partnership not only completed the Six Flags project but did so to great acclaim.[71] In fact, this moment marked a passing of the guard in the fledgling theme park industry. As Wood's company faded into oblivion, RDA surged, winning the lion's share of new contracts. In the 1960s and 1970s, it oversaw the design work for numerous themed attractions: AstroWorld (Houston), Magic Mountain (Valencia, CA), the Universal Studios Tour (Universal City, CA), Six Flags Over Georgia (Atlanta), Lion Country Safari (Irvine, CA), Opryland (Nashville), and Marriott's Great America (Gurnee, IL). After a rocky start, the regional theme park industry had stabilized itself and was here to stay.[72]

By the early 1970s, the theme park had joined the beach and the national park as popular vacation destinations. In 1972, the *Wall Street Journal* interviewed Dave Brown, a vice president at the Marriott Corporation, whose job it was to explore existing theme parks to "scout ideas" for his employer. "The average American is finding himself with more leisure time and a higher standard of living," Brown informed the reporter. "He is seeking a way to spend his money that is fun." He would not need to seek for long. That was because Marriott and other corporations, the article explained, were opening "fancy new parks" intended "to relieve the average American of his money." In the last year alone, Brown counted ten new parks that had each cost between $6 million and $30 million to build. These new parks were *not*, he stressed, "traditional amusement parks." Venues that "offered little more than thrill rides and cotton candy" were "closing."[73] In one regard, the *Journal* article irked John O. Hershey. The author announced the company's intention to build Hershey's Chocolate World, which, though technically true, misled readers. The company did plan to build an educational venue by this name to teach visitors about chocolate making (see chapter 7). However, the article implied that the new theme park would be named Chocolate World, which was false.[74] This error notwithstanding, the *Journal*'s reporting assured Hershey executives that, by choosing to build an expensive theme park, they had made a smart choice.

They had also selected a propitious time to do so. The industry had substantially matured since the freewheeling era of C. V. Wood. Gone were the days when a dreamy developer had no choice but to partner with the mercurial Wood and would likely face bankruptcy within a few years. In the 1970s, a prospective client could work with Randall Duell, the nation's leading expert in theme park design, aside from Disney. Ira West, who worked with RDA from 1965 to 2001, explained how the theming work of RDA and Disney differed. Walt Disney "did national themes" in his parks, West said, "and we did the regional." That said, RDA followed Walt Disney's example when it came to hiring Imagineers. "Randall Duell picked people out of motion pictures, particularly out of MGM," West said, because "they knew how to design and build period buildings." West himself was an outlier at RDA in that he did not possess a Hollywood background. He had studied industrial design at UCLA and worked for an interior design company before joining RDA. After Hershey chose RDA, Duell tapped West and his colleague, Ralph Bowerman, to coordinate the Hershey renovation.[75]

Designing Hersheypark

In 1971, Ira West and his RDA colleagues met with Hershey executives to form a preliminary plan. The redevelopment would take place sequentially, not all at once, in six phases over five years.[76] According to one RDA designer, most clients simply "wrote the check and let the experts take care of everything."[77] That was not the case here: Hersheypark would emerge out of a collaboration between the two sides. Though they got along, each brought a different knowledge base and set of priorities to the relationship. For this reason, Hersheypark would emerge out of a creative tension. Throughout the process, the Hershey people's preferences would be tempered by RDA's knowledge of what worked in the theme park industry. Conversely, Hershey's preferences and budgetary constraints would hold RDA's artistic vision in check. There was, in West's words, a "give and take between client and designer."[78]

Before the two sides could understand each other, two things had to happen. First, the Hershey people needed to learn something about theme parks by examining several examples. In the summer of 1972, they visited Disney World (Orlando), Cedar Point (Cleveland), Opryland (Nashville), and Six Flags Over Mid-America (St. Louis). West accompanied them on some of these tours. Along with studying the theming, this group scrutinized the nitty-gritty aspects of theme park management: height requirements for rides, effective strategies for queues, restroom layout, landscaping, employee dress and hair length, laundry systems, and chewing gum policy (the best practice: do not sell gum because it will wind up underneath guests' shoes).[79]

Second, RDA needed to study the situation in Hershey. When West made his first of many visits to Hershey in 1971, John Hart gave him a guided tour of the facility. "It was a rickety old park," West observed. "Most rides were made out of wood, and since Hershey gets a lot of rain, they got worn out." West also frowned on the free and open policy of the park, which he thought attracted the wrong element: people who did not spend money or, worse, those who planned to cause mischief. "You get lots of loitering" and "undesirables," both of which "keep families away." After forming an overall negative impression, West witnessed a couple of alarming sights. At one ride, the operator was "sprawled out fast asleep, his legs blocking the entrance." Embarrassed, Hart fired the employee. Even worse, at the

Comet rollercoaster, a reckless operator decided to join the passengers for a ride. As the coaster left the station, the young man was, astoundingly, "hanging on to the last car, not sitting down and not belted in!" "You cannot have this at a theme park!" West insisted emphatically. For West, the incidents epitomized the "difference between an amusement park and a theme park." Simply put, a theme park aspiring to the Disney standard cannot tolerate irresponsible or lackadaisical employee behavior.[80]

At some point, West sat down with John O. Hershey, John Hart, and Bruce McKinney to share the main tenets of RDA's philosophy. First, RDA favored imaginative theming over thrill rides. Of course, Disney's example had demonstrated conclusively the magical allure of themed environments. Yet West offered a more practical reason that he could sum up in one word: *families*. Since teenagers loved thrill rides, the easiest thing to do was to "buy a coaster from Germany." West cautioned against this approach. "Too many coasters drive away little kids and the elderly," he explained, and "it does not make good business sense to overbuild for one age-group and neglect others." Thus, a park that invested heavily in coasters catered exclusively to one demographic, when its goal should be to entertain the whole family. Disney's insight, which West agreed with, was that all generations—from grandparents on down to small children—enjoy themed attractions. Therefore, parks should invest in theming.[81]

What kind of theming worked best? Before enlightening his new clients, West offered his frank opinion regarding the *least* effective theme: the future. Though it was fun to dream about "rockets, space travel, jet packs," and "homes of future," theme parks that depict the future inevitably regret this decision. Since "no one knows what the future will look like," West explained, designers have to guess and invariably get it wrong. Though the inaccurate forecast does not matter in the *short term*, it causes a serious *long-term* problem. As the years roll by, the present eventually catches up with the park's depiction of the future. When the futuristic area is proven to be "way off target," it becomes obsolete. In the end, the theme park finds itself stuck with a costly curiosity—a three-dimensional representation of an alternative future that never happened. Though Disney's Tomorrowland succeeded, it represented the exception, not the rule. With deep pockets, Disney could afford to modify attractions, keeping them up to date with the latest prognostications in science and technology. As for Hershey, West offered strong advice: avoid the future and focus on the past.[82]

RDA favored historical themes for four reasons. First, the past was free. A park did not need to pay a motion picture studio for the rights to borrow concepts and characters from a popular movie.[83] Second, a park that adopts this strategy "fosters intergenerational interaction," West explained, "as parents use the architecture around them to explain what the past was all about to children." In short, the past advanced RDA's family-centered vision. Third, West agreed with John Hench's contention that people sought reassurance at theme parks. Historical attractions succeeded, in West's opinion, because "people feel comfortable and safe with the past." Fourth, historical themes worked well with the type of visitors a regional theme park could expect to draw: people who lived within a drivable radius. West pointed out that most parks designed by RDA "trade on their region and on history." RDA even owned a library well stocked with books about regional history so that its designers could study a location and present clients with accurate sketches.[84]

These reasons, especially the last one, dovetailed with a key priority of the Hershey people: the need to convince the local community to accept change. In one respect, the challenge in Hershey exceeded in difficulty what Walt Disney faced in the 1950s. Since Disney built his theme park on an orange grove, he was in essence starting with a tabula rasa. He did not need to bulldoze landmarks that had a history anyone cared about. In contrast, Hersheypark would be erected on top of Hershey Park—a beloved space, a locus of community memory, and the site of countless Perfect Hershey Days. If the new park did not possess a sensitive design, the danger was that the community's smoldering resentment might undermine—or worse, sabotage—the redevelopment. "How to transition the patrons" who were accustomed to a park dating back to 1906 was, in Bruce McKinney's view, "a difficult, difficult process."[85]

To facilitate that tricky transition, the new park would emphasize history and heritage. Ned Book, speaking broadly about this "era of change in the community," claimed that the Hershey interests made changes "cognizant of the preservation of the traditions and history of the community."[86] In theming the new park, the Hershey people sought to apply this principle.

Fig. 9 RDA artistic rendering of Hersheypark. Courtesy of HCA.

"We tried to maintain Hershey traditions and heritage in the new park," said McKinney, who urged RDA to "pay attention to Pennsylvania Dutch traditions and history."[87] In sum, historical theming both fit with RDA's design philosophy and enabled the new park to honor the past during a time of tumultuous change. With this general agreement, the two sides hashed out a master plan, and RDA started generating maps, architectural plans, and artistic renderings of themed attractions (fig. 9). The "new park," announced Jim Bobb, president of Hershey Estates, "will highlight the cultural and historical aspects of Hershey and the surrounding areas of Pennsylvania. We intend to theme the new Hersheypark along these cultural and historic lines."[88]

Interestingly, this plan would allow Hersheypark to accomplish more than merely pay tribute to the past. Recall that Walt Disney imagined Disneyland as a 3D movie that could strengthen guests' emotional bond to American history and values. In similar fashion, Hersheypark would place guests inside a larger narrative—a journey through time. For community members in particular, this 3D story had the potential to assist their psychological adjustment to a new era. That story would begin across the Atlantic

Ocean, where two themed areas located near the entrance, Tudor Square and Rhineland, would depict the Old World cultures, England and Germanic Europe, that exerted heavy influence on Pennsylvania (see chapter 5). Guests would next encounter Carrousel Circle, a celebration of Hershey's small-town past (chapter 4). Narrative momentum would carry guests next to a Pennsylvania Dutch area, a themed section designed to showcase the agricultural and artisanal culture of the Pennsylvania Germans (chapter 6). Visitors would then migrate over to the Pennsylvania Mining Town, where the theming would honor the coal mines that contributed to the industrial revolution (chapter 7). Finally, a Contemporary area, filled with technologically sophisticated attractions, would inspire excitement for the modern world (chapter 7).[89] How would this progression through historical stages facilitate psychological adjustment? Community members would "see transition in the architecture of the park," McKinney explained, "and be comfortable with change in their world."[90]

It is important to state here that this community-oriented objective was not the highest priority of Hershey executives. Theme parks exist to make money. Period. However, a park can pursue an ancillary objective so long as it complements the primary goal of profit-making. This was certainly the case with Disneyland, where "commercialism," according to Margaret King, constituted "only one intention" and not the "whole raison d'etre." Walt also pursued the "humanistic" goal of creating a "living museum of American history and symbols."[91] Similarly, Hersheypark aspired to achieve a nonmonetary objective. Executives sought to ease Hershey residents into a new phase of their town's evolution—one characterized by less dependency on the company. In short, Hershey executives believed that the new park could be designed *both* to attract tourists *and* to cater to the needs of the local community.

The Community Reacts

One change proved harder than others for the community to accept: the erection of a fence around the park. Gone forever were the days when guests could stroll in from multiple points, enjoy a leisurely picnic, and perhaps drop a few dimes on rides. Under that free-and-open system, community members had perceived the park as existing *for them.* In its new incarnation, the park would follow a different model, one that would fundamentally redefine its relationship to the community. Parkgoers would enter through a single gate, with an impenetrable fence preventing ingress from other locations. At the gate, all visitors, regardless of where they came from, would pay a single admission fee that covered all rides and attractions. Hershey would also discontinue the popular tradition of picnicking, which for decades had kept the outing affordable for families on a budget. Under the new system, guests could only eat park food purchased on the premises. These structural changes were, of course, necessary if Hershey hoped to meet the Disney standard. Nevertheless, they sent an unmistakable signal to local residents: the park no longer existed for them. If Hershey Park had symbolized the compact in the town's collective consciousness, it remained to be seen what Hersheypark would come to represent.

It was the job of John O. Hershey to prevent negative associations from forming. The best way to accomplish that goal, he believed, was to be proactive and transparent in communications with the community. Toward this end, he gave John Hart and Bruce McKinney a tough assignment: to hold information sessions open to the public. "We needed the backing of the community," McKinney recalled, "but we also wanted them to know that they could no longer enter the park with a dollar on a Saturday and leave with that same dollar."[92] In December 1971, the two men held an event at the Hershey Theatre with the following theme: "Come and see and come and ask." As McKinney watched from the balcony (where he was glad to be), John Hart took center stage. Armed with colorful visual aids, Hart began to describe "the new Hersheypark," trying hard to make the changes seem "as positive as possible" to a group predisposed to reject them. Partway through, Hart "got a coughing spell" and called for McKinney to "hustle" downstairs to take his place. Fortunately for McKinney, someone handed Hart a glass of water that allowed him to recover his voice and resume his presentation. "I didn't have to face that group," a relieved McKinney recalled. Though Hart perhaps wished he were anywhere else, he soldiered through the event. He did not, in McKinney's retelling, rush through his presentation, "close the door," and "run away."[93]

Despite such efforts, many in the community reacted negatively to the renovation. Some people complained about the likely increase in noise and traffic. Others worried that youth, no longer able to afford the park, would run wild in the streets.[94] However, the most common protest targeted the new admission system. Cy Little, who managed entertainment at Hershey Park, described the old park as "completely open," with "free admission" and "no fences around it." "Resistance" to the new system, though regrettable, was inevitable in his view because people accustomed to "getting a free ride . . . now have to pay to get in."[95] Little was correct; people did object to paying for something that previously had been free. It was partly for this reason that residents had decried the end of the compact. That said, Little perhaps overestimated the role of money in the community's resistance. People's outrage did not flow solely out of their frugality; it also came from a place much deeper in their psyches. And it did not take long for this outrage to locate its target.

Angry residents fixated on the fence. "The fence went up," recalled Ned Book, and "that was trauma for the community."[96] "The community . . . didn't like the fence going up," agreed McKinney. "There were a lot of people within the community who felt that their park had been taken away from them."[97] "They've moved away from the community ideal," many remonstrated. "They're shutting us out!"[98] Such people were not shy about griping to John O. Hershey, who, according to McKinney, was on the receiving end of their "wrath."[99] "Gosh, I'm just getting letters and phone calls from people in the community," an exasperated Hershey said, "with the terrible thing that I'm doing by closing off [the park]."[100] Many asked why they were made to "suffer" in order "to accommodate people from all over the country."[101] For those who objected to change in Hershey, the fence became a powerful symbol. It stood for corporate greed, the abandonment of community, and the death of Mr. Hershey's dream.

Conclusion

Not everyone reacted negatively to the new park. Though hard to discern amid the wailing from Hershey's Greek chorus of critics, some residents voiced optimism. Early in 1973, a local newspaper weighed the pros and cons of the new park. The article conveyed the negative viewpoint of those who, predictably, argued that the swarms of out-of-towners would worsen traffic, leave behind trash, and invade their privacy. That said, it also captured the perspective of local businesspeople who saw the new park as a boon. This positive group asserted that the park would employ Hershey residents and bring in droves of "potential customers" for local restaurants, shops, and hotels. These happy tourists would then "carry praise for Chocolate Town" all over the country.[102] A different paper carried the nuanced opinion of one resident who, while appreciating Hershey the way it was, accepted that change was inevitable. "We have to give into progress," he explained. If the park had to be renovated, he would "rather have Hershey do it . . . than some outside concern" because "they'll do it right." "They're not," he insisted, "indifferent to the community as many people believe."[103]

This resident was right. As one reads the oral histories of former Hershey executives, one is struck by the concern they felt for the community during this difficult transition. "In regard to the community," remembered Ned Book, "what we tried to do is become much more open in our communication . . . and let them know what our plans were."[104] "The community did not realize that the situation was dire," Bruce McKinney reflected years later. "The park would either change or shut down" because "continuing was not an option." His group ultimately chose "to keep the park alive by transforming it." This was "a community friendly gesture," he insisted, "but people didn't realize that."[105] Many residents also did not realize that, to clear space for new themed areas, many long-standing landmarks and beloved structures would have to be removed.

Chapter 4

Demolition and Preservation

In the early 1970s, Bruce McKinney's job taxed him. "I mean it was Saturday, Sunday, it was seven days in a row," recalled McKinney, who would go months without enjoying a day off with his family. What was making work so hectic? Hersheypark, of course. Newcomers to the theme park business, McKinney and his colleagues found themselves riding a steep learning curve. "We were all trying to adjust," he said, "and talking about advertising and talking about sales and talking about admissions and talking about buying new rides." Making matters more stressful, McKinney's group faced hard deadlines. An unforgiving schedule called for a soft opening in the 1972 season, with the true unveiling set for 1973. Since the park would still be under construction in 1972, visitors would encounter a space suspended halfway between the amusement park of the past and the theme park of the future. Amid the incessant hammering and the whirring of drills, guests could catch a glimpse of Hersheypark in a state of becoming. What exactly was it becoming? Some executives were not quite sure. Ned Book referred to the park as "the million-dollar mystery," a derisive joke that irritated McKinney. "We're . . . pouring our hearts out," an exasperated McKinney said, "and he thinks it's a million-dollar mystery."[1] Unfortunately, a doubting colleague was the least of McKinney's problems.

At 6:00 a.m. one June morning, McKinney received a phone call from a panicking John Hart. "Bruce, you've got to get over here," he said. "We are in serious trouble." Hurricane Agnes, after creeping up the Atlantic coast for days, was now pounding the area relentlessly with torrential rain. Spring Creek, which snakes through the park, had overflowed, leaving low-lying

Fig. 10 Rains from Hurricane Agnes flooded Hersheypark. Courtesy of HCA.

areas flooded. “That was one of the most sorrowful things that you can imagine,” recalled one employee. “The park had spent over a year working up to this . . . wonderful new Hersheypark,” and now some parts lay sixteen feet underwater. Though the flooding threatened multiple attractions, everyone recognized the animals as the most immediate concern. Without a rescue effort, most would perish. Personnel manager Jack Silar and Raleigh Hughes, the zookeeper, led Cocoa, the baby elephant, out of the park and into a temporary home in the Hershey Sports Arena’s box office. Other animals were also herded to safety. However, it was the two dolphins in the Aquatheatre, Dolly and Skipper, that posed the greatest challenge. As muddy water poured into their saltwater tank, the confused creatures swam in what looked like chocolate milk. To get them out, employees waded into the tank as the trainer coaxed the dolphins onto canvas stretchers. At this point, the employees carried the dolphins, each weighing 250 pounds, up a rocky hillside to a nearby pool. “That was terrible,” said Harold Sitler, an electrician, who remembered “slipping and sliding” while people hollered,

"Don't do this. Don't do that." For two tense days, the dolphins survived outside a saltwater environment before subsiding water levels finally allowed for their return to their tank. As for the rides, most incurred damage that could be repaired—but not all. Beyond saving was the Lost River, previously named the Mill Chute, a ride introduced by M. S. in 1929. Though worn with age, the ride had maintained its popularity, and so ambivalent park officials had not been able to decide whether to refurbish or demolish it. Hurricane Agnes made the choice for them (fig. 10).[2]

No one blamed park officials for failing to save the Lost River. However, the community was less forgiving when it came to other cherished landmarks inside the park that Hershey Estates had condemned to clear space for new themed attractions designated by the RDA. In the early 1970s, a series of demolitions tested the company's already fragile relationship with local residents. A handful of old structures and places saw their demise, a group that included the Picnic Pavilion and the Bandshell (the Starlight Ballroom followed in 1977). These venues, tied as they were to the town's history, had evolved into sites of community memory. For many residents, they had come to symbolize childhood innocence, a simpler past, and a company that cared about the community. Their erasure radically changed Hershey's landscape and proved to be emotionally jarring for many local residents. Fortunately, not every meaningful structure got destroyed. RDA and Hershey Estates elected to preserve the Comet and the Carrousel, ensuring in the process that the community could enjoy tangible links to its past.

Demolishing the Past

In the early 1970s, the landscape in Hershey changed dramatically as a handful of landmarks built back in M. S.'s day were reduced to rubble. In most cases, these structures were situated inside the park and had to be removed to create space for new attractions. The exception was the Cocoa Inn, which was located downtown. The demolition of this beloved hotel and restaurant in 1970 provoked strong feelings in the community. In doing so, it provided Hershey executives with a preview of the emotional reaction that was sure to follow when, one by one, several of Hershey Park's beloved structures met their ends too.

Constructed in 1910, the Cocoa Inn had served residents and out-of-town guests for over sixty years. Schoolchildren and teenagers on dates regarded its soda fountain as a favorite hangout, and adults praised the Oyster Bar Restaurant for offering the best food in town. Nationally famous musicians performing at the Starlight stayed in its guest rooms.[3] Ben Hogan, the legendary golfer, took up temporary residence there when he became a golf pro at the Hershey Country Club in 1941.[4] With its storied past, the hotel had evolved into a node of community memory. However, by 1970, safety concerns prompted Hershey Estates to question the famous inn's future. Specifically, the building failed to meet the minimum standards required by modern fire and safety codes.[5] Tastes were also changing. In the 1970s, middle-class families—the sort counted on to visit Hersheypark—desired larger and more modern rooms than those offered at the inn. For the inn to have a future, remodelers would need to knock down walls and add amenities. The brutal truth was that only a massive renovation could transform the local treasure into a safe and commercially viable business—and those renovations promised to be costly.[6] One resident remembered the "dilapidated" state of the Cocoa Inn in the 1960s. "The walls were slanting," she recalled, "and even when you slept in the beds, the beds slanted." However, it was her next recollection that rendered the whole debate moot: "You know there was a sinkhole there."[7]

Sure enough, directly beneath the inn's foundation, a sinkhole threatened its structural stability.[8] The building's fate was sealed. Looking back on the choice confronted by Hershey Estates—to renovate or condemn—Ned Book recalled the decision as being obvious from a business standpoint: "If you would have invested any amount of money in the building and then have a sinkhole open up on you, you'd really be in trouble."[9] Though Book's logic was impeccable, that did not make the decision any easier for the community to accept. Stella Cake of the *Hummelstown Sun* predicted that the demolition would inflict the most emotional pain on older community members. "The early residents of Hershey will sorely miss these original landmarks," she wrote, before piping in a note of optimism: "But progress means change, which is occurring in this community."[10] Yet to longtime residents, Cake's bromide—"progress means change"—provided little consolation. Several weeks prior to the scheduled demolition, Hershey Estates received a curious piece of mail. Composed by an anonymous older resident, the handwritten letter conveyed a desperate plea for a stay of execution:

> What is wrong with this community that they want to tear all these buildings down and most of all the [Cocoa] Inn. Please we beg you fellows of the Board not to leave or close the place down till Spring, so we old people can come in there to eat anyway. Lots have no place to go. Think of these things please. It's not only a few people. There are quite a good many. . . . But everybody gets old, not just us. . . . Oh God in heaven. . . . Give these old people a chance. . . . We beg you.[11]

Her entreaty did not fall on deaf ears; the moving letter was read and filed. However, neither this nor any other outcry succeeded in halting the demolition. At 9:35 on the morning of December 29, 1970, the Cocoa Inn came down. Instead of using the painfully slow wrecking ball, Hershey Estates contracted an explosives expert, who collapsed the structure in mere seconds using dynamite and gravity.[12]

Many bemoaned the loss of the historic landmark. In covering the event for the *Harrisburg Evening News*, Roger Conner could not hide his displeasure. "Without any final requests or pleas for a reprieve," Conner wrote, "Hershey's famed Cocoa Inn was brought to the ground today by a one-man firing squad." By invoking an execution, Conner anthropomorphized the inn, likening it to the human victim of an unjust verdict rendered after a hasty trial. In this way, he conveyed his sense of betrayal: a rash decision was made without regard to the community's feelings. Waxing rhapsodically, Conner wrote that, in the seconds preceding the detonation, "the landmark stood majestically in an early-morning stillness as if energy and motion had paused to pay tribute to the building that served this community for so many years." A minute later, as plumes of smoke and dust curled over the rubble heap, Conner could only find solace in the hope that the building might live on in community memory: "Hersheyites will have to nourish the infinity of stories that will keep the building alive in their thoughts."[13]

With his emotional farewell, Conner conveyed the feelings of many Hershey residents. Later in life, Robert Raffensperger recalled the outrage that many felt. "A lot of people criticized tearing the Cocoa Inn down," he said, a decision that receives "a lot of criticism to this day."[14] Robert Rath, a longtime resident, agreed: "A lot of people were saddened when they dropped that building to the ground. It was a real landmark."[15] Ethel Foley cited the importance of the inn for the community. "Then they tore down the Cocoa Inn, which was a real downfall," she recalled. "It was one of *the* places . . . that people went."[16] "That was a terrific place," commented Dionisio Castelli. "I really felt bad when they tore it down." Castelli urged Hershey to build a replica.[17] John Shuey "hated to see the Cocoa Inn come down" for "sentimental reasons." While he understood the logic behind the decision, that did not make the loss any easier to accept. On demolition day, he positioned himself across the street and watched.[18]

The Cocoa Inn was only the first structure to disappear. In 1973, Hershey residents bade farewell to the Picnic Pavilion. But this venue was not demolished so much as paved over; it became a parking lot. A site of community memory, the Picnic Pavilion had occupied the first position in the Perfect Hershey Day, that oft-repeated myth lodged deeply in the town's collective consciousness (see chapter 1). For many families, an outing to the park had traditionally begun with a picnic. Since the Pavilion allowed parkgoers to enjoy this special day out on a tight budget, it came to symbolize a company that prioritized family togetherness in a community space over corporate profits. The absence of picnicking space at the new Hersheypark meant that guests would be forced to purchase expensive meals inside the fence. According to Robert Rath, this altered the "whole atmosphere" of the park. "It has just changed," he remarked, in that "it does not cater to the same crowd because obviously if you don't have that kind of money." Though Rath did not finish his statement, his meaning was clear. A special place with "a real family atmosphere" had vanished under a layer of asphalt.[19]

The death knell also sounded for the Starlight Ballroom. With an open roof that allowed guests to twirl under the stars, the Starlight had flourished during Hershey Park's golden era. Back then, it had served as the venue for nationally recognized big band performers, whose Saturday night concerts were broadcast over the radio. With its storied history, the Starlight figured prominently in community memory. If the Perfect Hershey Day began with a picnic, it ended with a night of dancing on the Starlight's expansive wooden floor. Looking back years later, Raffensberger expressed special fondness for the old ballroom. "My wife and I used to go down there . . . every Saturday night," he reminisced, before adding, "Yeah, things have changed." If Raffensberger could have one wish granted, it would be "to see the dance floor" one last time. Though Raffensberger missed the ballroom, he understood that his nostalgia was a function of age: "I'm old." Hershey, he realized, did not necessarily have his generation in mind when making decisions about the future.[20] Dick McCrone, who reported on Hershey's plan to demolish the ballroom, made essentially the same point. Since big band dances had "faded into oblivion," the Starlight was "the victim of a change in lifestyles." In addition to evolving tastes, a more practical reason doomed the Starlight: it occupied land needed for the park's redevelopment.[21]

Dick McCrone also witnessed the sad demise of another landmark—the Bandshell, which had been the site of countless summer concerts. When "they got rid of" it, one park employee said, it "broke a lot of people's hearts."[22] The Bandshell was demolished by a team of front-end loaders that rolled in, collapsed the structure, and cleared away the debris (fig. 11). "A piece of Americana that has stood proudly and slowly watched its heyday drift by the wayside," wrote a local newspaper, "was taken down this morning in conjunction with Hersheypark's expansion." Its destruction "marks the end of an era."[23] Roger Conner, on hand to watch the demolition, agreed. The razing of the Bandshell "marks the end of an era," he declared, and the "beginning of a new era already taking shape."[24] Though Conner mostly accepted the loss, McCrone was deeply troubled by it. The Bandshell belonged to what he called the "nostalgic era," a bygone time in which Hershey Park had occupied the center of town life. "Time was, not too many years ago, when Dad took the family to Hersheypark on a Sunday afternoon in summer and, while the kids rode the rides, their parents relaxed at the bandshell, listening to the brass bands as they tootled Sousa marches." Of course, what McCrone described here was *not* an account of an actual day at Hershey Park. It was another rehashing of the Perfect Hershey Day. Like the Picnic Pavilion and the Starlight, the Bandshell symbolized all that was good from the town's golden age. "Yesterday another symbol of the past began falling when workmen started to raze the park

Fig. 11 The beloved Bandshell was demolished to make room for new attractions. Courtesy of HCA.

bandshell," McCrone reported. "Slowly but surely, the landmarks of that era have been giving way to 'progress.'"

There was nothing accidental about McCrone's placement of quotation marks around "progress." He wished to imbue his sentence with a sardonic tone. That society had evolved to a state where it no longer had any use for band shells was not, in his view, progress at all:

> Many thousands of Central Pennsylvania music lovers can recall relaxing in the shade as they toe-tapped to the martial music that emanated from the ornate bandstand. But alas, TV watching has long since replaced the joy of a Sunday afternoon band concert. No longer are older Americans content to just sit in the shade, sip pop or munch on ice cream cones while enjoying stirring band music. TV has made us a nation of stay-at-homes. Unfortunately, today's younger generation has become so accustomed to the raucous beat of rock and roll music that they consider old-fashioned band music "square."

McCrone did not believe that new things were always better than old things, that technological change inevitably meant progress, or that the present was necessarily superior to the past. To make these points, McCrone established the Bandshell as his symbol of traditional American culture. He then shrewdly deployed television and rock and roll as countersymbols, stand-ins for modern culture, which allowed for a contrast. Whereas the Bandshell represented an *active* lifestyle in which people left their homes and "toe-tapped" to music together, TV encouraged a *passive* lifestyle, dominated by sedentary viewing. And compared with the richly *communal* activity of congregating at the Bandshell, TV was *atomizing*: it isolated people by turning them into "stay-at-homes." Finally, those who enjoyed band music demonstrated a healthy *reverence for the past*, tradition, and heritage. In contrast, those who vibrated to the "raucous beat" of rock music showed only a *disdain for the past* and a will to reject anything "old-fashioned." For McCrone, what started as straightforward reporting on a demolition darkened into a scathing indictment of modern society.[25]

Edwin Zechman also saw Hershey's lost landmarks as casualties of modern society. Like many residents, he harbored "happy memories" that tied him emotionally to these old structures. In the past, he had attended concerts at the Bandshell, donned his white linen suit for the Starlight, and enjoyed the food and sociability of the Cocoa Inn. Though he considered himself "broad-minded enough" to realize that "Hershey had outgrown some of those things," he (like McCrone) could not overlook television's pernicious influence in effecting their downfall. "With television," he asked rhetorically, "have you noticed how many people stay home in the evening?" Instead of interacting with the community, they "sit in front of the television with their mouth open." "I deplore that," he declared emphatically. Though Zechman missed his magical evenings at the Starlight, he understood that this venue, if it had survived, would likely be hosting rock and roll bands. To that prospect, he said, "no thanks." The "times they are a-changing," he said, quoting Bob Dylan. However, for Zechman, Dylan's lyrics failed to capture the magnitude of change in Hershey. Invoking Margaret Mitchell instead, he likened Hershey to the old South after the Civil War had swept away an entire way of life. "It's the old story," he said, "*Gone with the Wind*." Hershey's old way of life was "gone with the wind" too.[26]

The Psychic Cost of Symbolic Cleansing

The situation in Hershey was unique. That said, modernizing forces were transforming many places in the United States. In the 1960s and 1970s, developers tore down old buildings and historic structures to clear land for shopping centers, malls, parking lots, condominiums, and theme parks. Much of this construction followed in the wake of the new highways being built after the passage of the Federal Highway Act of 1956. That year, Robert Moses, the twentieth century's foremost urban planner, predicted that the new highway system would reorder American life. "This new highway program," he wrote in *Harper's Magazine*, "will affect our entire economic and social structure" and "leave a permanent imprint upon our communities and people." He was right. Tom Lewis, who has written extensively on highways, explains step by step how highways reorganized American life: "first, the Interstate; then the housing developments clustered close to the highway's exits . . . then a shopping center."[27] In short, the Highway Act unleashed a construction boom that altered America's built environment in a way that facilitated commerce and encouraged consumption.

However, hidden beneath all this economic development, society was paying a tremendous cost. This was the contention of the sociologist Orrin Klapp in *Collective Search for Identity* (1969). Klapp argued that the country, though growing rich *economically*, was growing commensurately poorer *spiritually*. What was causing this spiritual impoverishment? Klapp diagnosed America's ailment using a complex framework that applied to Hershey. He attached great importance to *place*, which for him was not simply a geographic location. He defined it as "a space with a sense of locality and identity" that has become an affirming "territory of symbols." In Klapp's framework, a mere *space* ascends to the status of *place* when, over time, individuals and communities project symbolic meaning onto its structures and features. Symbols matter, Klapp explained, because they provide people with the "reliable reference points" they use to "locate themselves socially, realize themselves sentimentally, and declare (to self and others) who they are." In other words, symbols allow an individual or a community to form an "identity." Without these symbol-rich environments, human beings cannot enjoy a stabilizing sense of "rootedness." Unfortunately, Klapp's places were rapidly vanishing in the 1960s.

In assigning blame, Klapp pointed an accusatory finger at "modernism," the villain in his narrative. He understood modernism as a conglomeration of aggressive forces—capitalism, consumerism, real estate development, advertising, media, celebrity culture, and machines. Though modernism was transforming American life in multiple ways, it was having its most devastating impact on places. "Modernism," Klapp stated bluntly, is a "destroyer of place." Needing a symbol to capture modernism's violence, Klapp chose the bulldozer, a metal juggernaut that relentlessly steamrolls places in reckless disregard to the consequences. As modernism systematically reconfigures the American landscape, it leaves people bereft of the symbols that had nourished their identities.

People do not passively accept these losses. As "bulldozers wipe away . . . the reference points that make local identity possible," Klapp wrote, people lash out in ways the modernizers cannot comprehend. The latter mistakenly believe that when a man refuses to "welcome the bulldozer," it is because he possesses excessive "sentimentality," harbors a "fear of the newfangled," or wishes to "hold up progress and turn the clock back." In truth, that angry man is behaving quite rationally. He opposes the "wiping away" of the "symbols that made *his* environment meaningful and *his* kind of identity possible." Moreover, that man lives "in a state of constant outrage" against the "inexorable tide of men and machinery" that is "confining his childhood memories in concrete." And yet, Klapp found, the "notion persists" among modernizers that you can obliterate a man's landscape, and "he will be the same man." He won't. The fear of being "robbed of identity," Klapp maintained, "applies to practically everyone in the United States."[28]

It certainly applied to Hershey. Had Klapp visited Hershey, he would have discovered a community reacting to the loss of landmarks in precisely the way he laid out. Over the years, Hershey residents had invested many structures with symbolic meaning. Though a given structure might represent something specific to a single person, taken collectively, the landmarks stood for M. S.'s compact with the community. In this way, the landmarks had contributed to people's identities and anchored them with a reassuring feeling of "rootedness." When the company demolished the Cocoa Inn, for example, it erased not just a hotel but a meaningful symbol, instantaneously snapping the thousands of invisible cords tying the structure to the community. How do we know that this symbolic damage was truly taking place? We can infer it from the powerful emotions expressed by residents in their oral histories. The demolitions provoked grief and outrage that were both out of proportion with the true severity of the event and far more enduring than one would expect. Indeed, that people continued to manifest anger and sorrow one to two decades later is evidence of psychic scarring.

Philomena Castelli reacted in this way to the loss of the Cocoa Inn. "It was a pleasant town to live in when we had our Cocoa Inn," said Castelli, deliberately using the past tense. "To us people that were raised and lived here all our life," she said, the demolition "destroyed Hershey." In her mind, the loss of a single building (one resting on a sinkhole!) had somehow ruined the entire town. Her exaggerated response seems to defy logic until we remember that residents like her had assigned symbolic value to the Cocoa Inn. More than a physical edifice, it represented all that was good and right about Hershey under the leadership of M. S., which she cherished: "Hershey did take care of his people." Therefore, the Cocoa Inn's removal meant the end of the town she loved. Interestingly, in losing one symbol, she gained another. If the Cocoa Inn had represented a patriarch who cared for his people, then its destruction could symbolically stand for the opposite: the abandonment of the community by M. S.'s successors. "They are not taking care of the people at Hershey," she said, issuing a stern rebuke. "They want tourism." In sum, cold, heartless greed had replaced a benefactor's warm and loving care.[29]

We see a similar dynamic in the memories of Mary Levens. As she began to recall the Cocoa Inn ("I loved that Oyster Bar"), her mind uncontrollably shunted to the demolition: "And why they ever tore it down, it's beyond me." In fact, it was not beyond her, because her very next thought supplied the answer. "That was the regime at that time," she said, elaborating that "things were done differently after M. S. Hershey died." In other words, the people who succeeded M. S. acted in disregard of the community's needs. At this point, she briefly returned to the Cocoa Inn, describing family dinners, excellent food, and the celebrities who stayed there. Unfortunately, her mind proved unable to dwell on these fond memories: "Why it was torn down, I'll never tell you." As the interview continued, the Cocoa Inn's demise led her to reflect generally on all the heart-wrenching demolitions: "Everything that was decent and fun and interesting and exciting in town is torn down." For Mary Levens, the combined effect of so many demolitions was devastating: "It's just sad to watch that. It was a feeling. Hershey was a feeling, a tremendous feeling. . . . What can I say? The feeling's gone. It's sad. I guess you have to go along with progress, but you don't have to destroy all of the landmarks and all those wonderful things that Mr. Hershey had built years ago." To Levens, Hershey was not merely a geographic location but a "tremendous feeling." In other words, Hershey was a meaningful place, in the Orrin Klapp sense of the word, and, as such, transcended physicality. That "feeling" was the sum total of hundreds of memories tying her to specific landmarks built by M. S. When his successors leveled the landmarks, the ties were severed, she experienced emotional pain, and the wonderful feeling that had been Hershey died. This fascinating passage helps us understand why Mary Levens could not accept the loss and move on psychologically. The Hershey she loved no longer existed.[30]

Nobody's memories fit Klapp's theory better than those of Mary Hubler. A longtime resident and former chocolate worker, Hubler started visiting Hershey Park in the 1920s. In her 1982 oral history, she shared six decades' worth of memories, many of which are set in Hershey Park. In organizing her memories, she used landmarks as signposts, attaching each memory to one of these cherished places or structures. Their demolitions sent a disruptive pulse through her memory, impairing her ability to reminisce with pleasure. Indeed, what is fascinating about her act of remembering is that it follows a clear pattern. As she started to describe a fond memory from the park, the demolition of a landmark would creep into her consciousness, and her mood would instantly darken. She would then abandon the memory, not yet fully fleshed out, and shift to her displeasure with the company.

Some of her favorite memories involved the park's Picnic Pavilion, Bandshell, and fountain (also torn down during the renovation). "Well, it was nice to walk to the park," she began, before immediately sharing one of the park's finest features: "You could take picnics there." Instead of reminiscing for a while on picnics of the past, Hubler lurched to the problematic present in her very next sentence. "Everything has changed," she said bitterly. "Now they made it into the tractor-trailer parking," *they* referring to Hershey Estates. She added that some people, unaware that the Pavilion is gone, pathetically show up and "try to have a picnic on the outside of the fence." This same pattern defines Hubler's memories of band concerts and the fountain. "We'd sit and watch the band concert," she recalled, and then "stroll around the park," eventually reaching the fountain: "Oh, you could . . . just enjoy sitting there with your lover and watching the fountain." But just as the happy memory of youthful romance started to glow, Hubler's mind abruptly doused it by shifting to the present. "So that was the end of that. They had so many nice things. Why they ever got rid of them, I don't know." Hershey Park "*was* an attraction with memories."[31]

Hubler's memories of the ballroom adhere to the same pattern. She began, "Then the dance hall there, that was—" but abruptly stopped mid-sentence as the recent demolition crashed in on her thoughts. "It's a shame that they tore that down. . . . Hershey doesn't want anything, it seems." Despite her first unsuccessful attempt to remember the dance hall, she circled back to it moments later. This time, her reminiscing gathered some momentum before the demolitions again intruded on the idyllic past:

> Benny Goodman, or I think Glenn Miller was there. . . . You could go in there and dance without paying, and it was so crowded. . . . Then they . . . opened up their roof for a starlight ballroom. . . . Oh, beautiful places. Why in the world they were sold and tore down, I don't know. One time in my younger years and later, middle years, this Hershey was a beautiful place, wonderful. But in my later years, there's too much being torn down, taken away.

The site of happy memories from different stages of life, the ballroom clearly played an important role in Mary Hubler's life. Though she wished to contemplate the lovely past, she was unable to block out the disturbing present. In this way, all of Hubler's memories were marred by scar tissue. She could not enjoy her most cherished memories, the ones that had contributed to her identity, because her mind inevitably funneled them into a larger narrative of Hershey as a paradise lost.

When one reads Hubler's oral history, one point becomes abundantly clear: her mind was adept at choosing structures and ascribing meanings to them. In other words, she engaged in the exact sort of symbol creation that Klapp discussed. For her, the Picnic Pavilion, Bandshell, fountain, and Starlight collectively signified family, youthful innocence, romantic love, and a caring company. Interestingly, her tendency to manufacture symbols did not stop in her advanced years. As demolition crews razed one landmark after another, Hubler struggled to understand the destruction of her past. "Well, why are they getting rid of this and that?" she asked her daughter. Her search for answers yielded a new symbol that carried a dark and cynical meaning: "Money, money, money." In her mind, the elimination of symbols had itself become a new symbol. It stood for corporate greed.[32]

Like Hubler, Levens, and Castelli, June Herr also cherished the Hershey of the past and revered M. S. for building it. "The people that lived here liked living here," she said, because M. S. had "the soul of the community at heart." Herr was especially fond of Hershey Park but, like Hubler, proved unable to stay on target as she tried to recount her Perfect Day:

> You could go on Sunday and have a picnic . . . walk right in, sit down and listen to the band concert [or] ride what you wanted. Then one year the fence went up. Now it's a theme park. They say [it] makes money. . . . They tore down the facilities, you know, the things that you needed. We have to pay our sewage bill to Pittsburgh, our water bill to somewhere else. Everything was town-owned, and if something happened, we all shared it together and put it back together again. These people have . . . we thought we could trust them, but we can't.[33]

Her lovely memory of Hershey Park led inevitably to the erection of the hated fence, which in turn triggered a chain reaction of negativity: the tearing down of beloved places, the termination of free utilities (a key part of the compact), the loss of community spirit, and the rise of new leaders who betray the people. Predictably, her thoughts shifted to the HMC, which in her view accelerated the town's demise. For this, she blamed those same untrustworthy leaders. They did not have to allow the HMC to "overwhelm the town," but they failed to stop it.[34]

These and many other residents viewed Hershey Park as a *place* in Orin Klapp's conceptualization of the word. It had been a zone replete with meaningful symbols that had shaped their identities. Thus, the erasure of these symbols inflicted psychic damage on the community. Though Bruce McKinney probably did not read Klapp's book, he intuitively grasped its thesis and agonized over the demolitions. McKinney observed correctly that local residents claimed *emotional ownership* of the landmarks, even though Hershey Estates possessed the *legal right* to do as it pleased with them. "It was *our* ballroom" and "*our* bandshell," residents would insist with a "sense of pride." They understood the structures as belonging to the community, not the company. When Estates razed the structures, local residents' "feelings and memories flowed to the surface."[35] They felt dispossessed.

Years later, McKinney pondered the possibility that two landmarks, the fountain and Bandshell, might have been spared. "Duell made the decision to tear [the fountain] down," McKinney recalled, with the plan being to build a new one outside the park. Sadly, the old fountain was destroyed, and the new one was never built.[36] Similarly, RDA designers wished to install a new ride where the Bandshell stood. Without any debate, they made the determination to demolish the structure: "Well, the bandshell's in the way. Got to go." Though uncomfortable with the peremptory decision, McKinney opted not to resist. He and his colleagues—who understood the community's emotional attachment—deferred to RDA, which did not. "We gave them the title of . . . experts," he recalled, and "bowed" to their will. In retrospect, McKinney regretted staying quiet. As a result, the local community "had to adjust to the bandshell leaving and the fountain going." This "added fuel to the fire of discontent."[37]

Transitional Objects

"People don't like change," remarked Ira West as he recalled the demolitions. "They want things to stay the same. It's about safety."[38] Fortunately, two structures did survive and enjoy new life in Hersheypark. Hershey executives and RDA agreed not just to save the Carrousel and the Comet but to feature them. This single decision increased the chances that the local community would accept the new park. Why was that the case? Of course, it mattered to residents that Hershey Estates chose to honor the community by preserving two pieces of park history. However, more than a mere tribute, the continuation of these rides touched a deeper part of the town's collective consciousness—something McKinney hinted at when he shared the rationale for keeping the Carrousel. The Carrousel, he explained, provided Hersheypark with an "attachment to the past" because it "symbolized

Hershey's traditions."[39] With so much of old Hershey Park vanishing, residents needed symbols to cling to as they transitioned to a new era. Just as Klapp sheds light on the trauma people feel when a symbol is destroyed, D. W. Winnicott illuminates the psychological benefit individuals derive from a symbol's preservation.

Winnicott published *Playing and Reality* in 1971, the same year the park commenced its renovation. A British pediatrician and psychoanalyst, Winnicott developed ideas about childhood that enjoyed widespread influence in the 1950s and 1960s. In this work, Winnicott explained the importance of play and playthings in assisting children as they made hard but necessary transitions through various developmental stages. According to Winnicott, human beings easily recognize the existence of the two worlds they inhabit simultaneously: the "inner psychic reality" of the mind and the "external world" of material objects. Far less obvious is a *third* experiential zone, which occupies an intermediate position somewhere between "inner and outer reality," or between the "me" and the "not-me." Winnicott called this third zone "potential space." He believed that children accomplish psychological work in this liminal space. Indeed, it is here that the child engages in "creative playing," "develops a use of symbols," and learns to work through problems.[40] Readers familiar with *Mister Rogers' Neighborhood,* which debuted in 1968, recall the Neighborhood of Make-Believe. Fred Rogers, who kept abreast of developments in child psychology, envisioned this imaginary playscape as potential space. After a trolley transports young television viewers to this realm, they confront an array of puppet characters, each of whom symbolizes different parts of a child's psyche. As these characters interact with one another, a problem introduced earlier in the program—in the real world—is resolved.[41]

According to Winnicott, infants use this third space as they prepare for the first major challenge of their lives: to transition from a "state of being merged" with the mother to a "stage of separating out the mother from the self." During play, the child will project symbolic meaning onto a blanket, doll, or stuffed animal. This "transitional object," a concept Winnicott first developed in 1951, comes to represent the mother in the child's mind. Clutching this soft and cozy symbol of Mom, the child needs the actual mother less and can begin to accept a new reality characterized by increased maternal separation. Without a transitional object, this separation might have seemed too daunting. Whatever the selected object is, it is heavily freighted with symbolic significance, and the mother intuitively recognizes its importance to the child. She "lets it get dirty," Winnicott observed, "knowing that by washing it she introduces a break in the continuity of the infant's experience, a break that may destroy the meaning and value of the object to the infant." Winnicott cited cartoonist Charles Schulz's famous character, the blanket-hugging Linus, as a popular example of the transitional object concept.[42]

The child eventually arrives at a developmental stage characterized by reduced dependency. Once they demonstrate confidence in the new stage, the transitional object's importance begins to fade. Ultimately, the object's fate is to be, in Winnicott's terminology, "decathected." Though "not forgotten" and "not mourned," the object has become divested of symbolic meaning because the child has successfully made the transition that had infused it with a special purpose. Interestingly, the process described here has vast long-term significance. For while it is children who first learn how to manipulate symbols while at play, this creative third space—potential space—is not the province of children alone. As children grow into adults, potential space in their consciousness does not shrink; rather, it expands. For "the baby, child, adolescent," or even "adult," Winnicott wrote, the psychological activity of "playing leads on naturally to cultural experience and indeed forms its foundation." Playing in potential space becomes the basis for adult culture—the arts, religion, literature, film, and television.[43] Or even a theme park.

Walking in the Past

Winnicott's theory helps us understand the importance of the Carrousel and Comet during the renovation of Hershey Park. However, it also sheds light on the experience of countless other Americans who, like those in Hershey, struggled to adjust to a rapidly modernizing world. In 1959, CBS aired an episode of *The Twilight Zone* titled "Walking Distance" that addressed this very theme.[44] Written by the show's creator, Rod Serling, "Walking Distance" shows the importance that a place and its symbolic objects can have for someone making a tough transition. The plot begins with a man in a business suit named Martin Sloan (Gig Young), who zooms into a rural gas station in a shiny convertible. The aggressive driving and the sports car itself convey information to viewers: Sloan leads a fast-paced lifestyle and has achieved financial success. Sure enough, Serling states in his voice-over that Sloan is vice president of a New York advertising agency. He has attained wealth and status in the modern world.

But not peace. Viewers next see a frazzled Sloan impatiently pounding his horn to get service from a gas station attendant who moves at a slower pace. Sloan quickly regains composure, apologizes, and discloses the reason for his spontaneous "exodus" from the city: "Yesterday, I just got in the car and drove. I had to get out of New York City. One more board meeting, phone call, report, or problem, I would have jumped right out the window." With a high-pressure corporate career and hectic urban life pushing him toward a breakdown, Sloan had made his escape. He is a fugitive from the modern world. As chance would have it, the gas station is located within "walking distance" of Homewood, the small town where Sloan grew up. As the attendant begins the oil and lube job, Sloan embarks on foot to Homewood, which he has not visited for over two decades. At this point, he passes into the Twilight Zone.

For Sloan, the Twilight Zone functions much like Winnicott's potential space. Existing neither in the actual world nor in Sloan's mind, it constitutes a third space where he can confront and work through his problem. Upon arriving, he meets not a Homewood that has evolved over time, but rather a town frozen in 1934—the summer of Sloan's eleventh year. At first, Sloan fails to realize that he has traveled in time, finding it "amazing" that a place can "look so exactly the same." For someone fed up with New York, the absence of modernity comes as a welcome relief. In Wilson's drugstore, his old childhood haunt, he orders a chocolate soda, the kind he used to slurp as a kid, and is astonished to learn that it still costs ten cents. The old drugstore, the taste of the ice-cream soda, and the "familiar" man behind the counter combine to trigger a flood of happy childhood memories. It is "funny," he reflects, "how many memories you connect with a place." For Sloan, the drugstore is a *place* in Klapp's sense of the word. As such, it is therapeutic. His move to New York, by severing all links to meaningful places, had precipitated his crisis. The restoration of those connections in the Twilight Zone starts to repair the psychic damage.

Rejuvenated, Sloan strolls to another meaningful place: the town square. In this wholesome world of yesteryear, a vendor sells cotton candy, ice cream, and balloons to children as music wafts out of the calliope of a carousel (called a merry-go-round in the show). In this idyllic place, the biggest problem is a boy climbing a tree who refuses to come down. After Sloan helps the mother retrieve him, he engages her in a wistful conversation about the innocent pleasures of a child's summer. Staring dreamily ahead, Sloan engages in symbol creation, linking the carousel and its calliope to his idealized vision of childhood. The young mother picks up on his train of thought and contributes additional delights—cotton candy, ice cream, and band concerts. Though her list supplies Sloan with still more symbols, we should note that for her, these things are not symbols at all—they represent only themselves. Ice cream is a frozen treat and nothing more. There is one other curious aspect to this scene. As Sloan reminisces on the joys of summers past, he is indulging in nostalgia. However, thanks to the strange magic of the Twilight Zone, those very features surround him as he speaks. Paradoxically, he is feeling nostalgia for his current time and place. It is at this very instant that Sloan's past and present abruptly converge. As Sloan recalls carving his name into the bandstand's post, he witnesses a boy performing this very act. Sloan is staring at his eleven-year-old self.

In most episodes of *The Twilight Zone*, the protagonist eventually discerns a moral purpose looming behind the altered reality. "Walking Distance" does not deviate from this formula: Martin Sloan's excursion to the Twilight Zone yields the wisdom that he needs to resolve his problem. That solution is *not* to remain permanently in the past, though this possibility does tantalize Sloan. In fact, Sloan only accepts the difficult truth that he must return to his own time after forcing interactions with both his parents and his younger self. After locating his old home, he confronts his mother and father; they are disturbed, not delighted, by his presence. They also disbelieve his outlandish claim to be their son. To prove his identity to his incredulous parents, Sloan spews obscure facts about the family that a stranger could not possibly know and hastily produces identification cards from his wallet. This effort earns him a slap in the face from his mother, which causes the wallet to slip from his hands. At this moment, he hears the music from the calliope and realizes that he must deliver an urgent message to his younger self.

The scene shifts back to the town square, where night has fallen. Young Sloan is seated on a carousel horse, eating popcorn and enjoying his summer. He is startled by the sudden appearance of a stranger in a business suit (his adult self) lunging toward him. Frightened, young Martin dismounts his horse and attempts to flee. Weaving through the oscillating horses to elude his pursuer, young Martin falls off the revolving platform and screams, "My leg!" Old Martin also howls in pain because the injury, rippling instantaneously through time, afflicts him too. The music fades, and the carousel slows to a halt. Older Martin approaches the injured boy, who is cradled in the arms of the ride operator, and delivers part of his urgent message: "Martin, I only wanted to tell you that this is a wonderful time of life for you. Don't let any of it go by without enjoying it." After young Martin is taken away to receive medical attention, older Martin completes his message, though he speaks now only to the darkness: "There won't be any more merry-go-rounds, no more cotton candy, no more band concerts." The combination of Martin Sloan growing up and America abandoning its small-town past, he implies, will bring about the end of this childhood paradise.

Later that evening, Martin's father, Robert Sloan, finds his middle-aged son sitting in darkness beside the motionless carousel. Having gone through the contents of Martin's wallet, the father now believes what earlier had seemed impossible: the stranger is his son, who has somehow journeyed from the future. During a brief but poignant conversation, the father dispenses the wisdom that his son needs to hear before he can return to his own time:

ROBERT SLOAN: You have to leave here. There's no room; there's no place. Do you understand that?

MARTIN SLOAN: I see that now, but I don't understand. Why not?

ROBERT SLOAN: I guess because we only get one chance. Maybe there's only one summer to every customer. That little boy, the one I know—the one who belongs here—this is his summer, just as it was yours once. Don't make him share it.

MARTIN SLOAN: Alright.

ROBERT SLOAN: Martin, is it so bad where you're from?

MARTIN SLOAN: I thought so, Pop. I've been living on a dead run, and I was tired. And one day I knew I had to come back here. I had to get on the merry-go-round and listen to a band concert. I had to stop and breathe, and close my eyes and smell, and listen.

ROBERT SLOAN: I guess we all want that. Maybe when you go back, Martin, you'll find that there are merry-go-rounds and band concerts where you are. Maybe you haven't been looking in the right place. You've been looking behind you, Martin. Try looking ahead.

In this exchange, the father accepts that something disturbing about the future has propelled his son into the past. Though sympathetic, the father knows that Martin cannot remain in the past because it is occupied by his boyhood self ("this is his summer. . . . Don't make him share it"). For this reason, he urges his son to embrace the future ("Try looking ahead"). Yet his advice is more nuanced than just this. For while Martin must live as an adult in the modern world, his father does not advise that he forget the past. On the contrary, he instructs Martin to seek out the wonder objects from his youth: merry-go-rounds and bandstands. These can provide him with joy, respite, and sanity in the modern world. In short, the weary time traveler can cure his malaise by preserving select aspects of the reassuring past in the bewildering present.

We do not know if Serling was aware of Winnicott's transitional objects. Regardless, his script lends itself to the application of this theory. The episode implies that the cause of Martin Sloan's breakdown is his inability to make difficult transitions—from boy to man, from small town to big city, and from the simple past to the complex present. Sloan never had potential space, a liminal zone where he could use symbols creatively to resolve his problem. Rod Serling's intervention, which sends Sloan into the Twilight Zone ("a fifth dimension"), grants Sloan temporary access to the potential space he needs. By revisiting meaningful places, like the drugstore and town square, he reconnects with cherished symbols from youth, such as the ice-cream soda, carousel, and bandstand. The Twilight Zone allows him to play with these symbols and assign meanings to them—but not for long. Winnicott's toddler does *not* use play to strengthen his resolve to remain permanently in his current developmental stage. Similarly, the experience in the Twilight Zone does *not* convince Sloan to dwell forever in the past. The child and the man must both make transitions. However, just as the toddler can cling to his teddy bear as he advances to the next stage, so, too, can Sloan carry aspects of the past into the present. He can select transitional objects (his father recommends carousels and band concerts) that symbolize his small-town youth. These enable Sloan to cope with modernity's challenges by keeping him grounded in the virtues of the past.

Do they work? Serling gives viewers reason to believe that Sloan will adjust. After the father departs, Sloan hops onto the carousel to enjoy one final spin. In a fluid match cut, the revolving carousel gives way to a spinning phonographic record in a jukebox. Sloan has returned to Wilson's drugstore to taste one last ice-cream soda before returning to his former life. He is surprised to discover that, since his earlier visit, the drugstore has changed. It is now a bustling hangout for teenagers. The rock and roll music signals that Sloan has exited the Twilight Zone and rejoined his own time. In other words, he has returned to the world that had originally pushed him into crisis. This time, however, Sloan does not find modern times so disturbing. After canceling his order for an ice-cream soda that he seems not to need, Sloan walks away from the counter with a noticeable limp. When the soda jerk asks if he had been hurt during the war, Sloan disabuses him. The limp, he explains, is the remnant of an injury sustained on the carousel when he was eleven. When the soda jerk informs Sloan that "they tore that down a few years ago," Sloan confronts the fact that the central symbol from his youth is gone. This revelation should upset Sloan—assuming he still has a psychological need for the carousel. However, as Sloan drives off from the gas station, his calm demeanor and positive attitude suggest he has made the necessary adjustment. He seems to accept that the past has passed, and he must find his way in the present.

Old Rides Made New

"Walking Distance" considered the critical role played by the past in determining one's psychic well-being in the present. If links to the past are severed, one feels a disorientating sense of alienation in the modern world. In this way, Martin Sloan's predicament reflected that of many Hershey

Fig. 12 Hersheypark's layout channeled all visitors to Carrousel Circle. Courtesy of HCA.

residents. As trucks carted off debris from the demolished Bandshell, we can almost hear the forlorn Sloan uttering his prophetic message: "There won't be any more merry-go-rounds, no more cotton candy, no more band concerts." Except that in Hersheypark, there would still be a merry-go-round. Guests to the newly renovated park would meet with two holdovers from the park's past—the Comet and Carrousel. For community members, these two old rides functioned as transitional objects, aiding them as they advanced into an uncertain future.

With the Carrousel, Hersheypark's designers knew they had a local treasure on their hands. Instead of dismantling the community's favorite heirloom or relegating it to some corner of the park, they erected an entire themed area around its revolving glory—Carrousel Circle.[45] Recognizing the Carrousel's age as an advantage, the park highlighted its antiquity in promotional materials, billing it as "probably the oldest carrousel still in use in America."[46] For visitors, Carrousel Circle was impossible to miss (fig. 12). According to Ira West, designers imitated Disney's strategy by channeling all foot traffic to this centrally located themed area. Just as Disneyland forced guests to experience Main Street, USA, so, too, did Hersheypark require visitors to behold the old carousel.[47] For community members, this act of preservation meant they could once again enjoy the same carousel that had enchanted their childhoods.

Except it was not quite the same because the Carrousel's context had changed. After Hersheypark opened, the Carrousel prompted a curious reaction from a couple from North Carolina who had visited the old park in the past. Writing to management after their visit, the couple asserted generally that the refurbished park represented "such an improvement over previous days." Though they preferred Hersheypark to Hershey Park, they singled out the Carrousel for praise. "The retention of the old carrousel," they wrote, "with its authentic music equipment is a joy for us."[48] On the surface, the couple's response appears to present a contradiction. After all, how can one assert the superiority of the new park and then, in the next sentence, select a relic from the old park as the most enjoyable feature? That the couple made this observation underscores an important point: the new context of a modern theme park had conferred fresh meaning to the old Carrousel.

For most of the twentieth century, Hershey's Carrousel had signified only itself: a musical ride that simulated horseback riding. Though the physical properties of the Carrousel had not changed since its assembly in 1919, the ride had, in a symbolic sense, acquired fresh meaning. In its new physical and temporal setting (the 1970s), it started to represent different things to guests: youthful innocence, the simpler days of yesteryear, vanished small-town life, and the way America was before nuclear weapons, the Vietnam War, and television. For local residents, the Carrousel also symbolized Hershey in its golden era before the sweeping changes of the 1960s. These layers of symbolism made the Carrousel enticing for guests. It had the power, if only for a fleeting moment, to transport them back in time. It was a revolving nostalgia machine.

The Seventies Nostalgia Wave

In this regard, the Carrousel played into a local and national trend. In both Hershey and the nation, the 1970s were awash in nostalgia. It was in this decade that Hershey residents started making the deliberate attempt to save items from the town's golden era. They missed Hershey's past and wished to own a piece of it. Robert Rath collected artifacts from Hershey Park as a way to maintain a tangible connection to a cherished past.[49] Similarly, James Stover brought home a bench from the Bandshell before it was demolished.[50] In 1975, Sam Hinkle, the former president of Hershey Chocolate, was asked about the "growing interest in Hershey memorabilia" and "Hershey nostalgia." The trend, he confessed, mystified him. "The fact that old Hershey Chocolate Company literature or containers or any other kind of memorabilia," he said, "has taken on value surprises me." In Hinkle's view, the objects people collected, all from the twentieth century, were not old enough to qualify as antiques, which he defined as items from before 1830. He then joked that, based on the collectors' criteria, "I'm an antique myself."[51]

Though Hershey residents had unique reasons for saving old things, their behavior reflected a national trend. Gary Cross, who wrote a book about Americans' nostalgia for old radio hits, TV shows, cars, toys, and other consumer goods, claims that this form of longing "matures after about 1970."[52] The 1970s witnessed an explosion of antiquing, as what had been the exclusive domain of professionals became a hobby for ordinary people. Shows, conventions, trade publications, and price guides emerged to serve the new antique enthusiasts.[53] Sports memorabilia collecting also spiked in popularity. Baseball cards, once seen as a boy's pursuit, started attracting adults. They formed clubs, attended conventions, and subscribed to collector magazines, which materialized to enable their new obsession.[54] Radio followed the same pattern. By 1971, three hundred radio stations had started broadcasting Westerns, game shows, comedies, suspense thrillers, and horror shows from the '30s, '40s, and '50s. More stations would follow as the decade wore on. Fans of what became known as "old-time radio" started forming clubs, joining radio preservation societies, attending conventions, and reading newsletters such as *Hello Again*.[55] In sum, there was no shortage of options for Americans wishing to revisit the past. In 1971, Gerald Clarke, writing for *Time* magazine, asked the salient question: "How much more nostalgia can America take?"[56]

It turned out, quite a bit more. The decade also featured television shows, movies, and stage productions that capitalized on the nation's sudden fascination with earlier eras. *Grease*, a musical about a 1950s high school romance, premiered in 1971, and the motion picture starring John Travolta and Olivia Newton-John followed seven years later. *The Waltons* (CBS), a wholesome show set in the Great Depression, made its debut in 1971 and aired for nine seasons. *Little House on the Prairie* (NBC), set in nineteenth-century Minnesota, premiered in 1972 and also lasted nine years. No actor hopped around historical periods more than Ron Howard. At the age of six, he journeyed back to the 1930s to play a small boy who converses with Martin Sloan in "Walking Distance" (1959). The next year, he started his eight-year run as Opie Taylor in *The Andy Griffith Show* (CBS), a popular sitcom that evoked nostalgia for small towns. Though it originally aired in the 1960s, the show enjoyed continued life in the 1970s through syndication. In 1973, Howard starred in George Lucas's *American Graffiti*, a film that captured the spirit of youth in the 1950s (though it was technically set in 1961). In 1974, Howard traveled back in time again for *Happy Days* (ABC), which for ten years fed the nation's nostalgia for the 1950s. On the lake of time, Ron Howard was a human skipping stone.

Along with producing new shows that harked back to earlier eras, networks in the 1970s also rebroadcast old shows from those times. Americans tuned in en masse to watch sitcoms like *Leave It to Beaver* (1957–63), *Father Knows Best* (1954–60), and *I Love Lucy* (1951–57). The decade was awash in reruns. Thanks to the "sheer volume of reruns," writes media scholar Derek Kompare, "the past had become as much a part of television as the present." Of course, reruns had existed before the 1970s. However, Kompare argues that Americans in the 1970s consumed them in a fundamentally different way, treating reruns as visual time capsules and enjoying them for their nostalgia value. He crystallizes this point by explaining that a viewer from the 1960s and one from the 1970s, while reacting with the same five words to an episode *I Love Lucy*, might convey opposite meanings simply by shifting the emphasis. Whereas the former derisively remarks, "*Look* at that old show!," the latter affectionately gushes, "Look at that *old show*!" The infatuation with fifties reruns frustrated Gary Deeb, who covered television for the *Chicago Tribune*. In 1977, news that a local station planned to air *I Love Lucy* episodes pushed Deeb into a state of exasperation. "Our nation . . . seems to be trapped in such a militant adoration of the 1950s," he vented, "that virtually anything belonging to the sleepy Eisenhower era is the automatic recipient of coast-to-coast hosannas." Sensing that nostalgia was driving viewing habits, publishers started churning out sentimental books on old shows.[57]

Other publishers exploited the nostalgia craze by launching new magazines devoted to the past. *Remember When*, a magazine about old movies, appeared in 1971.[58] That same year marked the advent of *Liberty: The Nostalgia Magazine*, a periodical with a unique business model. Instead of offering readers fresh content, the magazine reprinted old articles from the defunct *Liberty Magazine* (1924–50), which had competed with the *Saturday Evening Post* in its heyday. In the first issue, one could find a review of Orson Welles's *Citizen Kane* (1941), learn Greta Garbo's reasons for staying single, tackle a crossword puzzle from 1924, enjoy a short story by F. Scott Fitzgerald, and read Shirley Temple's New Year's resolutions for 1935. Even the advertisements featured retrospection. Most companies purchasing advertising space had existed for at least fifty years—Hertz rental cars, Kotex napkins, AT&T telephone, Plymouth automobiles, and Chesterfield cigarettes. They submitted both new ads and old ads from their archives to the magazine, which juxtaposed them on facing pages. Though America had seen the magazine's articles before, this content—like Hersheypark's Carrousel—was rendered new again by its altered context. Whereas previously the articles had satisfied readers' curiosity about their present, now they indulged the public's craving to revisit the past.[59]

In the 1970s, millions of Americans, channeling their inner Martin Sloan, tried to return to the past by tapping into the new nostalgia industry. But why? At least in part, Americans collectively turned to the reassuring past to escape the troubling present. Matty Simmons, editor of *Liberty: The Nostalgia Magazine*, said exactly this. "Let's face it," he wrote, "nostalgia is a form of running away from today and, so far, today hasn't been a very bad day to run away from" with its inflation, unemployment, and war.[60] Gerald Clarke of *Time* saw nostalgia as a strategy to "erase memories of assassinations, wars, racial hatred and student riots." While agreeing that there were problems in the present, he admonished serenity seekers that "there is no such thing as a golden age" because the "past is an illusion just as much as the future."[61] Writing for the *New York Times* in 1973, historian Richard Lingeman saw the nostalgia craze as motivated by a "yearning for stability and domestic tranquility and a return to traditional American values." Lingeman quoted a disc jockey who played hits from the fifties and understood the seductive nature of the past. "My audience wants to forget its problems," he said, "and return to . . . those happy times—the prom, no wars, no riots, no protests, the convertibles at the drive in." Lingeman contested the accuracy of the popular image of the 1950s on the grounds that it left out unpleasant realities like McCarthyism and the Korean War.[62] Two scholars, Douglas Miller and Marion Nowak, agreed that the present was causing nostalgia. "Excessive, sentimental nostalgia generally occurs during times of perceived crisis" and "widespread disillusionment," they wrote. "Such has been the case in the seventies." In 1977, the pair devoted an entire book to debunking their own decade's "distorted" depiction of the 1950s.[63] Looking for a safe haven from a disturbing present, Americans projected a halo onto the 1950s, giving it a warm glow of peace and serenity.

Fred Davis, a sociologist, tackled the nation's obsession with nostalgia in *Yearning for Yesterday: A Sociology of Nostalgia* (1977). Like his contemporaries, Davis observed that nostalgic people tended to cleave time into simple halves—"the beautiful past and the unattractive present." But *why* did they do this? It was true, Davis acknowledged, that worrisome current events rendered the past appealing: fuel shortages, Watergate, counterculture movements, urban blight, and the end of the postwar boom. However, Davis contended that nostalgia seekers were not simply trying to escape the present. Something psychologically profound was taking place. Davis posited that people are animated by a powerful "yearning for continuity." When "discontinuities and dislocations" interrupt their lives, they react with nostalgia. Nostalgia, he bluntly stated, "thrives on transition." Davis specifically pointed to three types: transitions in one's life cycle, historical change, and social change. Concerning life cycles, an individual progressing from childhood to adolescence or from adulthood to old age can feel nostalgia for earlier stages (a carousel, as a symbol of childhood, serves this kind of nostalgia).[64]

Historical change could also disrupt continuity. Davis listed the jarring historical events from the previous decade that had intruded on people's lives: the Vietnam War, urban riots, student protests, the Kent State shootings, and the assassinations of John F. Kennedy, Robert F. Kennedy, and

Martin Luther King Jr. "Consider for a moment what America experienced," Davis told readers, "and one can begin to appreciate the appeal . . . of the nostalgic wave." Davis expanded the concept of historical change beyond what one sees on the evening news, also addressing the psychological impact of significant demographic shifts. Earlier generations of Americans seldom left the small towns and agricultural communities of their youths. Their lives were therefore defined by "continuity," as they maintained unbroken bonds to home, family, community, traditions, and the land itself. But the twentieth century unleashed vast economic forces that, at a "frenetic pace," uprooted people and severed their ties to meaningful places.[65] "Walking Distance" probably resonated with viewers because America was filled with Martin Sloans.

Social revolutions also ruptured continuity. To demonstrate this point, Davis listed the profound changes to the American way of life that had occurred within just a few years: African Americans attained equal rights, homosexuality was decriminalized, abortion was legalized, casual sex and pornography were celebrated in magazines like *Playboy*, hippies embraced hallucinogenic drugs, youth regarded the Protestant work ethic with "scornful disdain," and adolescents learned to "denigrate authority" instead of respect it. Though most people today classify at least some of these developments as progress, Americans at the time struggled to adjust to these unprecedented social convulsions. "Millions upon millions of Americans," Davis explained, endured "the most wide-ranging, sustained, and profound assault on native belief concerning the 'natural' and 'proper' that has ever been visited on a people over so short a span of time." In the end, the upheaval left many of the bedrock certainties of American life "challenged, disrupted, and shaken."[66]

So many transitions eventually took their toll. Invoking Klapp, Davis contended that the country was suffering from a "*collective* identity crisis." To repair their fractured identities, Americans turned en masse to the past. Nostalgia, Davis posited, provided "the means for holding onto and reaffirming identities which had been badly bruised" amid the social tumult. Not merely an escape from the "radical discontinuity" of the modern world, nostalgia actually offered Americans a psychological strategy for coping with that discontinuity.[67] Is it any wonder so many adored a carousel?

The Meaning of the Carrousel

The Carrousel at Hersheypark could evoke nostalgia because, by the 1970s, this classic ride had become a universally recognized symbol. It stood for childhood innocence, America's small-town past, and the passage of time. Multiple artists and intellectuals understood a carousel's utility as a symbol. We have already seen Rod Serling project this meaning onto the carousel in "Walking Distance." Disney's *Mary Poppins* (1964) also features a carousel. As a symbol for childhood joy and imagination, the carousel was a natural fit for a movie about a stern banker (George Banks) who has grown distant from both his children and his childhood. In the movie, the titular character, Mary Poppins, functions much like the Twilight Zone: through mysterious magic, she creates the conditions that allow Mr. Banks to reconnect with his children, learn to laugh again, and rediscover his youth. Though he is not, at the movie's end, riding a carousel, he is engaging in a comparable innocent pleasure: flying a kite.

A carousel also figures prominently in *Everybody Rides the Carousel* (1975), an animated film about psychologist Erik Erikson's eight stages of life. John Hubley, a former animator at Disney Studios, and his wife, Faith Hubley, collaborated with the Yale School of Drama to produce this educational film. The Hubleys generated the script and artistic vision, and Yale's actors-in-training, a group that included Meryl Streep, supplied the voices. The film opens with the host, a mildly creepy harlequin, introducing the carousel as a metaphor for life. Life consists of eight developmental stages, he says, each of which is symbolized by a ride on a specific horse:

> And here we have the carousel of life! Eight rides for eight ages. Everyone is invited. An age for every rider on our cycle of life. Can you find your painted pony? Who will win the brass ring? Each ride is the beginning of a new way of being. One builds on the other—from genesis to death. Each ride has its own surprise, its pushes and pulls, ups and downs, its ons and offs, a throbbing pulsation of feeling, sometimes scary, sometimes joyous. Eight rides for eight ages. . . . Everybody rides on the carousel of life—if they dare.

The film begins with the infant stage and proceeds methodically through the next seven stages, ending with old age and death. For each ride on the carousel, the film explores the expected challenges and triumphs inherent in the corresponding life stage. For example, in the third stage, the preschooler strives to move from a state of dependency on his mother to one of greater autonomy (a transition Winnicott also studied). As the child tries to do things for himself, such as getting dressed, he experiences both pride in his newfound independence and frustration when he cannot achieve his goal. After each stage, the film returns to the harlequin and the carousel, so that a new horse can be mounted and a new life stage introduced.[68]

Ray Bradbury saw dark potential in the carousel's ability to symbolize the passage of time. In *Something Wicked This Way Comes* (1962), the ride possesses the power to accelerate or reverse the aging process. In the novel, a mysterious and, as it turns out, sinister carnival passes through a small American town. Two boys visiting the carnival, Jim Nightshade and Will Holloway, happen to see something incredible but forbidden: an enchanted carousel that alters the age of the rider. For each forward revolution, the rider's age advances one year; for each reverse revolution, the rider becomes a year younger. Thus, there is the potential for an adult to step onto the carousel and then either crawl off as an infant or hobble off as an elderly person. The hero of the story is Will's father, Charles Holloway, a man who got a late start at building his family. Now fifty-four, Charles feels too old to be the vigorous dad his son Will needs. Yet, when the satanic carnival people attempt to make Will one of their own, Charles must protect his son while resisting the allure of a carousel that can restore his youth.[69]

Unlike Ray Bradbury, Hershey residents did not project evil onto their carousel. However, they did pick up on the Carrousel's utility as a symbol relating to time. "It is a link to the past," observed Bruce McKinney. People enjoy saying, "I rode that carrousel in 1948 when I was 12 and it is still here."[70] Dina Willard was such a person. "Well, my memories of Hershey go back to being brought here by my Aunt Jenny," Willard said, referring to Hershey's golden era. "She would take us on weekends to Hershey Park, and my favorite ride was the Carrousel, and it has remained my favorite ride. But *it* was very, very different than *it* is now."[71] We cannot be certain what noun Willard intended as the antecedent of the pronoun *it*. If *it* replaced the Carrousel, then Willard was referencing this ride's altered meaning in its new context. *It* possibly referred to the park, transformed by the renovation. Finally, she may have been alluding to the times themselves, which clearly were changing. Regardless, when Willard contrasted the past and present, she saw the Carrousel as a useful symbol. It served as a reference point, helping her mark the passage of time.[72]

Keith Dittenhauer was also happy to see the old Carrousel enjoy new life. A self-described "Park Buff," Dittenhauer was saddened by the fact that many amusement parks were either destroying their carousels or dismantling them and selling the pieces to collectors who traded in nostalgia. He was "extremely glad," he wrote in a letter to John Hart, "that this beautiful one is being restored." The Carrousel's rebirth provided Dittenhauer with the opportunity to go back in time, so to speak, through research. Since Hershey lacked records on its own carousel, Dittenhauer immersed himself in the archives of the Philadelphia Toboggan Company, which built the Carrousel in 1919. He then shared his findings—such as the fact that the music came from a Wurlitzer organ—with John Hart so that Hart could use these details in promotional materials.[73] Hart did exactly that. Five weeks after Dittenhauer mailed his letter, information from it appeared in press releases and the *Lebanon Daily News*.[74] "All of the horses on the carrousel were individually hand-carved and no two are alike," the reporter wrote. "It is one of the oldest carrousels still in use in America, and features the nostalgic chords of a Wurlitzer organ."[75]

Doraine Mitchell experienced both the Carrousel and the Comet at different stages in her life. As a child, she recalled visiting Hershey Park every summer. When she was eight, her older sister let her ride the Comet—and then regretted the decision. "Once she got me on, she couldn't get me off of it!" Mitchell exclaimed. "I was hooked!" Later in life, Mitchell moved to Texas with her family. As an adult, she returned to Hershey after the renovation. She was elated to be able to "re-live my roller coaster experience on the historic Comet!" However, it was the continued operation of the Carrousel that affected her most profoundly. Mitchell felt "awed" when she saw the Carrousel frozen in a perfect state of preservation. Its restoration allowed her to venture back in time and reaffirm the blessing of her youth. "Thank you, Hershey Park [*sic*]," she exclaimed, "for helping make my childhood even more wonderful!"[76] Mitchell was not alone. Even Mary Hubler, who greatly resented Hershey Estates for demolishing cherished landmarks, grudgingly credited the company for doing a good deed with the Comet and Carrousel. But she did fault the park for failing to preserve the Miniature Railway also.[77]

Conclusion

As summer approached in 1973, park officials eyed the much-anticipated grand opening with excitement. That said, a troubling question nagged at them. What if the local community were to reject the new park? This was no idle concern. In the early 1970s, a cloud of negativity hung ominously over the once-happy town. In recent years, a proud community that had grown comfortable with its way of life had absorbed, against its will, a series of changes: restructuring at the chocolate company, the termination of the compact, a demographic shift effected by the HMC, and a series of jarring demolitions. In 1972, a correspondent from *Newsday* interviewed members of the community. "There are some residents who grumble quietly," he wrote, "that the company no longer cares for the people" and "is trying to shove down their throats a huge amusement park."[78]

Articles like this one gave park officials a sinking feeling because the new park's future rested on the community's acceptance. Should residents spurn Hersheypark, the consequences promised to be severe. Socially, the town would acquire an ugly dynamic if out-of-town tourists were to confront rude locals who resented their presence. Financially, Hershey Estates was depending on the local community to spend money at the new park. In fact, ERA had factored local patronage into its favorable forecast. "Economic characteristics of the population surrounding theme parks significantly affect attendance potential," the consulting firm informed generally before sharing the good news about Hershey specifically: "Per capita income of Hersheypark's resident market area is one of the highest in the East."[79] Yes, it was good news, but only if the community embraced the park. As 1973 approached, that loomed as a big *if*.

Chapter 5

Grand Opening

In early May 1973, life inside Hersheypark got hectic. With the grand opening just days away, workers made final touches on all attractions. On that day, the park would unveil two historically themed areas, Tudor Square and Rhineland. In previous months, RDA had taken painstaking measures to confer "pastness" onto these recreations of centuries-old English and German architecture. Specifically, RDA designed, sculpted, textured, and colored newly made structures and objects at these two sites to give them an aura of historical authenticity. In this sense, Tudor Square and Rhineland were the opposite of the Carrousel. If the Carrousel was an old attraction made new, then Tudor Square and Rhineland were new attractions made to appear old.

Away from the park, the public relations team implemented a multipronged strategy to entice guests and attract favorable media coverage. To excite the local market, it prepared "Welcome to Hersheypark '73," a twenty-page advertising supplement that would appear in a Sunday edition of Harrisburg's *Patriot-News*.[1] It also sent press releases and photographs to 3,800 newspapers as well as travel, tourism, and automotive magazines. Local TV stations in tourist markets that Hershey had targeted received a script and images to use in broadcasts. In this way, the PR office endeavored to "maximize the formidable publicity potential of the complete redevelopment of Hersheypark into *the* leading theme park of the Northeastern United States."[2]

When a media outlet receives a prewritten narrative, sometimes it cooperates by following the script. After all, that is the easiest thing to do.

Sure enough, in the summer of 1973, dozens and dozens of newspapers ran minimally altered versions of the PR office's prefabricated story, "How Sweet It Is . . . at Hersheypark." "Everyone knows all about America's favorite chocolate bar," the piece began, "but how many people know that Hersheypark is in the midst of a five-year redevelopment program?"[3] Sometimes, however, a newspaper rejects the script, choosing instead to craft its own narrative. That is what the *Philadelphia Inquirer* did, dispatching a reporter, Murray Dubin, to investigate Hershey. After talking with residents, Dubin homed in on the underlying story, which had nothing to do with exciting new attractions.

Hershey, Dubin discovered, was struggling through a difficult transition. To convey the essence of his story, he—like Hershey's PR office—used a chocolate-themed pun: "Chocolate Town in Midst of a Bittersweet Change." Formerly a "sleepy" place dominated by Germans and Italians, Hershey was now, he wrote, the site of a "$50 million hospital" and a "Disney-type" park. To assess the impact on the town, Dubin interviewed Jim McAree, a professor at a nearby college, who called Hershey a "company town that works." The chocolate company, McAree noted, has always "contributed to the community" without becoming a "Big Brother." These positive words aside, McAree doubted that residents would be able to adapt to the changes. The "old time Hersheyites are very self-satisfied," he went on, and think they are "the center of the universe." "They don't realize," he portentously added, that "this will never be a provincial little town again." As Dubin continued to snoop around, he located another source of tension beneath the town's placid surface—the new residents. The HMC, Dubin reported, "has caused blacks, Jews and Democrats to move into Hershey for the first time." Though African Americans remained a tiny percentage of the population, Dubin found one to interview. Fletcher Rainey, who had moved from Baltimore in 1972, viewed Hershey as a "beautiful town and a good place to raise kids." That said, he harbored the unsettling feeling that "something is amiss." He found it unnerving that people gave him cold looks in the street. Rainey felt as if he stuck out like a "sore thumb." To get a white perspective, Dubin spoke to Robert Gite, a factory worker who had grown up in Hershey. Gite noted that, as recently as five years earlier, you did not see "black faces" at either the factory or the park. Now you did. Though he did not comment either positively or negatively on the town's increasing diversity, he did bemoan its worsening traffic. As for Hersheypark, he declared his intention to never go there.

Dubin's piece was not exactly an exposé because it did not reveal anything truly shocking. Thus, it probably inflicted little or no damage to the town's reputation. Regardless, it certainly was not what Hershey executives wanted Philadelphians to read. As the park prepared to welcome thousands of tourists for its grand opening, the article set the wrong mood. Instead of igniting enthusiasm for the park, it ominously portrayed the town as unwelcoming to new residents, unable to adjust to change, and unwilling to embrace its theme park. Hershey came across as a town on edge.[4]

As the grand opening approached, Hershey executives were on pins and needles. After all, there was a lot riding on this single day. Indeed, this was the day that would end the built-up suspense by answering many lingering questions. Would tourists have fun in a way that boded well for the future? Would the press provide a favorable review of the new park? And perhaps most crucially, would the local community embrace the park—or reject it?

Unveiling Hersheypark

Preparations

Randall Duell liked to say that "behind each successful park, you'll find one man who's totally involved." He is willing "to live it, walk it," and "pick up the paper cups."[5] For Hersheypark, that man was Bruce McKinney. As McKinney reconnoitered the park grounds weeks before the grand opening, he spied a problem. It had nothing to do with the creative side of the business, such as the historical theming. The issue he identified was purely practical: the park's trash removal system was inadequate. How could McKinney detect a fatal flaw in a system that had yet to fail? He used his imagination. As he strolled about, he tried to visualize the facility hosting twenty thousand people at once. In his mind, he could see the trash receptacles rapidly filling during peak hours with disposable cups, plates, napkins, and utensils. Though each one would have to be emptied at regular intervals, at present, the only way for staff to remove garbage sacks was to lug them across the park *within sight of guests*. For a park that aspired to Disney-level cleanliness, this was unacceptable. Adept at problem-solving,

McKinney devised a solution. The park would theme a small fleet of flatbed scooters with fiberglass animals. Employees would drive the scooters to the receptacles, quickly stash the garbage bags behind the cute animals, and whisk them away.[6]

As this anecdote suggests, the success of a theme park depended as much on nuts-and-bolts concerns as on its creative design. For this reason, RDA trained its designers to think practically as well as creatively. "Our architects are entertainment-oriented," Ira West commented, but they also "ensure . . . that basic needs are met." A shortage of toilets or parking spaces will diminish someone's experience, West added, "even if the entertainment is stellar." To illustrate the point, West shared an anecdote from the summer of 1973. While walking through Hersheypark, he approached a men's room, only to find his path blocked by a woman. "You're not going in there," she defiantly informed him. "We took over!" After West reported the problem, the Hershey people started hovering outside restrooms with stopwatches, timing people as they entered and exited. The data convinced them to install additional toilets and sinks in the women's rooms.[7]

Long queues at rides could also ruin a guest's experience. When visitors were standing in line, two bad things were happening: they were not making purchases, and they were growing frustrated. To prevent this problem, a park obviously had to possess sufficient ride capacity. How much capacity was enough? When working with any client, Randall Duell trained his designers to start *not* with a creative vision but with the park's mathematical profile. In other words, RDA designers did not begin by saying, "We're going to put a coaster" or "a water ride in." Rather, they started by analyzing ERA's market projections. They progressed "from the economic figures to the rides," Duell explained, "and not vice-versa." Specifically, a designer would input just two data points into a mathematical formula: first, the number of people expected to visit the park on a typical day during peak season and, second, the park's total population at the busiest hour on this day (between 2:00 and 3:00 p.m.). At this point, the designer had what they needed to determine ride capacity because RDA already knew, using data from other parks, that the typical visitor enjoys 1.5 rides per hour. To be on the safe side, West recommended that parks roughly the size of Hersheypark install enough attractions to allow ten thousand people to enjoy two rides within sixty minutes.[8]

As opening day approached, park managers endeavored to train and prepare the roughly 850 new employees hired for the summer season.[9] Hershey executives had visited Disney's parks and come away impressed by its spiffy, cheerful, and professional uniformed army. They hoped to transplant the "Walt Disney Look" to Hersheypark.[10] Toward this end, managers composed a *Hospitality Handbook* to teach proper conduct. The "Dress and Grooming" section (which parroted Disneyland's policies) stipulated that male employees' hair must not exceed shoulder length and mustaches and sideburns must be kept "neatly trimmed" (rules prohibited beards and muttonchops). The handbook also explained how to interact with guests. With a far-reaching advertising campaign, Hersheypark expected to attract more minority visitors in 1973 than in any previous year. In anticipation of diverse patronage, park managers taught employees, most of whom were white, how to handle people who looked different from them: "This summer, people of all races, all sizes, all manners of dress and attitudes will visit Hersheypark. They will be looking to you to provide the fun they have come to enjoy, not damage what could be a 'Happy Experience.' During the course of a busy day, you may be tempted to say or do something foolish. Restrain your emotions; you could trigger a minor incident into a serious situation." John Hart, who delivered what amounted to a pep talk, hammered home the same message. "People are 'funny,'" he said. "No two are alike." This being the case, he promised his staff that they would acquire useful wisdom and experience: "You'll be dealing with all of them, and in so doing, will be gaining valuable insight into just what mankind is all about."[11] Thinking specifically of African Americans, Hershey executives circulated among themselves a trade-journal piece titled "Racial Balance Poses No Deterrent to Carowinds." According to the article, African Americans accounted for 30 to 50 percent of visitors to Carowinds, a recently opened park in North Carolina. Carowinds reported no difficulty in hiring African Americans or pleasing them with affordable, family-oriented entertainment. Hersheypark hoped to provide African Americans with a comparable experience.[12]

The Preview Event

Opening day was set for Sunday, May 20, 1973. The day before, the park held a preview event for elected officials, special guests, radio and television personalities, and members of the local and national press. To entice the latter, the PR office sent formal invitations to *Time, Newsweek, Fortune, Better Homes and Gardens*, and the *New York Times*. Each invitation came with a free Samsonite travel bag and encouraged the journalist to bring the whole family. PR also arranged for the cast of *The Waltons* to make an appearance, since this TV series projected the wholesome family image Hersheypark coveted.[13] Disney World executives also received an invitation but declined to attend, citing their own busy schedules.[14]

Hersheypark also welcomed the entire local community to the preview event.[15] In truth, no one knew what to expect from this group. Some executives feared that Hershey residents would collectively signal their discontent by shunning the festivities. Others predicted solid turnout for the following reason: after two years of agonizing demolitions and incessant construction, curious residents would want to see the source of so much controversy. But these were only guesses. No one successfully predicted what actually happened.

On the morning of the preview event, employees made final preparations. Over at the Craft Barn, a brand-new attraction, workers furiously applied one last coat of paint.[16] When the park officially opened, attendance exceeded even the wildest expectations: more than twenty-two thousand people showed up outside the fence.[17] The tremendous "throng" first massed around a stage to watch the ribbon-cutting ceremony. There, Ernie Kline, Pennsylvania's lieutenant governor, cut more than just a strip of colored tape. In the spirit of theme park fun, he cut in half the wife (and assistant) of the park's resident magician, Mark Wilson. As she continued to smile and wave during her bifurcation, the crowd "gasped in astonishment," wrote a reporter for a local paper. After the ceremony, the park gates opened and the "mass of humanity surged through them." Not wishing to deal with such commotion, the reporter decided to leave and come back later, when the crowds had subsided. They never did. She returned at 9:00 p.m., only to discover that the lights were still "twinkling," and the local residents were continuing to enjoy themselves.[18]

The preview event was not without challenges. The crowd exceeded what Hersheypark could realistically accommodate, and so it overwhelmed rides, vending, and food services. "The huge crowd that hit the park on May 19," wrote a trade journal, "created queue lines reminiscent of peak days at Disney World." Ordinarily, a theme park could interpret a comparison to Disney World as a compliment. But this journalist intended his as an admonition: "Opening day pointed out to management several factors that need improvement." Bruce McKinney, who spoke to the journalist, explained the problem as "growing pains."[19] He later recounted how the immense crowd had caught him by surprise. "The people were pouring through . . . all at one time," he recalled, and the "honest aspect of it was we weren't prepared for twenty-some thousand people." As a consequence, the "food lines were long and the service was very, very slow."[20]

Long queues notwithstanding, McKinney judged the day a resounding success. For two years, he and his colleagues had tried, through formal presentations and casual conversations, to explain the renovation to the local community. For the first time, residents who were used to the deteriorating old park could see the finished product. "The people from the community were absolutely in awe," McKinney recalled, with some even remarking, "This is like Disneyland." At Hershey Estates, phone calls and letters poured in, praising the redevelopment. On the next day, which was the park's true opening, the rain never stopped. A meager seven hundred people paid for admission and entered the park. However, this drenched opening hardly mattered. The smashing success of the preview event had marked a turning point and seemed to promise a bright future.[21]

Music, Magic, and Animal Attractions

By signing Mark Wilson and other performers, Hersheypark was adhering to the Disney model. At Disneyland, a family that needed to take a break from walking, standing, riding, and screaming could enjoy a show. The same was true at Hersheypark. Wilson and his wife, Nani Darnell, were nationally known performers, thanks to their weekly television show, *The Magic Land of Allakazam* (1960–65). The show was truly pioneering. Prior to its airing, TV viewers could see magic only in short segments on variety shows. Wilson and his wife were the first to demonstrate that people would tune in to see a show exclusively about magic.[22] For Hersheypark, Wilson designed an entirely new act tailored to the theme park experience.

He was joined by Al Alberts, formerly of the fifties pop band the Four Aces, who performed three times daily in the newly built Amphitheater.[23]

Once a teen icon, the aging Alberts had wisely reinvented himself and found a new demographic to entertain—children. To succeed with this audience, Alberts adopted a clean-cut style that fit perfectly into Hersheypark's family-oriented entertainment. "A Special Thanks for the Al Alberts Show," wrote a father who had taken his family to Hersheypark. "Boy, it does us good to see such a bunch of wholesome people, performing for all the family." In his view, the show was a "beautiful sign of a healthy future for America."[24]

In addition to offering wholesome entertainment, Alberts helped the park in another way—he provided television exposure. Each week, the Philadelphia native hosted an hour-long, televised talent show featuring young performers. The syndicated *Al Alberts Showcase* aired on Saturday afternoons in the vast Philadelphia viewing area, as well as in fifteen other cities, including Pittsburgh and Washington, DC. For thirteen weeks over the summer, Alberts taped his show from inside Hersheypark.[25] According to Cy Little, who managed entertainment, the show was "produced at different places throughout the park."[26] This meant that, each week, the estimated six million viewers saw the park's rides and attractions in both the show and Hersheypark's two minutes of commercials.[27] In this way, Alberts's television presence helped to advertise Hersheypark in the region. When Joe Sharkey of the *Philadelphia Inquirer* visited Hersheypark, he focused on Al Alberts's televised show, which exemplified modern media, and the Carrousel, a "relic from the park's earliest days." Hoping to capture the essence of Hersheypark, Sharkey contrasted the two. "A contradiction, nonetheless, is this pleasant big amusement park," he wrote, "where a hand-carved carrousel" can "exist side-by-side with the blazing television lights and the squeals of children in love with the summer."[28]

Children were not the only ones squealing, as Hersheypark also featured animals. In the Animal Garden, guests could meet baby pigs, donkeys, goats, and sheep. This area differed from a zoo because visitors could touch, pet, and feed the animals (fig. 13). "It's a real education," a press release explained, "for children to actually experience the world of animals in the flesh." In this "animal-contact area," children and adults could "mingle and play" not just with typical "barnyard animals," but with more "exotic breeds."[29] Guests could pat a llama, shake hands with a monkey, and befriend Cocoa, the baby elephant that had survived Hurricane Agnes.

Fig. 13 Visitors interacted with animals in the Animal Garden. Courtesy of HCA.

A couple of times each day, the resident trainer would lead the animals in performances before gathered spectators.[30] A different kind of performance took place over at the Aquatheater. There, the two dolphins, Dolly and Skipper, headlined a popular water show that, thanks to the knowledgeable trainer, taught guests about marine life.[31] "The perpetual dolphin smile and obvious intelligence make the show exciting and fun," wrote a nearby college student. "They flip, sing, applaud themselves and the audience and jump through hoops of fire."[32]

Tudor Square and Rhineland

Can Designers Manufacture Symbols?

Magic shows, musical performances, and animal acts aside, the success of Hersheypark would hinge on its historical theming. RDA's core conviction was that three-dimensional representations of history would lure people from large metropolitan areas who sought comfort and reassurance in the past—a temporary respite from modern life. What is more, by showing respect for local history and heritage, such attractions would also soothe Hershey residents upset by change. The Carrousel served this vision beautifully by invoking both America's small-town past and Hershey's golden era. However, the vision required more than a relocated carousel. After all, the goal was to enable guests to "taste, touch, and feel" *multiple pasts*, not just one.[33] For the 1973 season, Hersheypark opened two areas themed according to history: Tudor Square and Rhineland.

The hope among Hershey executives was that residents who had treated the old Hershey Park as a symbolic landscape would do the same with Hersheypark. In other words, the local community would embrace the new themed areas in the same way they had the Bandshell, Starlight Ballroom, and Picnic Pavilion. Those landmarks had come to represent many things in the town's collective consciousness: the compact, a benevolent patriarch, childhood innocence, family togetherness, and a simpler past. Indeed, residents regarded the demolitions as emotionally jarring because they cleared away so much of the town's symbolic ecosystem. Though the Comet and Carrousel survived as transitional objects, the rest of Hershey Park emerged from the destruction as a blank slate on which to build. The challenge facing RDA designers and Hershey executives was to repopulate this space in a way that would render it meaningful again. That was the hope. However, creating new symbols proved to be tricky. After all, the lost structures had attained meaning naturally and over time. For example, the Bandshell had signified nothing other than itself when first constructed in 1914. It had only started to glow with communal significance after the fond memories of thousands of residents had attached themselves to the structure. The question was whether Hollywood-trained designers could engineer the sort of meaningful symbolism that typically had to evolve organically over several decades.

Orrin Klapp was skeptical. The "problem of creating meaningful common symbols," he stated bluntly, "has not been solved." In his view, the failure of architects to erect symbolic landscapes had nothing to do with effort—for they were trying hard. However, he contended that it was human "interaction" over time that conferred meaning onto a structure. In other words, symbolic significance came to a place through gradual accretion and could not be conferred instantaneously through the "designer's will."

Try as they might, designers simply could not know "what a significant design is" for a given community. Of course, their lack of local knowledge did not prevent them from making attempts. Yet these efforts inevitably yielded something lacking in authenticity—what Klapp called a *pseudo-place*. He explained that a pseudoplace was "a lot of ingeniously arranged concrete that creates the illusion of somewhere one has been." Disneyland exemplified the pseudoplace. Klapp admitted that, as a "children's mecca," Disneyland might be "fun to go to." However, in the end, a replica of a place or historical era would always fail to satisfy people's deeper psychic needs. A pseudoplace "robs identity," Klapp stated succinctly, while a genuine place "nurtures it."[34]

If RDA's designers had read Klapp's book, they probably disputed his claim. That was because, in their opinion, Walt Disney and his Imagineers had achieved the very objective Klapp dismissed as impossible. Visitors did regard Main Street, USA, Frontierland, and Tomorrowland as embodiments American values and aspirations. In other words, Walt Disney succeeded in creating flash symbols—structures that acquired meaning instantly and did not need to marinate in time. If Disney could do it, then there was cause for optimism in Hershey. Historical theming that honored local heritage could convince people to abandon their resistance to Hersheypark. That, anyway, was the hope.

The Old World in the New Park

Tudor Square and Rhineland allowed parkgoers to explore two Old World cultures—English and German. Tudor Square presented the architecture of England during the reign of the Tudors (1485–1603), a dynasty that ended with the death of Queen Elizabeth, who had no heirs. It was an eventful period, one that included the Protestant Reformation; the defeat of the Spanish Armada; the blossoming of England's science, literature, and arts (e.g., William Shakespeare); and its first colony in the New World—the short-lived settlement on Roanoke Island. Though tumultuous, the period of Tudor rule saw the rise of England as a world power intent on exerting its influence in North America generally and Pennsylvania specifically (though William Penn received his royal charter to found the Pennsylvania Colony after the Tudor dynasty). Hersheypark's Tudor Square, therefore, celebrated England during its remarkable years of ascendancy, when it acquired the ability and determination to imprint its culture on the New World.[35]

Rhineland, which recreated traditional German architecture, represented a different origin story. For much of the 1600s, the central European territories bordering the Rhine River were characterized by strife, bloodshed, and dislocation as the result of the Thirty Years' War (1618–48) and the frequent French incursions of King Louis XIV in the late 1600s. This prolonged period of instability provided the German-speaking inhabitants with plenty of incentive to migrate elsewhere. But who wanted them, and where could they go? Enter William Penn. When Penn made his two visits to the Rhineland in the 1670s, the beleaguered Germans saw him, in scholar Russell Gilbert's words, as a "ray of hope." "In this dark chapter of European history," Gilbert wrote with dramatic flair, "Penn's promise appeared as a distant, beckoning light." Penn's "Holy Experiment" in Pennsylvania offered prospective emigrants the chance to plant crops in fertile soil, ply their artisanal trades in towns, raise families in peace, and practice religion without persecution. The opportunity proved irresistible.[36] If Tudor Square honored the Old World civilization that heavily influenced the United States and Pennsylvania, then Rhineland paid homage to the origin culture of the Pennsylvania Germans.

As the summer of 1973 got underway, Hershey used advertising to generate excitement for these new attractions. To whet readers' appetites, advertisements highlighted the park's ability to simulate time travel: "How often has one wished to be able to turn back the hands of time, or maybe just wonder what it would be like to actually see a lifestyle as it was in the past? Hersheypark has made that wish a reality."[37] Even if one did not hold this wish, the park's layout rendered a visit to old Europe inescapable. Visitors to the park met first with Tudor Square, situated right at the entrance; after paying admission, they passed immediately into Rhineland. By seizing control of the visitor's experience in this way, Hersheypark sent essentially the same message that Disneyland had with Main Street, USA: the past has much to offer the present.

Tudor Square sought to recreate old England through architecture, costume, food, and music. Indeed, as visitors made their approach to Hersheypark, their first sensory experience was an audible one, as the "tunes of merry old England" wafted from the speaker system.[38] After crossing two

Fig. 14 Tudor Square carried visitors back in time. Courtesy of HCA.

artificial lakes on a cobblestone path, parkgoers next encountered an elaborate "replica" of an English town (fig. 14). "A great deal of time and special effort," commented Ralph Bowerman, RDA's chief architect for this project, "has been taken to insure a faithful reproduction of the precise Tudor Style." One structure, the "castle tower," included "crenellated parapets similar to those used by the master's archers as lookouts and shooting sites." Bowerman went on to praise builders from the Tudor era for producing such "sophisticated work."[39]

The buildings were sophisticated. A confluence of factors allowed RDA to build not artificial-looking fiberglass structures, but faithful replicas of Tudor architecture. First, Bowerman discovered that real stone, close to what Tudor masons had used, was available nearby. Of course, local quarries were of little use if no one possessed the skills to work with stone. Here again, Bowerman enjoyed good fortune. Hershey was located in close proximity to Lancaster County, where Pennsylvania Germans had kept alive many of the old artisanal trades. Bowerman found a stonecutter able to do the job. The last challenge, generating historically accurate architectural blueprints, was an easy one. RDA's team included Hollywood set designers experienced in

Fig. 15 After passing through Tudor Square's gates, visitors entered Rhineland. Courtesy of HCA.

making period reproductions for movies. Proud of Tudor Square, Ira West declared, "Disney would not have done a better job."[40]

Tudor Square delivered more than old English architecture. RDA designed the costumes to reflect the Tudor-era wardrobe. According to a press release, visitors could meet "shopkeepers dressed in the garb of the period" who sell "goods and services typical of 17th century England."[41] There were no rides in Tudor Square (or in Rhineland), and that was by design. According to West, the themed areas were intended not to elicit screams, but to immerse guests in history and, in the process, foster intergenerational interaction within families. "A father visiting Tudor Square with his son can point things out," West explained. "This is how architecture once looked in England. This is how they baked bread."[42]

Many of Tudor Square's offerings were edible. As impressive as the structures and costumes were, the themed area also provided visitors with a culinary experience. At the Tudor Cremes Shop, they could find "ice cream, sundaes, sodas, and soft drinks." Though the image of Queen Elizabeth slurping fizzy cola through a straw presented an anachronism, the menu at the Tudor House Restaurant included "definitely English fare" such as dishes named "Queen Anne's Ladle," "Royal Armada," "Mid-Summer Dream," and "House of Lords." There was also chocolate. Visitors hankering for chocolate could find it inside Tudor Square, where its English roots were stressed. "Highlighting the tour of Tudor Square is The Chocolate House," explained a promotional article, "where children of all ages can shop for chocolate products and drinks . . . in much the same way as their forefathers did some 300 years ago." Offering a history lesson, the article went on to credit England's chocolate houses with wrestling chocolate away from the "aristocracy" and spreading it to the "millions." Though the narrative never mentioned M. S., visitors could infer the chocolate baron's crucial role in consummating this populist fable through the mass production of the Hershey bar. Thanks to his vision, all could now enjoy the pleasurable experience of consuming chocolate.[43]

After purchasing admission at ticket booths that formed a part of the Tudor Castle, visitors passed through the gates and entered a second facsimile of the Old World—Rhineland. "When you enter the park," tantalized promoters, "you have to blink twice to be sure you haven't walked back through time to find yourself at a peaceful village along the Rhine River. Ancient maples and elms tower overhead, their graceful branches providing shade and giving the scene a genuine touch of the Old World" (fig. 15). Much like Tudor Square, this small "German village" offered historically themed architecture, music, costumed people, and food. Guests could dine on bratwurst and sauerkraut in Das Wurst Haus and then enjoy a treat in the Black Forest Sweet Shop. However, more than merely depicting German culture, Rhineland paid tribute to it. Rhineland "honors the origin of the Pennsylvania Dutch, who settled in and around the Hershey area." Members of the local community—many of whom had German ancestry—would feel as if their heritage were receiving proper veneration.[44]

Symbols of What?

RDA designers and Hershey executives hoped that Tudor Square and Rhineland would form important parts of a new symbolic landscape. When taken individually, each realm stood for something fairly obvious. Tudor Square represented the Old World country that had most influenced the United States. Rhineland stood for the European culture that had shaped central Pennsylvania. Though we might stop here, the problem is that Hersheypark encouraged visitors to link the two themed areas—to see them as a binary. In every important aspect, the two were paired: they were part of the same phase of the redevelopment, designed by the same architects, constructed simultaneously on adjoining plots, and promoted as a single experience comprising two parts. In short, Tudor Square and Rhineland were joined at the hip. They even possessed a historical tie in the person of William Penn. It was during the English Quaker's trips to the Rhineland in the 1670s that he identified this region as a promising source of colonists. In the 1680s, a migration stream from the Rhineland started to flow into Pennsylvania, one that did not abate until the mid-nineteenth century.[45]

When viewed in tandem, Tudor Square and Rhineland took on added meaning. They symbolized contrasting cultures coexisting in a beneficial state of tension. Tudor Square represented the point of origin for America's most dominant cultural stream, the one that had powerfully shaped the legal, political, scientific, and economic frameworks of colonial America and, later, the United States. Over the centuries, America's English-inherited values favoring order and rationality had helped drive the country's progress. However, if unbalanced by a counterweight, English values threatened to create a society that was efficient and productive, but also coldly machinelike. Fortunately, in Pennsylvania, that healthy counterweight was provided by the Germans—a group rivaled only by the English in terms of the state's population. The Pennsylvania Germans organized their communities around a different set of virtues and priorities: piety, modesty, honesty, family, tradition, craftsmanship, and closeness to the earth. This cultural mixing is what set Pennsylvania apart from the English-dominated colonies of Massachusetts and Virginia. "Pennsylvania has a unique position in American history," wrote Russell Gilbert. As the "abode for peoples widely different in language, nationality, and religion," Pennsylvania became America's first "melting pot."[46] The larger message implied by Tudor Square's juxtaposition with Rhineland was encouragingly optimistic. Just as English and German themed areas existed side by side in Hersheypark, so, too, had Pennsylvania harmonized its cultural and ethnic heterogeneity.[47]

Finally, Tudor Square and Rhineland symbolized the passage of time. Hersheypark organizers tried hard to sell guests on the illusion of time travel conjured up by these European-themed areas ("How often has one wished to be able to turn back the hands of time?"). This possibility of time travel appealed, but in different ways, to two types of park visitor. For the out-of-towner from a large metropolitan area, time travel would have been especially attractive in the summer of 1973 and beyond. With the continuing Vietnam War, a worsening Watergate scandal, and a populace still recovering from the tumultuous sixties, the country seemed to lack a clear direction. In short, the ship of state seemed adrift in turbulent waters, rudderless, and without a steady hand at the helm. According to Ira West, a major advantage of the historical theme was that it offered a temporary refuge from anything new and disturbing. "People don't like change," he observed. "The reason you go to a park is to forget your problems."[48]

In that case, Tudor Square and Rhineland offered something miraculous: the chance to rewind the tape of American history, so to speak, all the way back to two hopeful moments of genesis. For these themed areas depicted not just England and Germany, but—crucially—those countries as they might have looked to emigrants on the eve of their embarkation to the New World. From the perspective of these courageous people on the cusp, the vast continent across the Atlantic beckoned as a wide-open land of boundless promise, as yet unsullied by strife, division, or corruption. In sum, Hershey's Old World attractions offered guests the chance to renew their faith in the American experiment.

If out-of-town visitors sought refuge from the present, local visitors enjoyed a different experience. Inside Rhineland, they could celebrate a way of life that had not only flourished in the New World but was also not responsible for the present predicaments. Indeed, as such visitors ambled through the cluster of brown and white timber-framed structures, they found themselves amid a congratulatory architecture. Here were good values. Here was sanity. Such guests might privately comment to themselves that the larger American culture was threatened by discord, dishonesty, and division. However, the Pennsylvania German way of life—with its emphasis on faith, family, and farming—had yet to fail and had much to offer (see chapter 6).

Reaction from the Public and Media

John Hart wanted to know what people thought of the new park. What attractions did they most enjoy? What about the experience could be improved?

During the summer of 1973, he frequently strolled through the park in his coat and tie (no matter how hot the day), wearing on his lapel a big badge that read, "John Hart, General Manager." He would then hunt for guests who seemed willing to share their impressions. "Young man," he would say, "what do you think of my park?"[49] Hart's informal chats provided one channel for feedback. The park also gathered opinion systematically by conducting a survey. When executives reviewed the data, they found it encouraging. The single-price admission policy received approval from 87 percent of visitors; apparently, most people liked avoiding the constant hassle of producing coins in the old pay-by-the-ride system. With respect to the rides themselves, 96 percent rated them as either "excellent" or "good." As for service, almost three-quarters of guests found employees to be both polite and professional in appearance. These positive numbers aside, the feedback also indicated areas that could be improved. The park needed additional dining facilities and more benches located in the shade for the elderly.[50]

Letters from parkgoers largely corroborated the survey's data. As the mail poured in during the summers of 1973 and 1974, Paul Serff, a park manager, responded to each one. Numerous people commented favorably on both the cleanliness of the park and the courteous behavior of employees. One woman, whose letter could stand in for dozens, shared that she "was *MOST* impressed with the polite, considerate, relaxed yet conscientious manner of the ride operators." She added that her husband appreciated the girls who swept up trash "as it hit the ground." In response to letters like this, Serff always trotted out the same phrase: he was glad, he wrote again and again, to provide "a little hospitality in the Hershey tradition." In the few cases where patrons complained about rude employees, he would deploy the same phrase. We strive "to provide our guests with what we call hospitality in the Hershey tradition," he wrote to one angry patron. "Apparently you came in contact with some of our employees who do not share this motto," and "for this I apologize." Not surprisingly, letters focusing on employee behavior and park cleanliness invariably came from adults. When children wrote, they tended to express enthusiasm for rides. "I loved all of the rides," wrote one elementary schooler. "Most of them were scarey [*sic*]." Another child, in addition to praising specific rides, offered Hersheypark encouragement with regard to its attendance. "At the rate you are working," he wrote, "you will have as much people as Walt Disney."[51]

Newspapers and magazines also reviewed Hersheypark. Impressed by Disneyland's neat appearance, park managers had placed a premium on landscaping and cleanliness. That effort paid off. A writer for *Holiday* magazine who attended the preview event went on to write a major article on theme parks in 1974. He called Hersheypark "one of the cleanest and greenest [theme parks] around."[52] Bruce McKinney was ecstatic that, "because of that day," a magazine had "called us the cleanest and greenest."[53] The public relations office picked up on this quote, "cleanest and greenest," and incorporated it into press releases.[54] As a result, the magical phrase reverberated across local and regional newspapers. Lost in all the repetition was the fact that *Holiday* had called Hersheypark "*one of* the cleanest and greenest." When the quotation appeared in print, it looked as if judges had awarded Hersheypark first prize in a nationwide contest. "Clean is the word to describe Hersheypark," wrote the *Hanover Evening Sun*. "Holiday Magazine listed Hersheypark as *the* cleanest and greenest theme park *in America*."[55] Some exaggeration notwithstanding, Hersheypark truly was a well-kept and environmentally responsible facility. As evidence of that fact, it received an ecological award from the United States Department of Agriculture.[56]

In addition to *Holiday*, the park also garnered other favorable reviews. *Recreation Management*, a trade journal, labeled Hersheypark "one of the best theme parks in [the] United States today."[57] However, the park received its best endorsement from *Better Homes and Gardens*. In 1973, the magazine dispatched writer Gordon Greer to dozens of theme parks around the country. His task was to review all "logical contenders" and then submit a list of the top fifteen parks. When Greer visited a park, he always brought children to ensure his evaluations included the perspective of youth. When he reached Hersheypark, Greer picked up on its intriguing temporal dynamic: "For its first 60 years . . . Hersheypark was a monument to tranquility and ease, a green, gauzy dreamworld from whose romantic old ballroom the music of Paul Whiteman and Rudy Vall[é]e serenely floated. . . . Thankfully, what was pleasant then remains so today . . . even in the middle of an ambitious five-year program to transform the old amusement section into a gleaming, modern theme park." Hersheypark, Greer correctly observed, was attempting to harmonize nostalgia for the park's past with excitement for its modern future. In the end, he did place Hersheypark in his top fifteen, a prestigious group that included Disneyland, Disney World, and two Six Flags parks (Texas and Georgia).[58] Not surprisingly, Hersheypark's PR office highlighted the honor in press releases, and many newspapers ran the story.[59]

But not all. Some newspapers chose to craft their own narratives. These were often, but not always, negative. Writers who disliked the park tended to come from the area and harbor strong feelings for the old park. However, unlike Greer, they did not use nostalgia to offer readers an innocent stroll down memory lane. Rather, they deployed nostalgia as a rhetorical weapon, as the following editorial makes clear: "To those of us who spent many happy hours as children . . . at Hershey Park, the memories still have the ability to tug, ghost-like, on our minds. Hersheypark then meant a day of happiness, a day spent strolling through every child's dream of wonderland. . . . Now, however, it seems that the cold hand of the corporation has been laid over fairyland." The author, though disliking Hersheypark generally, objected specifically to the price of admission. With it, Hershey had erected a barrier to anyone not from the "affluent class." In the past, working-class people could still afford a Sunday at Hershey Park. However, the "cold hand of the corporation" had eliminated this innocent and inexpensive pleasure. "There are thousands of people," he asserted, "who can now never take in the sights of the wonderful Hershey Park" because "there is just no way in Hell they can afford it." In the end, he blamed Hersheypark for inflaming the class divide.[60]

If that article were not bad enough, a worse one appeared in the *Paxton Herald*. Written by Curtis Demmy, it recounted the Hersheypark experience of "Jim and Marr." After growing up in the area, the two moved to Indiana and started a family. Returning to Hershey to visit Jim's parents, the couple decided that their five kids should experience the free-and-open park of their youths. "I'll never forget the fun we had there when I was a boy," said Jim. "I'd like to have the kids see how we used to enjoy picnics there." After packing a basket with sandwiches and lemonade, the family happily headed over to Hersheypark. "No one prepared Jim," Demmy wrote, "for the shock he was in for." At the gate, they were told both that outside food and drink were prohibited and admission would come at a steep cost. Unwilling to pay, Jim led his family away in a huff. Since the park's advertisement had made no mention of any admission charge, he accused Hershey of "trickery."

Later that evening, Jim discussed the abortive outing with his parents. Jim's father invoked M. S. as a way to criticize the park's profit-oriented model. He wondered what M. S. would have done had he overheard someone at the ticket booth utter the plaintive words, "But I don't have five dollars. I just wanted to walk around the park a little, sit down and relax, buy a hotdog and some chocolate milk and enjoy the people." At this point, Jim asked his kids to gather around. "If you're ever to realize the joy of a family or church picnic," he informed them, "we'll have to find a place that . . . resembles the old Hershey Park I knew as a boy." He then painted a "word picture" of the park before the "hatchetmen" had ruined it. Predictably, he listed nearly every highlight from the Perfect Hershey Day: a picnic, a baseball game, a pie-eating contest, swimming, arcade games, a concert at the Bandshell, and ballroom dancing. After the children inquired what happened to the old park, Jim supplied the tragic answer. The people who run the company "no longer have any regard for the things Milton S. Hershey believed in," he said. "They use his name to promote something which he never . . . dreamed of in his philosophy."[61]

It was a devastating article that spoke for a segment of the local community that could not be prevailed on—not even once—to pay the admission fee and enter the park. Margaret Clark, a resident, was adamant in her refusal. "Now you pay $7 just to get in," she said in 1975. "I'll tell you something, they never got $7 from me. Oh, no they never will." When asked why not, she insisted that "Mr. Hershey wouldn't like that." At this point, her nostalgia kicked in, and she, like Jim and Marr, started to reminisce about the Perfect Hershey Day. "I would go and sit in his park," she remembered, and "when I was younger, I rode the roller coasters and swam in the pool. I did all those things." But not anymore. Now the hated fence "enclosed Mr. Hershey's park."[62]

Demmy's article did present one silver lining. Its extreme negativity prompted one reader, William Houck, to send in a rebuttal. The Hershey employee who clipped Houck's piece from the newspaper scribbled "better than the previous article" on it before handing it to John O. Hershey. Though he was right, he had understated the point: *it was demonstrably better*. Houck contended that the old amusement park had become "dumpy" and needed a "transfusion" to again become a place "we can . . . be darn proud to recommend." Should the park succeed in evolving into a "miniature

Disney World," that would improve the local economy. Houck also appreciated the new admission system because kids no longer have to "dig out money from ride to ride." And the much-bemoaned loss of picnics meant there was no garbage "scattered around by inconsiderate people." All that said, Houck confessed that he, like Demmy, preferred many aspects of the past to the present:

> I like to sit back and remember when things were different; like when a farmer could plant what he wanted; when the aged were cared for by their children; when a life sentence in jail didn't mean parole in 5 years; when our flag was respected abroad as well as at home; when a father went on welfare out of desperation and got off as soon as possible; when the doctor's first question was, where does it hurt? rather than, do you have insurance? When taxes were a nuisance rather than a burden; when Father and Mother were respectfully answered, Yes Sir! Yes Ma'am!

With this list, which he jokingly called the "Remember Whens," Houck captured the feeling of those resisting modern change. Though he understood their complaint, he did not endorse it. Change was inevitable, after all, and so not worth fighting. What is more, some change was good. Houck reminded readers that Hershey Park, had it failed to modernize, would surely have joined the list of "Remember Whens."[63]

Houck was correct. Thanks to the renovation, Hersheypark would escape that sad fate. In fact, it clearly had a future. After just one summer, it gained substantial traction not just in the region but also among town residents. In total attendance, the park surpassed one million visitors in 1973.[64] The following year, the number would rise to 1.2 million.[65] Though these figures failed to reach ERA's projections (the firm had predicted 1.3 million people for 1973), McKinney attributed the problem to ERA's rosy forecasting, not the park's performance. "One of the problems with ERA," McKinney realized later, was that "they projected unrealistic figures . . . for the first couple years . . . and so we weren't making them."[66] Though McKinney viewed the 1973 season as a smashing success, he knew that something was missing. Before Hersheypark could claim to offer Disneyland-style entertainment, it would need to make one key addition.

Furry Tales and Product Characters

As Hershey executives digested the feedback from 1973, they formed plans for 1974. Thinking of children, they recognized that conspicuously absent from the park was perhaps the most kid-friendly attraction of all. "We decided to have, as most other parks had, theme characters," McKinney recalled. But what theme would Hershey choose? Candy-themed costumed characters presented the obvious choice. After all, kids would surely love to see goofy, foamy, oversized versions of their favorite Hershey's treats. Unfortunately, Hershey Estates, which operated Hersheypark, did not own the rights to the famous candy brands. Those belonged to Hershey Foods, which was fiercely protective of its brands. When Hershey Estates asked for permission to create product-based characters, Hershey Foods flatly refused. Though this decision to pass on the opportunity to receive free advertising seems counterintuitive, the chocolate manufacturer had its reasons. First, it feared that the public would view chocolate-themed characters as a brazenly shameless attempt to promote its product line. Second, Hershey Foods worried that guests who had a negative experience in Hersheypark would blame Hershey Foods. In other words, the park was new and unproven, and Hershey Foods did not wish to risk imperiling its brands.[67]

Unable to trot out seven-foot Hershey bars, park officials needed an alternative. As they did with most decisions, they looked to Disney for inspiration. For almost twenty years, Disneyland had delighted children with strolling versions of the studio's beloved anthropomorphic animals: Mickey and Minnie Mouse, Donald Duck, Goofy, and others. Though these "walk-around" characters had become fixtures in Disney's parks, they did not figure in Walt's original plan. He initially intended for Mickey and Minnie to play only a cameo role: they would lead the parade at Disneyland's grand opening in 1955. "The walk-arounds' success," recalled John Hench, "persuaded us that they had to move into the park permanently." Since the first costumed characters appeared ridiculous with their bulbous cartoon heads and normal human bodies, Walt tasked Hench and other Imagineers with "sculpting full-body costumes" that would allow the anatomy of Mickey *the walk-around* to match that of Mickey *the animation*. Walt also expanded the role of costumed characters in the Disneyland experience. "The demand for the walk-arounds grew as time passed," Hench noted, "which meant that we had to devise special places for them to appear."[68] When Hershey

Fig. 16 Starting in 1974, the Furry Tales provided Hersheypark with Disneyesque strolling characters. Courtesy of HCA.

executives visited the Disney parks in the early 1970s, they did not overlook the important role played by costumed characters.

For the 1974 season, Hersheypark attempted to replicate this formula. An internal report stated that Hersheypark, recognizing the success of "costumed characters popularized by Walt Disney," would be introducing its "own exclusive costumed fantasy." The Furry Tales were born.[69] A trio of animal characters, the Furry Tales were designed by Scollon Productions, a company founded by Allie and Bill Scollon that specialized in mascot costuming. In 1968, Scollon had created the costumes for *The Banana Splits* children's television show. The 1974 season at Hersheypark introduced guests to Dutch the blue bear, Violet the purple skunk, and Chip the brown chipmunk (fig. 16). Like Disney's characters, each Furry Tale possessed a pronounced personality trait that the costumed actor had to perform.[70] "We really get into our parts," remarked Heather Noll, a college senior who played Dutch. Noll, who sometimes forgot to drop the Dutch act when out of costume, admitted to "waving at everybody" and "acting like a nut" when she was dressed in her street clothes outside the park. Inside the park, she enjoyed being a magnet for children. "When we're in our suits," she said, "everybody loves us," and the kids "run up and pet you."[71] All summer long, the Furry Tales would stroll about the park, posing for photographs and making children laugh with their "clowning and antics."[72] In addition to perambulating, the three characters entertained guests with a variety of ten-minute stage shows that consisted of catchy music, choreographed dancing, and slapstick prop comedy.[73] They also made appearances at area hospitals to cheer up sick children.[74] "Mickey Mouse may be the Big Mahoff at Florida's Disney World," wrote Scranton's *Sunday Times* in 1974, "but it's guys like Blue Bear and Purple Skunk that run things at Pennsylvania's Hersheypark." "Perhaps Mickey Mouse," the article warned in jest, "had better stay on his side of the Mason-Dixon Line."[75]

Perhaps he had better. However, the true challenge to Furry Tales' supremacy arrived that same year, and it did not originate in Orlando. "Hershey Chocolate products come to life," announced a press release in 1974. "Strolling chocolate characters such as the Hershey bar, Reese's Peanut Butter Cups, Krackel Bar and the Hershey Kiss are a sweet delight for Hersheypark's guests."[76] The candy characters had arrived at last (fig. 17). Why did Hershey Foods, which had adamantly opposed the idea just months earlier, reverse its decision? The simple answer is that Hersheypark, by exceeding one million visitors in 1973, proved itself to be a worthy partner. Hershey Foods also came to see the wisdom of exploiting a Disneyesque corporate synergy: Hersheypark could function as a colossal advertisement for Hershey Foods' products, with every wrapper reminding consumers of the fun that could be had in Hersheypark.[77]

Despite this reasoning, the two sides did not move beyond their impasse without outside help. In other words, the partnership required a catalyst, and that catalyst had a name: Bill Scollon. He had been brought in solely to create the Furry Tales. Acting on a whim, Scollon asked McKinney if he had considered characters based on Hershey's candy brands. Shaking his head, McKinney informed Scollon that, sadly, Hershey Foods had "no interest in having their product replicated in the form of a Hersheypark character." Scollon suspected that the decision-makers at Hershey Foods had rejected the idea because they had contemplated it only in the abstract. In other words, they were failing to imagine the magical potential

Fig. 17 Product-themed characters, including the bizarre two-headed Reese's Peanut Butter Cups, appeared in 1974. Courtesy of HCA.

of product characters because they could not see and touch them. Acting on his own initiative, Scollon constructed a Reese's costume, which he showed to McKinney. Impressed, McKinney invited Scollon to the next Rotary Club meeting. After the meeting concluded, McKinney escorted the unsuspecting group to a backroom, where Scollon awaited in costume. As astonished club members beheld the comical orange and brown mascot, they were delighted—none more so than Robert Reese, the son of H. B. Reese. McKinney next conveyed the costumed Scollon to Hershey Foods, where executives took an instant liking to the character. "It was Scollon's persistence and willingness to make the costume," McKinney recalled, "that was the start of the change at the chocolate company."[78] As resistance melted away, Hershey Foods authorized the product characters, and the park changed forever. "We started to chocolatize Hersheypark," said McKinney, converting a noun into a verb. "We Hersheyized everything."[79] The advent of ambulatory chocolate products, though rendering the Furry Tales somewhat redundant, did not spell their doom—not immediately, at least. The woodland animals and candy characters coexisted in harmony into the 1980s.[80]

Conclusion

With robust attendance and mostly favorable press coverage, Hersheypark was off to an auspicious start. It was succeeding as a revenue-generating theme park. Profits aside, recall that Hershey executives had a secondary objective, which was to help local residents accept the changes sweeping through the town. The hope was that Hersheypark, as a symbolic landscape, could play a role in this process. Thanks to RDA's theming, guests found themselves immersed in a historical continuum that started in the Old World (Tudor Square and Rhineland), the point of departure for many settlers in Pennsylvania. The tour across time did not end there. Guests moved next to Carrousel Circle, a celebration of Hershey's small-town past, before proceeding to a fourth themed area called Der Deitsch Platz. If Rhineland captured the culture of German emigrants on the eve of their departure, then Der Deitsch Platz brought to life the next chapter in their story: the world they made in Pennsylvania. This themed area taught guests about the contributions made by the Pennsylvania Dutch to the state's agricultural and artisanal past.

Chapter 6

Honoring Agriculture

On July 17, 1955, ninety million Americans, or just over half of the population, turned on their television sets to watch *Dateline Disneyland.* A televised spectacle, *Dateline Disneyland* provided Walt Disney with a national platform on which to unveil his new park. Throughout the broadcast, Walt would shuttle from one themed realm to the next to read prepared statements. "Before you enter this realm," he said while standing outside the wood-plank fence enclosing Frontierland, "I'd like to read the dedication." He proceeded to define the realm as a place where "we experience the story of our country's past—the color, romance, and drama of frontier America as it developed from wilderness trails" to "railroads" and, eventually, to "civilization." In Disney's telling, Frontierland amounted to a "tribute" to the traits and values of the pioneers: "faith, courage, and ingenuity." After Disney finished, the broadcast shifted to a waiting Ronald Reagan, microphone in hand, positioned at Frontierland's entrance. "Walt Disney has created a frontier village," he stated reverentially, "that could have been carved out of the wilderness a hundred years ago by the pioneers themselves." At this point, the gates to Frontierland dramatically opened, actors dressed as soldiers fired a multigun salute, and a wagon approached, conveying a group of park visitors. They, Reagan proudly announced, were "the first visitors to travel through the gates of time and into our very historic past."[1]

With Frontierland, Walt Disney had taken a chapter of American history and brought it to life. In the early 1970s, Hershey executives were eager to exploit a different chapter—one that Disney had not touched. After various concepts were bandied about, Rufus Hollinger raised eyebrows with his novel idea. Hollinger was not a member of Hersheypark's top brass. For many years, he had taken care of students at the Milton Hershey School while working in different capacities for Hershey Estates. He was also the chief organizer of Dutch Days, an annual weeklong festival that showcased the handicrafts and farming culture of the Pennsylvania Germans. It was Hollinger's positive experience with Dutch Days that inspired his big idea: build a spacious barn and fill it with craftspeople. In short, Hersheypark might celebrate Pennsylvania's agricultural heritage.

Reaction to Hollinger's idea was divided. Some people dismissed it, bluntly telling Hollinger, "You're crazy." Others were intrigued. To settle the matter, the Hershey people placed a long-distance call to California to broach the idea with RDA. After hearing them out, the RDA designer hesitated to decide one way or another. He could not "speak very authoritatively" on the matter, he explained, because he did not quite grasp the concept and needed a way to visualize farm-themed entertainment. As luck would have it, Hershey was, at that very moment, celebrating Dutch Days. "Come in right now," the Hershey people urged, so "you can see what it is." After flying to Pennsylvania, the RDA designer experienced Dutch Days—and came away convinced. "He took one look at that," Hollinger remembered, "and decided this was something that Walt Disney didn't have." RDA approved the idea, and the Craft Barn was born. Visitors who stepped inside would encounter a variety of artisans making things by hand, just as people did on farms before the industrial revolution. If Frontierland could transport visitors back to the rollicking Wild West, Hersheypark would reproduce an equally important, though less riveting, chapter of American history—the nation's agricultural past.[2]

But was farming as a way of life truly gone? Americans disagreed on whether modern life had rendered farming obsolete or more relevant than ever. Instead of picking a side, Hersheypark mirrored the nation's ambivalence in its presentation of farm life and crafts. It sometimes classified the agrarian way of life as historical, a chapter of the nation's storied past that, like the frontier, had vanished. A visit to these attractions, therefore, allowed one to enter a time machine and witness America *the way it was*. At other times, the park reversed the message by suggesting that guests could see a lesser-known part of America *as it currently is*. Indeed, many of the craftspeople employed by Hersheypark hailed from vibrant Pennsylvania

German communities that still embraced farming culture. By showcasing these people's values and skills, Hersheypark preached the virtues of farm life and underscored their continued relevance in a modern society struggling with excessive television viewing, disappearing communities, rampant consumerism, and a spiking divorce rate. In sum, Hersheypark portrayed agrarian culture as restorative—an antidote to modern society's sickness.

Farming's Ambiguous Status

What was the status of farming in America and Pennsylvania in the 1970s? Was it rising, declining, or holding steady? These simple questions prompt the muddiest of answers. In 1970, if one were to survey developments in American agriculture that had taken place since 1950, one would confront a paradox: farming was simultaneously flourishing and failing. Indeed, between 1950 and 1970, American agriculture steadily hemorrhaged its workforce, and the total number of farms dropped precipitously. Yet during the same two decades, farms became larger and their soil far more productive. To make the point with statistics, a farmer in 1950 could expect to harvest on average nineteen bushels of wheat or forty bushels of corn from a single acre of land; by 1970, that same acre's productivity had nearly doubled, yielding thirty-six bushels of wheat and eighty bushels of corn. In other words, agriculture had enjoyed twenty years of stunning growth *in terms of output*; however, farming *as a way of life* had entered into severe decline. Based on statistics, one point was abundantly clear: the agricultural sector of the economy was undergoing a radical reconfiguration.[3]

Three major developments were driving the transformation of agriculture: the advent of new machinery, the introduction of new chemical inputs to the soil, and the rural electrification movement. Concerning machinery, the gasoline-powered tractor had, by 1950, replaced the horse on all but a few farms. However, it was the harvesting combines that most dramatically revolutionized husbandry. In his study of American agriculture, Paul Conkin calls combines "the supreme implements in contemporary agriculture." "No other machine," he asserts, "with the possible exception of the mechanical cotton picker, has displaced so many farmworkers, so lowered the unit cost of crops, and so directly affected the structure of farming in America." As these iron and steel giants harvested crops with startling efficiency, the soil in which the crops grew became both more fertile and more resistant to threats, thanks to chemical compounds developed in laboratories during and after World War II, including fertilizers, insecticides, herbicides, and fungicides. And finally, the New Deal's rural electrification program, by making lighting and appliances possible on farms, helped farmers modernize and systematize their operations. While only 11 percent of American farms had electricity in 1935, by 1960, just 3 percent of farms remained off the power grid. For most farmers within this tiny minority, the absence of electricity amounted to a deliberate choice, not a lamentable deprivation.[4]

Of course, all these improvements required abundant capital, something that not every farmer had. According to Conkin, farm operation became so "capital intensive" and "specialized" as to discourage new entrants into agriculture and force out smaller and less efficient farmers who "could not compete."[5] Even if a farmer did possess sufficient capital, he might not have owned enough land to justify making large expenditures in costly machinery and chemical inputs. Indeed, such investments only made sense on large farms that could expect to harvest crops in high volume. In the end, that small farmer faced a fateful but inescapable decision: either expand his land holdings dramatically or exit the business.

Many chose the latter option. As small farmers sold their land to larger farmers with more capital, and as those larger farms increasingly replaced human hands with mechanization, the countryside witnessed a mass exodus. "Farmers . . . have been forced out of business," observed an alarmed James Abourezk, U.S. senator from South Dakota, in 1973. "Communities and towns have been broken up and abandoned—and an entire rural culture is disappearing."[6] The census backed up what Abourezk had witnessed with his own eyes. As farms shed workers, the agricultural population plummeted from roughly twenty-three million in 1950 to fewer than ten million in 1970. In an era marked by consolidation, the total number of farms also dropped, falling from over five million in 1950 to under three million in 1970.[7] Historian David Danbom sums up the revolution: "What agricultural reformers had desired for nearly a century—that farming would become an enterprise requiring a specialized technical knowledge and that farmers would be accomplished, self-confident, and respected professionals—increasingly became reality after World War II."[8] By 1970, farms had become large, farming had become scientific, tools had become technological and expensive, and farmers had become professional. And there were far fewer of them.

In several ways, Pennsylvania mirrored the nation. After the war, the state witnessed a swift decline in the number of farms, an expansion in the size of the average farm, a dramatic reduction in the population of farmworkers, and a surge in per-acre productivity.[9] What is more, the machine, as it had in other agricultural states, made its bold entrance into the bucolic Pennsylvania garden. In 1947, visitors to the Pennsylvania Farm Show, an annual exposition devoted to agriculture, could not fail to make one observation: the age of the horse was passing away, and the era of mechanized agriculture had arrived. Before the event, Miles Horst, state secretary of agriculture, explained that "farm machinery was never so important to the stabilization and economic development of Pennsylvania." He proceeded to allocate an unprecedented 60 percent of the main hall's exhibition space to machines—tractors, grain combines, corn pickers, and corn shellers. In Pennsylvania farming, mechanization had seized center stage.[10]

Yet while most Pennsylvania farmers either embraced the new methods or quit the vocation altogether, one population found a third way: the Pennsylvania Germans. Since they played a key role in Hersheypark's agricultural entertainment, readers should know a few basic things about them. Scholars divide Pennsylvania Germans into two groups: *church people* and *sectarians*. The former consist mostly of the descendants of the Lutheran and German Reformed immigrants from German-speaking regions in Europe. In the words of Bernard Bailyn, this group "quickly acquired American characteristics" in nearly all aspects of life—language, technology, religion, and culture. In contrast, the sectarians remained apart from mainstream society. These Old Order Amish and Mennonites deployed "fiercely self-protective devices," Bailyn explains, to "help perpetuate their group identity over succeeding generations," allowing them to preserve their "distinctiveness." Specifically, sectarians adhered to "strict rules" in their religious lives, practiced "austerity and self-denial," and shunned worldliness.[11] In farming, this group resisted modern agricultural techniques and machines, choosing instead to have the horse pull the plow. Sectarians also used language as a barrier, speaking a tongue that the outside world could not comprehend.

That dialect, "Pennsylvania Dutch," was "derived from nonstandard forms of German," writes Mark Louden, "and contained vocabulary borrowed from English." Though Pennsylvania Dutch blended German and English languages, neither German nor English speakers can understand it.[12] John Hostetler, an authority on the Amish, summed up this group's stand. "They have refused to go along with civilization," he wrote in 1968. "They are a slow changing, distinctive cultural group who place a premium on cultural stability rather than change." With its vast industrial farms coexisting with smaller Amish farms, Pennsylvania evinced a striking contrast of modernity and tradition.[13]

The novelist John Updike reflected on Pennsylvania's agricultural transformation in *Of the Farm* (1965). Raised in rural Berks County, Pennsylvania, Updike understood the importance of family farms to the state's identity and, thus, the poignancy of this transitional period. The novel begins when thirty-five-year-old Joey Robinson, having been summoned by his widowed mother, arrives at the Pennsylvania homestead of his childhood. Like Martin Sloan from *The Twilight Zone* (see chapter 4), Joey Robinson represents modern man, embodying, for better or worse, the changes transforming the nation. Raised in a small farming community, Robinson has almost the same job as Sloan. He works as an advertising executive in—where else?—Manhattan. What is more, Updike makes it clear that Robinson's big-city lifestyle has shaped his morals, priorities, and expectations. Though his parents had dutifully labored to keep their imperfect marriage intact, Robinson is already divorced, estranged from his children, and remarried to a woman who brings to the relationship a son from her earlier failed marriage. Attending church for the first time in years (he has dropped religion, too), Robinson experiences intense discomfort as he feels the eyes of the congregation, families he recognizes from his youth, judging him with moral disapproval.

If Robinson represents modernity, the farm on which his mother lives symbolizes the great change in American agriculture. The place is a paradox: a farm on which absolutely no farming takes place. When mealtime approaches, the characters must drive to the grocery store to buy the sorts of foods a farm should produce. With his overall depiction, Updike suggested a larger point about agriculture: this period witnessed the decline of the small farm and a way of life centered on agriculture, family, church, community, and tradition. This being said, Updike deliberately included one group of people who buck the trend by continuing to believe in small-farm life—the Pennsylvania Germans. They creep silently across the novel's rural landscape as nameless background characters who never intrude on the plot. Updike nevertheless implied that they do not intend to abandon farming any time soon. In fact, we are to assume that, when Robinson's mother dies, the sale of the farm will attract eager bidders from the Amish and Mennonite communities.[14]

With *Of the Farm*, Updike composed an elegy for a way of life that, once pursued by millions, had entered into decline. With the dramatic growth of cities coinciding with the rise of agribusiness, Americans in 1970 would have spoken of farms using the same kind of epochal language that Frederick Jackson Turner employed in describing the vanished frontier back in 1893. "The frontier has gone," he wrote, "and with its going has closed the first period of American history."[15] By 1970, one could simply remove the word *frontier* and insert *small farm* because the era of small farms had seemingly gone, and with its passing had closed the agricultural experience in American history. Foodstuffs would now be purchased from grocery stores after having been trucked in from vast farms, located far away, that the average consumer would never see and seldom contemplate. Updike's novel resonated among readers because it played to their collective nostalgia for a bygone era.

Der Deitsch Platz

Though many Americans associated farming communities with an earlier era, not all did—a point Updike underscored with his inclusion of Amish and Mennonite husbandry. In the 1970s, these sectarians refused to consign farming to the misty past. Instead, they tenaciously clung to farming as essential not only in the present but also in the future. In their view, farming transcended time because it presented human beings with the best possible way of life. Thus, it never grew outdated. While farming possessed so much merit that it was certain to endure, some Pennsylvania Germans, the Old Order Amish in particular, were not so sure about the world around them. Indeed, some of them looked at many modern developments—crime-ridden cities, nuclear submarines able to annihilate civilization, television bombarding children with advertisements, and a rising divorce rate pushing families into crisis—and shook their heads in disgust. Exactly which way of life deserved the label "dead end"?[16]

So, had farming vanished into the sepia-toned past, or did it form a robust part of the future? That this single question could prompt different responses from different groups suggested that, as a way of life, farming exhibited ambiguous temporality. And this ambiguity presented Hersheypark with an opportunity in the 1970s. It could design Der Deitsch Platz (the Dutch place), home of the park's farm-themed entertainment, in a way that satisfied the needs of different constituencies simultaneously. Urban tourists who associated farming with the past would flock to Hersheypark to experience the sights and smells of what they considered a bygone way of life. In doing so, they could play the role of Martin Sloan by escaping their hectic modern existence for a few pleasurable hours and immersing themselves in the past. Local residents, though no longer farmers themselves, could see in Der Deitsch Platz a recreation of an important chapter of local and regional agricultural history. Though largely in the past, the farming way of life was not considered obsolete by them. That was because it had produced admirable values and traditions that modern society sorely lacked. Finally, sectarians among the Pennsylvania Germans visiting Der Deitsch Platz could contest the very assumption that the sun had set on those who wished to till the soil. From their perspective, Hersheypark had not erected a paean to a vanished way of life. On the contrary, it honored a superior culture that, far from fading into oblivion, promised to endure in perpetuity.

Pennsylvania Germans did not just visit Der Deitsch Platz—they played a starring role there. In an effort to ensure authenticity, Hersheypark officials turned to the Pennsylvania Germans, with whom they had strong ties, thanks to the success of Dutch Days. As noted above, Dutch Days was a weeklong summer festival dedicated to the crafts, folk art, dialect, foodways, storytelling, and music of Pennsylvania Germans. Rufus Hollinger had played a key role in organizing the popular festival since its inception in 1949. Through him, Hersheypark enjoyed relationships with area blacksmiths, quilters, weavers, sign painters, potters, and broom makers. The mutual benefit of this relationship was eloquently captured by Governor Milton Shapp when he proclaimed the opening of Dutch Days in 1976.

"The people of the Pennsylvania Dutch communities," Shapp declaimed, "have given of their traditions and talents to this great State and have contributed much to our . . . cultural heritage." As for Hersheypark, it has reciprocated by presenting an "original tribute to the Pennsylvania Dutch with an outstanding program each year highlighting their culture." In short, the relationship was symbiotic in that both sides benefited.[17] From the perspective of Pennsylvania Germans, the alliance with Hersheypark allowed craftspeople who wished to share their knowledge to plug into an established commercial nexus. Indeed, both Dutch Days and the attractions within Der Deitsch Platz provided platforms on which they could demonstrate their artisanal skills, exhibit their wares, and secure access to a vast regional audience. In this way, a people of tradition could avail themselves of the abundant resources that only a modern corporation could offer.

As for Hersheypark, it benefited from the partnership in two ways. First, Pennsylvania Germans could help the company with its local problem. By devoting an entire themed area to the Pennsylvania Germans, Hersheypark could honor the heritage of area residents, many of whom were of German descent. In this way, the park hoped to appease a skeptical community that had viewed the company with distrust ever since the termination of the compact. The presence of Pennsylvania Germans sent a reassuring message that even during a time of great change, the company held fast to a core set of values: family, community, and tradition. It signaled to local residents that Hershey had not lost its soul. Second, the Pennsylvania Dutch played a crucial role in enhancing the experience for tourists from metropolitan areas and their surrounding suburbs. Since Dutch Days had attracted tour buses from New York and Philadelphia, the park had good reason to believe that guests from urban areas enjoyed agriculturally themed entertainment.[18] To borrow from Aesop's famous fable, Town Mouse wished to visit Country Mouse to experience his rustic lifestyle. Recognizing this fact, Hersheypark used Der Deitsch Platz to broker urban and suburban America's pleasant encounter with rural America.

To play the role of Country Mouse, Hershey tapped the Pennsylvania Germans, many of whom hailed from nearby Lancaster County. In his study of Lancaster, David Walbert explained its symbolic power in the American imagination. As "the Garden Spot," Lancaster seemed to embody the best of "rural pride and agrarian ideals" and came to represent "all that was right and good about traditional rural America." In the popular imagination, Lancaster's farmers epitomized Thomas Jefferson's mythic yeoman farmer, the self-reliant individual who leads a sober life of godly virtue by tilling the soil, raising his family, and voting his conscience. Though the yeoman farmer has long since vanished from the American scene, urbanites enjoyed believing that a remnant lived on in Lancaster County. They happily cast Pennsylvania Germans—especially the Old Order Amish—in this role.[19]

More than other Pennsylvania German groups, the Amish captured the imagination of urban Americans—and did so without even trying. John Hostetler studied this group "microscopically" in his seminal work *Amish Society* (1963). He argued that mainstream Americans viewed the Amish in one of two ways, both of which were flawed. Some shook their heads with patronizing "pity" at a hidebound group that "will not modernize" or adopt the "convenience of twentieth-century ways." But more common were those who placed the Amish on a pedestal, nominating them for "sainthood." Tourists "come in here and think we are angels," one Amish man informed Hostetler, "and expect to find us floating several feet off the ground."[20] Curiously, mainstream Americans idealized a people whose clear policy was to shun them.

Hostetler saw modernity as the key to understanding this dynamic. In his view, the Amish showed Americans what they had sacrificed in the twentieth century's massive bargain—when society traded tradition for modernity. On the positive side of the ledger, modernity brought about a transformation that verged on miraculous: medical science cured diseases, modern agriculture reduced hunger, and new technologies conferred convenience onto daily life. However, hidden behind these stunning gains lay severe losses. "Without preachment," Hostetler explained, the Amish "have taught us something of the human cost" of modernity. He went on to enumerate those costs: there is a loss when an "agrarian community" is converted into a "mechanized, agricultural business," when urban living divorces humanity from the earth, when "old values are cast away," "when parents are alienated from children," "when neighbors are treated as strangers," and "when man is separated from his spiritual tradition."[21] Simply by standing pat with their traditional way of life, the Amish proved useful for Americans who wished to measure the steep cost of modernity.

The folklorist Simon Bronner articulated mainstream society's strange psychological attachment to the Amish in succinct language: "If they did not exist, we would have to invent them."[22]

Upon initial inspection, urbanites appear generous in ascribing morality, purity, honesty, and self-sufficiency to Lancaster's farmers. Yet this reverence exacts a toll. As Walbert explains, the terms of this city-country dichotomy are always controlled by the urbanites, who "identify rurality with the past." By doing so, they sever the "ties" between "rurality" and the notion of "progress." In other words, the dominant perception is that progress takes place in cities alone, and never in the countryside. Rural America remains in a state of perpetual stasis, frozen in time. Of course, staying put means falling behind. That is because relative to urban America—where modern values propel society onward toward new scientific, technological, and social horizons—farm life appears to recede further into the past. In short, Pennsylvania Germans got to play the part of Jefferson's venerable farmer; however, in accepting this role, they were instantly sent spiraling back in time.[23]

This past-present dynamic unfolded within Hersheypark. From the perspective of Hershey executives and RDA's design team, the success of the redeveloped park hinged on the satisfaction of urban and suburban tourists. If such people wished to visit America's agricultural and preindustrial past, then the park would deliver the illusion of time travel. The following press release from 1975 clearly sold Der Deitsch Platz as an excursion into the past: "Imagine in this space age of technology that Hersheypark guests can actually visit a 19th century Pennsylvania Dutch village, with a village blacksmith, a cigar maker, and a dozen other craftsmen."[24] In the eyes of tourists, the presence of Pennsylvania German craftspeople could effect instant aging in this newly fabricated themed area—transforming something new into something old. Thus, these craftspeople had to tolerate promotional materials that consigned them to the 1800s. They became human artifacts on display in a living history museum.

The Craft Barn

John Zerbe crisscrossed the country in airplanes. Brought in to serve as operations manager during the redevelopment, Zerbe needed to observe other entertainment complexes of a comparable size to see how these were organized. Toward this end, he joined other park managers in touring Disneyland, Disney World, Sea World, and Opryland.[25] Yet Zerbe derived the most benefit from his visit to Colonial Williamsburg. "As a result of that trip," he recalled, "we made a slew of changes" that "brought the whole maintenance program to a new standard."[26] Featuring blacksmiths and cobblers rather than roller coasters and flume rides, Williamsburg might not, upon first glance, appear relevant to a theme park manager. Yet Williamsburg taught visitors about colonial America, a historical period in which production had taken place on the small farm and in the artisan's workshop. It did so by encouraging interaction: guests could meet the craftspeople, ask questions, and handle tools and finished goods. Hersheypark aspired to the same kind of educational experience, though on a smaller scale. It did so with the Craft Barn.

Located in Der Deitsch Platz, the Craft Barn fostered interaction in the Williamsburg style (fig. 18). No generic red barn, the Craft Barn was a faithful replica of a "bank barn," an iconic architectural form that had graced Pennsylvania German farms since the 1800s.[27] "If it were out in a field," Hollinger said of its authentic look, "you would not have known it from another barn." In this way, the Craft Barn linked Hersheypark to the region's agricultural roots and its German heritage. Inside this spacious structure, the entertainment adhered to the proven formula of Dutch Days. That was because the Craft Barn was an extension of Dutch Days, and most of the exhibitors whom Rufus Hollinger recruited had previously participated in that festival.[28] Working within stalls, the craftspeople explained their handiwork and invited guests to ask questions and handle objects, all of which were available for purchase (fig. 19). It was a tactile experience. Guests who gathered around Dorothy Lota learned that "the art of doll making is not something you can learn in 10 easy lessons," but is instead "an old German art."[29] Some people formed relationships with Brian Varker, the candlemaker. "Many of the people who watch me work here in the Craft Barn," he commented, "invite me to their homes."[30] Salome Eberly, who had rolled tobacco since 1918, enjoyed explaining her "ancestral art" in the Craft Barn. "I like being around people," said a smiling Eberly, "and this way I get to teach them something most people never get to see." Adults (but not children) could buy her cigars.[31] One could also purchase the unique

Fig. 18 The centerpiece of Der Deitsch Platz was the Craft Barn. Courtesy of HCA.

Fig. 19 Lois Garrison, the rug hooker, showcased her skills in the Craft Barn. Courtesy of HCA.

jewelry made by Joseph McCormick, a former coal miner, after observing the remarkable process he "kept alive." "I take lumps of coal and slice it down," McCormick explained, "and then . . . I make the fancy jewelry that is shown here at Hersheypark." McCormick liked to joke that, if visitors wanted true antiques, they could find none older than his "black diamond" jewelry, formed from anthracite coal over 250 million years old.[32]

While hewing to this interactive model, the Craft Barn was animated by a larger mission. Rufus Hollinger explained its rationale: "We had women quilting; we had the blacksmith blacksmithing. . . . The entire barn was filled with real honest-to-goodness craftspeople. . . . That's what we were—the whole idea . . . was to preserve as heritage these things, because . . . anything is only one generation away from death. . . . We attempted to keep people spinning and weaving and all that sort of thing."[33] With the seemingly redundant observation that the "blacksmithing" was done by a "blacksmith," Hollinger was making an important statement: the artisans were genuine. Though regular park employees assigned to Der Deitsch Platz would don "authentic Pennsylvania Dutch garb," the exhibitors themselves were not costumed teenagers. They were authentic craftspeople, mostly from nearby Pennsylvania German communities, who had inherited skills from their forebears. These were skills that, Hollinger claimed, verged on extinction in a modern world flooded with machine-made goods. Hersheypark sought to preserve these vanishing skills by providing craftspeople with a platform to teach the public about them.

Hollinger saw the Craft Barn through a preservationist's lens. He believed the venue could help to forestall a tragic crafts extinction. In this way, he comes across less as a manager at a theme park and more as a curator in an anthropology museum. His dire reading of the situation prompts a question: had modern production methods really pushed traditional crafts to the brink of annihilation? To be sure, there was plenty of evidence supporting Hollinger's portrayal of crafts as endangered. Factories that employed mass-production techniques had succeeded in displacing the artisan's workshop as the primary locus of production. However, by the 1970s, the transformation of the American economy had long since played out. The economic forces that might have killed traditional crafts had done their damage—yet craftspeople remained. Something was keeping these skills alive.

Traditional crafts survived behind a solid firewall—the Old Order Amish. According to Hostetler, sociologists ominously forecasted around 1950 that the Amish would be "absorbed" into the "dominant society" within a quarter century. "The predictions," Hostetler declared in 1980, "were wrong." In fact, in the very period predicted to bring their extinction, the Amish defied the doomsday prognostication by doubling their population.[34] Far from going extinct, the Amish were witnessing a renaissance. And since the Amish way of life promised to endure, there was no reason to believe crafts would vanish anytime soon. Though Hollinger framed the Craft Barn as a noble effort to preserve skills facing imminent annihilation, the exhibitors themselves viewed their mission in a different light: to showcase a viable lifestyle for the future. In this way, the Craft Barn inspired opposing opinions regarding the status of traditional crafts.

Right or wrong, Hersheypark's stated mission to preserve craft traditions helped it please the two groups its designers cared most deeply about—area residents and regional tourists. Betsy Rupe, a local reporter, explained the benefits of this preservationist mandate:

> Historic crafts have become a part of Hershey's heritage. The Hersheypark Craft Barn and Pennsylvania Dutch Days have brought the hand arts to the attention of both townspeople and thousands of tourists. Since Hersheypark has come to be known as a theme park, such features as original arts and crafts exhibits have achieved new emphasis. The Craft Barn, for instance, gives recognition to the important role that crafts have played in the development of America. . . . These people . . . are artisans preserving for today and tomorrow some of the beauty and craftsmanship of yesterday.[35]

From Rupe's description, we can see how the Craft Barn (and, as will be shown, Dutch Days) performed important work for Hershey by pleasing two different audiences simultaneously: "both townspeople and thousands of tourists." For the latter, the Craft Barn offered the much-coveted trip back in time by featuring the mode of production so crucial for "the development of America." As tourists watched the blacksmith bend red-hot iron just taken from the forge, they saw an eighteenth-century American artisan, not a present-day resident of Lancaster County. For this visitor, temporality (i.e., time travel) trumped both geography and ethnicity in defining the Craft Barn experience.

The Craft Barn succeeded in a different way with area residents (Rupe's "townspeople"). These were local residents who perhaps distrusted the company after its reorganization and were left embittered by the broken compact. Recall that Curtis Demmy had captured this distrust with his scathing newspaper story imputing to Hershey's "hatchetmen" only a base desire to extract money from guests (see chapter 5). Returning to the Craft Barn, we can see how Hershey's embrace of the worthy cause of preservation helped to nullify accusations of corporate greed. After all, how could anyone indict a company that worked so passionately to keep artisans employed and crafts alive? It was for this reason that two Hershey executives, John O. Hershey and Bruce McKinney, favored a vision for Hersheypark that preserved the area's "rich heritage." Such a focus, they believed, had the power to remove the "stamp of negative feeling" from the community.[36] The Craft Barn offered an element of redemption.

While disarming disgruntled locals, the Craft Barn also allowed area residents to stroll through the agricultural chapter in their collective history. If Rhineland depicted the point of departure, then Der Deitsch Platz presented the next chapter in the story: the blossoming of Germanic people and culture in the New World. Sufficiently retrospective to appeal to regional tourists hungry for time travel, the Craft Barn satisfied local visitors by nodding respectfully to their heritage. Crucially, it did so without implying that this heritage was obsolete. Indeed, the Craft Barn tantalized visitors with the possibility of future relevance. Now more than ever, modern America needed its past, and Hersheypark's Craft Barn helped keep this important linkage secure. As Rupe wrote, the park was "preserving for today and *tomorrow* some of the beauty and craftsmanship of yesterday."[37] Able to entertain, placate, and honor different constituencies at once, the Craft Barn provided Hersheypark with an attraction of rhetorical utility.

Tapping into a National Trend

With the Craft Barn, RDA and Hershey executives hoped to capitalize on a trend in tourism: a surging national interest in crafts. In 1972, Mark Jury covered the phenomenon for *Parade* magazine. For the article, Jury interviewed Nancy Hanks, chairperson of the National Endowment for the Arts, appointed by President Richard Nixon. Hanks confirmed Jury's suspicion that a crafts explosion was taking place. "Crafts are going right through the ceiling," she informed him. "Everywhere you go, people are deeply interested in crafts and it's absolutely marvelous. People who never thought they could be skilled are finding they can use their hands."[38] These were not hollow words from a public figure, hastily tossed to a journalist in need of a quote. By 1972, Hanks had fixed her gaze squarely on crafts. In a general sense, Hanks had always given crafts attention because they fit squarely into Nixon's overarching wish that the arts be more inclusive. If NEA programming could reach a wider audience, Nixon believed, the endowment could silence critics who complained that it mainly supported stuffy arts institutions. To advance what she called Nixon's "populist" initiatives, Hanks reliably supported nonelite arts programs: jazz concerts, urban sculptures, graffiti art, as well as folk arts and crafts.[39]

This populist vision notwithstanding, something else was driving the NEA's embrace of crafts in 1972. That year, an unexpected flurry of activity from Hanks indicated that she had lifted crafts out of the general pool of supportable arts and elevated them to the top of the endowment's agenda. Without being asked, Hanks approached the American Crafts Council to inquire how the NEA might better advance its mission. Without waiting for the Council to respond to her generous offer, Hanks proceeded to scrutinize the NEA budget to locate hidden pockets of money that could be sent, that same year, to various crafts organizations to support their programs. "In looking through the Endowment Programs," Hanks wrote to a member of her staff, "I saw bits and pieces of money we might be able to steal to get a bit more going *this* year." Quite unexpectedly, crafts organizations that had not requested financial assistance found themselves receiving exactly that—unsolicited NEA funding. At the same time, Hanks issued the following mandate to program directors operating under the NEA umbrella: "It is my wish that crafts be given equal billing with other arts in all appropriate phases of your programs."[40]

What loomed behind Nancy Hanks's sudden interest in crafts? It was politics, of course. Earlier in 1972, Hanks had learned that Congress was seriously considering establishing a National Folklife Center that would join the NEA and NEH (National Endowment for the Humanities). Of course, Hanks opposed the formation of a third endowment that would draw resources away from the NEA. Since crafts could fall into either category—arts or folk culture—Hanks viewed them as a contested area and, thus, as of strategic importance. With this political backstory, Hanks's preemptive funding strikes make sense. By aggressively channeling NEA resources toward the crafts movement, she was staking her claim to crafts. If she could demonstrate conclusively that crafts constituted a vibrant part of the NEA's sphere, she could block the creation of a rival endowment.[41] In this way, the enthusiasm for crafts conveyed by Hanks in her interview with Mark Jury had more to do with federal politics than anything else.

That said, the crafts boom that Hanks spoke of was real, not a trend contrived in Washington. In his attempt to isolate the deeper cause of the phenomenon, Jury identified a pervasive will among Americans to hold onto their cultural heritage. He cited Dutch Days as the quintessential example of a festival that revolved around this principle. At this crafts festival, he wrote, "a cross-section of America comes to watch demonstrations of coopering, spinning flax, rug hooking, candle-dipping and dozens of other skills of yesteryear." He then quoted Rufus Hollinger, who predictably linked the crafts renaissance to Americans' collective desire to "to postpone the abandonment of the crafts of our forefathers for a few years." People supported crafts, Hollinger believed, to delay the artisanal extinction.[42] Though Jury did not challenge Hollinger, he perhaps sensed that there was something unsatisfying about his explanation. For sure, the growth of mechanized factory production had worked to the detriment of the artisan's workshop; no one would debate that point. However, for Hollinger's theory to be correct, one had to believe that Americans were witnessing in the 1970s the final stage of an ongoing economic war in which the outcome was no longer in doubt: mass production's victory over artisans was both assured and imminent. This theory certainly explained the Arts and Crafts movement from the turn of the century, which truly had been a cultural reaction to factory production. However, by the 1970s, that war had been over for decades. If Americans were not engaged in a last-ditch effort to shield artisans from mechanization's coup de grâce, why were they turning to crafts?

Though Hollinger was no doubt sincere, Jury continued probing to find the true cause. To obtain a psychological perspective, he interviewed Dr. Robert F. Green of Fort Wayne, Indiana, whom he described as "a psychiatrist who is also deeply involved in a craft" and "has an answer." "The mechanization of society," Green asserted, "spawned the banality and the triteness—the throwaway society—that is a reflection of the illness of man." Humanity, Green elaborated, was motivated by a wish "to return to something with a greater degree of permanence." In his opinion, Americans increasingly saw in traditional crafts the antidote to a modern society that was polluting their lives with junk, reducing meaningful human interaction to superficiality, and making America sick.

Green's theory bore some relation to Hollinger's in that both pointed an accusing finger at modernity. However, the former had a couple of advantages. First, and most obviously, Green's theory did not require that there be an ongoing war between artisans and factories in its final phase. Accepting mass production's triumph to be a fait accompli, Green expressed concern about the long-term aftereffects this outcome was having on people's psychologies. Second, Green's theory did not require ascribing philanthropic motives to festivalgoers, unlike Hollinger's preservationist argument. People were making things with their hands, Green asserted, because they perceived this activity as having therapeutic benefit, not because they wished to forestall a crafts extinction. They genuinely believed that crafts helped them ward off or repair the deleterious effects of modern life by offering a tangible link to the preindustrial era.[43]

Should Americans ever cut that link, either through apathy or neglect, they did so at their own peril. At least, this was the conclusion drawn by Gordon Greer, whose article in *Better Homes and Gardens* told Americans where they could find a crafts fair in the summer of 1974. This was the same Greer who, in a different article, included Hersheypark in his list of America's top fifteen theme parks (see chapter 5). Like Jury, Greer attempted to explain the crafts vogue. Adept at selecting symbols, he observed that "homemade apple butter and hand-cranked ice cream" have now been replaced by "frozen TV dinners." With this precooked, tinfoil-encased, compartmentalized meal that could be consumed in front of a TV (and that even bore a visual resemblance to one), Greer wielded a potent symbol. For him, the TV dinner stood for the erosion of cooking skills, the fragmentation of the family at mealtime, the rise of passive consumption, and television's pernicious influence. In other words, TV dinners stood for what was wrong with modern life.[44]

Greer also used vocations as symbols. He pointed out that "blacksmiths and basket makers and weavers and wood-carvers" now find themselves "outnumbered by media managers and system analysts and computer programmers." With this comically absurd understatement, Greer committed the same fallacy as Hollinger. He suggested that the tide was just now turning and artisans were starting to lose ground in the great economic game. Regardless of whether Greer believed this faux narrative, he clearly found it useful. Through it, he could zero in on the hidden meaning he perceived behind the crafts boom: Americans were reacting against modernity. "The craftsmen you encounter when you attend these festivities," Greer wrote, "are often people bypassed by the headlong rush of 'progress.'" Like all authors who placed the word *progress* in quotes, Greer viewed much of the modern world with cynicism. What is more, he clearly mourned the loss of the agricultural way of life that "progress" was replacing. Knowing that he was not alone in holding this view, Greer interpreted the crafts resurgence as a manifestation of Americans' collective desire to return to the values of simpler times and reject the objectionable elements of modernity—impersonal cities, rampant consumerism, and passive television viewing (accompanied by TV dinners). In Greer's opinion, an unhealthy modern lifestyle was conferring renewed relevance on the traditional virtues he associated with an earlier agricultural way of life.

For Greer, those virtues provided the key. In fact, he deemed the crafts themselves to be less important than the virtues they fostered. In articulating what he gathered to be the primary mandate of a crafts fair, Greer stated succinctly, "To celebrate the virtues of an earlier era." Those virtues, Greer explained, resided in the craftsperson. If a crafts festival preserved craftspeople by providing them with a commercial zone in which to sell their wares, then the craftspeople themselves constituted a second preservation site. Craftspeople are "repositories not only of ancient skills," he wrote, "but of some of the better elements of the native American character which, in cities where greater power and publicity are concentrated, have suffered concurrent neglect." What were these "elements"? Greer listed "optimism, integrity, pride in craftsmanship," and "good humor." Though he invoked Abraham Lincoln as someone who appreciated artisans, his endorsement of the agrarian lifestyle strongly suggests Thomas Jefferson as his true intellectual forebear. Like Jefferson, Greer harbored a deep distrust of cities, concentrations of "power and publicity" that inveigh against the virtue of the individual. Through atrophy and neglect, urban dwellers had lost touch with the virtues of America's agricultural past.

Where could urbanites find these lost virtues in a hectic modern world? Martin Sloan must wander inadvertently into the Twilight Zone. Greer presented a far easier solution: Americans needed to exit their cities and head to the countryside, where the craftspeople host their fairs. "It does the heart good," he advised, "to spend some time in their company, under the warm summer sun of some delightful rustic setting, with maybe a leg of barbecued chicken in your hand and the happy strumming of banjo music floating across the fields from the candy-striped tent where the square dancing is in progress." By locating a crafts festival, one could reaffirm one's connection to the past, replenish depleted stores of agrarian virtue, find psychic renewal, and cleanse one's soul of the toxins of modern life.[45]

Dutch Days

If one lived near Hershey, one did not have far to look: Greer highly recommended Dutch Days. Hershey's crafts festival had flourished since its inception in 1949. Back then, Hollinger, the festival's organizer, had planned a relatively limited showcase of Pennsylvania German culture. In fact, the inaugural Dutch Days took place on a single day. "It was a Saturday afternoon affair," Hollinger recalled, "and most of the activity was in the bandshell" inside Hershey Park. Expecting a modest turnout, Hollinger was not prepared for the crush of humanity that descended on the park all at once—twenty-five thousand people. The traffic caused by out-of-town cars clogged the roads and overwhelmed local police.[46] To accommodate this demand, Dutch Days expanded in ensuing years, evolving into a week-long summer festival. In the 1960s, Dutch Days activities, though still centered inside the park, also happened in various places around town (a strolling band would march from the town to the park).[47] The opening of Dutch Days also became a major event, accompanied by pomp and circumstance. Guests heard speeches by politicians, listened to a Pennsylvania German oompah band, and applauded the ceremonial ribbon-cutting. As the event grew, it never sacrificed its distinctive local flavor. One year, the ribbon cutting was replaced with the slicing of a five-foot-long Lebanon

Bologna. As far as food was concerned, organizers eschewed expected festival fare—hamburgers, hotdogs, and potato chips—and opted instead for traditional Pennsylvania German dishes like chicken corn soup.[48] After the park's renovation in the early 1970s, park leadership relocated Dutch Days to the spacious Hershey Arena, home of the Hershey Bears minor-league hockey team.[49]

Visitors came in droves to Dutch Days, eager to plunge into the colorful culture of the Pennsylvania Germans. Guests who picked up the program received a framework for understanding the crafts demonstrations. "Stop for a chat with Mr. Houpt, the Pennsylvania Dutch Days blacksmith," urged a friendly invitation, "you'll be glad you did." Guests would be glad, but not just because Houpt offered friendly folk wisdom. The program intimated that people like Houpt, remnants of a bygone way of life, would not be around much longer. "Once one of the most important craftsmen in frontier America," noted the program, "the Blacksmith is fast disappearing from the American scene."[50] This ominous language, the sort usually reserved for endangered wildlife, allowed Dutch Days to promulgate a narrative of impending extinction. Why would a festival promote such a gloomy thought? One clear reason is that Hollinger, as we have seen, believed that mass production was rendering traditional crafts obsolete. That said, by imbuing Dutch Days with moral urgency, the impending extinction narrative also created a role for the guest. By patronizing Dutch Days, the visitor helped the craftsperson, a vanishing species, stave off annihilation. In sum, the narrative transformed visitors into agents of preservation.

Interestingly, the program's narrative was inconsistent with the message that many of the exhibitors shared with newspapers and guests. Art Howes, who painted the colorful signs that adorn Pennsylvania German barns ("hex signs"), described these ornaments as part of "an artistic heritage that was brought to this country" from the Rhine River region and "preserved." In the twentieth century, this craft had nearly vanished, "kept alive only by a few." Howes professed great relief that this folk art was now "gaining a wide following" and becoming "established" again as people recognized its decorative value.[51] A craft that had been pushed to the brink was enjoying a resurgence in the 1970s.

Howes was not the only exhibitor to observe a rising interest in crafts. Tim Gastler, a woodworker who enjoyed "working in front of people," also offered a hopeful message. Instead of dying, traditional crafts were gaining in popularity. In fact, it was the current crafts revival that had inspired him to learn a new skill (which was, of course, a very old skill): he carved wooden hay forks. When interviewed at Dutch Days in 1974, Gastler explained that, until very recently, "there was virtually no interest in the past, in tradition, or in the crafts around which the people had built their lives." Fortunately, the national attitude toward crafts had undergone a remarkable reversal as of late, and Gastler had a theory as to why. Many people were tiring, he explained, of the "artificial, mechanical," and "fast" aspects of the "modern lifestyle." At the same time, they felt "a sense of loss" when contemplating the disappearance of older skills. For such people, crafts presented the answer, allowing them to "return to natural rural life" while also consummating their "rejection of the modern style."[52]

On the question of whether crafts were gaining or losing vitality, Dutch Days offered inconsistent messages. Both sides, however, reached consensus on one crucial point: modernity was disfiguring American life in a way that was augmenting the relevance of crafts. Rufus Hollinger saw modernity as an economic juggernaut that, by systematically destroying crafts, had compelled people like him to take up the cause of preservation. Gastler and others offered a slightly different interpretation. For them, modern life had become so unsatisfying for people—socially, intellectually, and spiritually—as to ignite a quest for an alternative. Helen Fruhwirth, the quilter, said that "people today want to go, go, go." She promoted quilting, which offered a "calm, relaxed, and accomplishing way to live," as an antidote to the hectic pace of modern society (fig. 20).[53] The festival's program also mounted a mild protest against modern life. To convey the virtues of Andrea Schreiner, the basket weaver, the program alluded to the wasteful habits of present-day consumerism: "Before our current 'throw away' packaging came into vogue, every family owned several baskets which served many purposes." Schreiner's baskets, crafted by hand and made to last, symbolized an older way of life, one that contrasted sharply with the disposable society of the present. Other exhibitors celebrated production before the machine age. At a time when homeowners turned to electric vacuums to suck up dirt and dust, the program instructed visitors to consider the role of brooms and observe how they were once made: "Don't miss Mr. Nissley and the fascinating step by step creation of brooms on equipment over a hundred years old."[54]

Fig. 20 Helen Fruhwirth (*left rear in white dress*) demonstrated quilting at Dutch Days. Courtesy of HCA.

Though broom-making and its equipment were both old, the actual broom that Nissley made in front of guests was brand new. Or was it? Dutch Days shrewdly left the status of the broom—and all the other handcrafted objects—in a state of advantageous ambiguity. This question of newness versus oldness mattered because these objects were all for sale. The practice of selling artisanal creations had not always been a Dutch Days feature. In the festival's early years, the craftspeople were permitted only to display their wares, with sales strictly forbidden. Yet according to Hollinger, "we soon learned that people wanted to buy the things that these people made." By lifting the ban on sales, Dutch Days organizers unleashed a torrent of pent-up demand. "Somebody like the broom maker," Hollinger recalled, "could work his fool head off and people bought 'em as fast as he could turn 'em out."[55] For many visitors, the opportunity to take home the very item one had just seen handcrafted proved irresistible. Noting the appeal, Hersheypark adopted the same policy for its Craft Barn. Guests took home handcrafted objects to remind them of their happy day in Hersheypark.[56]

More than a mere souvenir, this object possessed a larger symbolic function. Referring to the creations of the artist who painted animals and rural scenes on wooden barrels, the program urged visitors to "Own a Piece of the Past."[57] Of course, the individual who purchased a painted barrel could not legitimately claim to own a "piece of the past," as that object was made the same day it was purchased. However, an object manufactured on century-old equipment by an artisan using ancient techniques did acquire an enchanting aura of oldness. At least, in the mind of the beholder, it did. As a result, these barrels, brooms, baskets, ceramic wares, and barn signs existed as tangible oxymorons: *they were instant antiques.* As such, they performed a symbolic function inside the home. Mr. Nissley's broom quietly emitted a soothing message of homespun wisdom and traditional values.

At Dutch Days, it was not just the objects that seemed old. Dutch Days programs sometimes consigned the craftspeople to the hoary past. Visitors enjoyed observing Ethel Fuehrer, a weaver, as she worked her loom. Though Fuehrer made cloth for her Pennsylvania German community, the program situated her in a history lesson. "The loom was one of the necessities which our forefathers carried with them as they settled in the wilderness," the program explained. "The ladies of the home and children were skilled in the use of equipment."[58] In this way, the program muted Fuehrer's German ethnicity and relocated her to the past so that tourists could associate her with early European settlers.

She was not alone. Mindful of the fact that many visitors enjoyed the illusion of time travel, Dutch Days sometimes encouraged a historical gaze instead of an ethnographic one. This was especially true in 1976, the bicentennial year, when organizers amplified the event's retrospective focus. Craftspeople came across more as actors from the nation's storied past and less as skilled artisans from living communities. For this reason, Mr. Johnson, the cooper, found himself shunted into a time warp: "Mention the name John Alden and most Americans will think of Miles Standish and his fair lady Priscilla. But did you know that John Alden was the first one to practice the craft of coopering in the new world? Serving as the 'resident cooper' aboard the *Mayflower* on her voyage to America, he decided to stay in the colonies and produce the items which were necessary for survival. . . . See coopering being demonstrated by Mr. Johnson during . . . Pennsylvania Dutch Days."[59] Whereas the program left the details of Ethel Fuehrer's early American connection nebulous, it explicitly associated Mr. Johnson with one of America's favorite origin stories: the Pilgrims at Plymouth Rock. Interestingly, there were at least three different ways to view Dutch Days craftspeople. Out-of-town tourists consulting their programs perhaps projected a New England Pilgrim's identity onto them. Other visitors, especially those from the area, might have contemplated the contributions of artisans from small farming communities to the history and identity of Central Pennsylvania. Finally, visitors from Lancaster County would likely have disputed the entire notion that craftspeople were at all historical; if anything, their skills proved the surprising resilience of tradition-minded Pennsylvania Germans in the modern world. In this way, Dutch Days presented visitors with a Rorschach inkblot test. Was one witnessing a depiction of America's *colonial past*, Pennsylvania's *agricultural past*, or *contemporary life* within a Pennsylvania German community? The answer lay in the eyes of the beholder.

Though different constituencies experienced Dutch Days in different ways, all visitors encountered essentially the same core set of values. In other words, whether one thought they were seeing Pilgrims from the 1600s, Pennsylvanian artisans from the 1800s, or Amish craftspeople from the 1970s, the implicit values were the same. That was because those values were *agrarian values*, which transcended time, geography, and ethnicity. According to David Walbert, the same Amish lifestyle that the mainstream viewed as exotic in the 1970s would not have stood out as "unique" as late as the early twentieth century. Back then, Amish attitudes toward community, family, agriculture, and technology "had much in common with other American family farmers." For example, barn raisings, a communal event associated with the Amish, had once been a common practice among all farming families.[60]

Since the entire festival exuded agrarian values, most visitors could infer them without being told. Regardless, Dutch Days organizers presented them in distilled form in the "Farmer's Creed," an oath dating back to 1915 printed in programs:

> I believe a man's greatest possession is his dignity and that no calling bestows this more abundantly than farming. I believe that hard work and honest sweat are the building blocks of a person's character. I believe that farming, despite its hardships and disappointments, is the most honest and honorable way a man can spend his days on this earth. I believe that farming nurtures the close family ties that make life rich in ways that money can't buy. I believe that my children are learning values that will last a lifetime and can be learned in no other way. . . . I believe that true happiness comes from watching your crops ripen in the field, your children grow tall in the sun, your whole family feel the pride that springs from the shared experience.[61]

With the Farmer's Creed, organizers extolled time-honored virtues associated with an agricultural way of life: honesty, dignity, hard work, closeness to nature, and family. It portrayed these as flowing naturally from the earth and sun and into human beings who tilled the soil. What is more, the Creed implied the continued relevance of these traditional values in the modern world.

That was because the values could still inspire. Through Frontierland, Walt Disney advanced a set of values in response to a perceived problem—the global threat of communism. That themed realm unabashedly promoted American individualism as a foil to Soviet collectivism. While Hershey's agricultural values did not speak to the exigencies of the Cold War, they did address a different danger: modernity. In an overt reference to consumerism, the Farmer's Creed contended that farm life could "make life rich in ways that money can't buy" and that the values children internalize could "be learned in no other way." Though the Creed probably did not convince any visitors to drop their vocations and pick up a hoe, it nevertheless struck a chord during a time rife with unnerving change. Indeed, it spoke meaningfully to those concerned about the rising divorce rate that broke families apart, the passivity of children glued to their televisions, and the excessive consumerism pervading society. "As the world becomes more complex, insecure, and stressful," Hostetler portentously wrote, "many more seekers will be attracted to the Amish way of life."[62] Their lifestyle seemed sane by comparison.

With traditional crafts holding broad appeal, it should not surprise us that Hersheypark would continue to support Dutch Days and construct the Craft Barn to render permanent the festival's showcase of artisans. Like the Carrousel, Dutch Days was chosen to cross the divide and play a role in the reconfigured park. If the Carrousel provided visitors with a transitional object, then Dutch Days exposed them to transitional people—a colorful array of artisans who somehow subsisted in the modern era *despite* their unwillingness to relinquish a traditional way of life. Or was it *because of* this refusal? After all, was not the lesson learned by Martin Sloan that one needed to use the past to keep oneself anchored in the present? And did not these craftspeople live and breathe this very principle? For anyone who took this lesson to heart, a visit to Dutch Days or the Craft Barn presented one additional advantage. Those transitional people were in the business of manufacturing transitional objects—new things representing older virtues. From its position leaning against the fireplace, Mr. Nissley's broom could provide a family with a talismanic counterweight to the noisy television hawking products in the next room.

Conclusion

Der Deitsch Platz offered visitors a temporary refuge from modernity. Inside the Craft Barn, visitors could admire the Pennsylvania Dutch, purchase their handmade goods, acknowledge their role in state and local history, and support the preservation of their culture. This themed area, along with Dutch Days, was imbued by the organizers with a subtle critique of modernity's worst aspects—humanity's separation from the soil, the erosion of traditional values, the loss of artisanal skills in an era of mass production, and the wasteful throwaway society. However, the purpose of Der Deitsch Platz was not to encourage visitors to dwell in the past. Quite the contrary, it inculcated the implicit message that agricultural traditions, values, and skills helped people meet the challenges of the modern world. In other words, Der Deitsch Platz, despite its celebration of an older way of life, had a forward-looking orientation. In this way, it aligned with the park's grand narrative and prepared visitors for the final historical stages: the industrial revolution and the modern world.

Chapter 7

Industrial Challenges and Modern Wonders

In 1977, Hersheypark tried something new. Instead of buying the rights to a prepackaged musical show, park organizers commissioned an original production for its Music Box Theater. Everything about *Heyday USA*—the script, music, choreography, set, and costuming—was new except one thing: the theme was old. The show, reported a local newspaper, offers a "nostalgic look" at turn-of-the-century America. Capitalizing on nostalgia, its skits and musical numbers were set in the sorts of places older Hershey residents remembered from their town's past—the trolley, gazebo, ballroom, and ice-cream parlor. Like Martin Sloan, park visitors could escape into the past.

For performers, the director tapped New York's inexhaustible supply of talent, hiring young people from Broadway and Columbia University's drama department. To gather a behind-the-scenes perspective, local newspapers interviewed these actors. Some spoke about the strain the show placed on them. Because theme parks are supposed to be happy places, often relentlessly so, the actors felt pressure to "keep smiling." "It's such a relief," one confessed, "just to relax your face muscles" when backstage.[1] If incessant glee was not tiring enough, another performer stressed the importance of stamina when a compressed schedule stacked five shows between 4:30 and 9:00 p.m. "You have to keep yourself up for five hours," she elaborated, "whether you feel like it or not."[2] Since the job was taxing, the actors depended on the audience's enthusiasm to give them a boost. Most of that, observed one actor, came from the "older members of the audience," who derived the most "enjoyment" from the show. While appreciating applause, the performers recognized that their production was not the primary magnet pulling people to the park. The sooperdooperLooper, they agreed, "gets top billing."[3]

Like *Heyday USA*, the sooperdooperLooper was designed exclusively for Hersheypark. However, the similarity ends there because the two occupied opposite ends of the pleasure spectrum. If the nostalgia-laden musical elicited wistful sighs from the elderly, the modern Looper provoked screams in the young. A marvel of engineering, the Looper was just the second rollercoaster in modern times, and the first in the eastern United States, to feature a terrifying vertical loop. It caused a sensation when it debuted in 1977. As tourists and locals stormed the park to experience the steel leviathan, attendance surged. Though lines were long, the wait delivered anticipatory pleasure as parkgoers worked up their courage. When the ride was over but the euphoria had not yet worn off, guests celebrated their victory by purchasing T-shirts that reassured a nervous world that they had "survived the sooperdooperLooper."

More than any other attraction, the Looper epitomized modernity. As we have seen, Americans and Hershey residents alike viewed modernity with ambivalence. Yes, they associated it with innovative technologies, scientific discoveries, and medical breakthroughs. However, they also recognized its dark side: a rising divorce rate, the erosion of traditional values, excessive consumerism, impersonal cities, weakening communities, and passive television watching. In fact, the Looper, just like the modernity it symbolized, possessed a Jekyll-and-Hyde personality: it constantly broke down and even caused a death.

Hersheypark added other avatars of modernity in the 1970s: the Giant Wheel, Kissing Tower, and the Monorail. Taken collectively, these four attractions represented the park's last historical stage, one that RDA called "contemporary" America. It concluded the historical progression that had begun in the Old World (Tudor Square and Rhineland), advanced through America's agricultural phase (Der Deitsch Platz), and celebrated the small towns of yesteryear (Carrousel Circle). However, if the historical sequence had ended there, it would have been missing an important link. After all, it was the industrial age that bridged America's agricultural and small-town past to the contemporary era. Industry was represented in part by Hershey's Chocolate World, located just outside the park, which replaced the popular factory tours in 1973. Inside the park, guests discovered two rides themed to honor coal mining, significantly fewer than promised at the start of the redevelopment. Indeed, the original plan called for an entire area themed on coal—the Pennsylvania Mining Town. However, budgetary constraints forced Hershey Estates to postpone this and other projects. The weak economy of the 1970s adversely affected the finances of all the Hershey corporate entities and colored all decisions relating to the park. This chapter begins with a look at the economic forces and financial realities that shaped the executive-level decisions that were made about the ongoing redevelopment.

Hershey's Grim Finances

On the surface, Hersheypark appeared to be thriving. With attendance over one million, the park recorded strong profits for the 1973 season. In 1974, attendance rose to 1.2 million, an increase of 17 percent.[4] Unfortunately, these numbers did not convey the complete financial picture. Behind closed doors, executives fretted about money. Phase 2 of construction had gone $1.5 million over budget. The worrisome financial situation forced park leaders to appear before Hershey's board of directors to explain the problem and propose a solution.[5] This involved an unpleasant termination. In 1973, John O. Hershey reluctantly fired John Hart, who left with bitter feelings. The board also pumped the brakes on the redevelopment. In a meeting with RDA, Hershey executives took out a red marker and drew lines through some of the attractions planned for coming phases. The ambitious vision for Hersheypark was being scaled back.[6]

Even if construction expenses had stayed within the budget, some degree of downsizing was inevitable because rocky shoals lay ahead. The 1970s presented a strange economy that required an adjustment from businesses and consumers alike. After World War II, the United States enjoyed over two decades of economic growth. Many Americans, especially those too young to remember the Great Depression, naively expected the postwar boom to last indefinitely. In October 1973, an event jolted them out of complacency. A group of oil-producing Arab nations, angry at the United States for supporting Israel in the Yom Kippur War, launched an embargo. The price of oil skyrocketed, increasing by 350 percent. As the higher energy prices rippled through the U.S. economy, they inflicted multiple forms of pain. Of course, Americans paid more at the gas pump; however, they also saw an alarming spike in the cost of nearly all goods. This inflation, combined with stagnant economic growth, created a disturbing new economic reality that was unprecedented and required a new word. America, economists declared, was in the grips of *stagflation*. According to Beth Bailey and David Farber, Americans found the times "disorienting, frustrating, and frightening."[7] With stagflation and high gas prices, Americans in the mid-1970s felt poorer than they had before. Many cut back on their summer vacations, a fact that depressed Hersheypark's attendance.

Hershey Estates (renamed HERCO in 1976) was not the only company entity in Hershey to struggle. A different economic trend, the rising price of specific commodities, hurt Hershey Foods specifically. Cocoa beans, which had cost $250 per ton in 1965, steadily rose during the latter half of that decade. By 1970, the price had more than quadrupled, topping $1,000.[8] Though the increase affected all chocolate producers, it hit Hershey especially hard. After all, Hershey sold mostly solid chocolate products in which cocoa was the key ingredient; Mars, which used chocolate as a coating, was less affected. With the Hershey bar in particular, the company found itself wedged between a rock and hard place. Dependably priced at five cents for seven decades, the nickel bar had become a national icon, as American as apple pie. Hershey Foods understandably resisted a price hike that would upset loyal customers. However, as the cost of cocoa soared, the company could hold the price at five cents only by shrinking the bar—which it repeatedly did. The Hershey bar proceeded to get smaller and smaller and smaller.[9]

The candy's embarrassing size finally forced Harold Mohler's hand. On November 24, 1969, Mohler did the unthinkable: he discontinued the nickel bar. The only option for someone who craved Hershey chocolate was to buy the ten-cent bar. Sales plummeted immediately as consumers punished the company for the perceived betrayal. "We couldn't win," said one executive. "In the consumer's mind, the Hershey bar was a nickel." Period. When customers had to plunk down a dime, "all hell broke loose."[10] People objected to the ten-cent bar for the same reason that they decried the fence that went up around Hersheypark: they wanted things to remain the same. But things never would be the same. In the 1970s, the price of cocoa spiked again, reaching a staggering $5,700 per ton in 1976.[11] Compounding the problem, sugar, which had cost ten cents per pound in 1973, soared to sixty-six cents in 1974.[12] These increases forced Hershey to raise the price of the Hershey bar again. "Less than a decade ago, a candy-loving child on a tight allowance could budget a nickel for a daily chocolate bar," the *New York Times* wrote after the price hit twenty cents. "But those days have gone."[13]

The sacred nickel bar would not be the only causality of the adverse economic environment. In 1972, as Harold Mohler studied his dismal balance sheet, he concluded that Hershey Foods was headed toward an unprecedented event: it might report an annual loss for the first time in its history. Of course, poor fiscal years are not uncommon in the business world. Many companies view such setbacks as unfortunate but not devastating because they can rebound the next year. At Hershey, however, the stakes were higher because the fortunes of the Milton Hershey School were tethered to chocolate sales. "All of us know we're working for more than just profit," said Dearden, citing the needs of the 1,300 orphans. Desperate not to fail the school, Mohler resorted to drastic measures to avoid reporting a loss: he cut the advertising budget.[14] When newer employees heard the news, they were apoplectic. Mohler, after all, had hired them to bring modern business practices to Hershey, which they had done. What is more, the advertisements had succeeded in boosting sales. And now the company was killing a strategic initiative that was working. It defied logic. "That was probably the blackest day of my entire work career," recalled Bill Suhring. In Suhring's view, advertising was not a choice; it was a necessity. "You can't turn an advertising spigot on and off."[15] Actually, you could, and Hershey did, much to the delight of its rival. Sensing Hershey's vulnerability, Mars decided to pounce. It ratcheted up its national advertising, an aggressive move that generated increased sales. In 1973, Mars surged past Hershey in terms of market share for the first time in history.[16] As for Mohler, his drastic solution did ensure another year of corporate profits. However, the results were hardly worth cheering about. Between 1972 and 1973, Hershey Foods' net income fell from $19.6 million to an anemic $13 million.[17] This grim economic picture provides the backdrop for the decisions executives made regarding Hersheypark.

Deindustrialization

Though stagflation and the oil crisis were awful, Americans could take some comfort in knowing they were temporary. More worrisome was a larger tectonic shift in the nation's economy that manifested itself most forcibly with deindustrialization. With coal mining, steel manufacturing, and railroads, Pennsylvania had made a robust contribution to America's industrial revolution through World War II. During the postwar decades, however, its manufacturing and mining sectors entered decline. The state witnessed numerous plant and mine closures, resulting in lost jobs and desolate towns.

The story was truly depressing. The hollowing out of American industry first became glaringly visible in the 1970s, but its origins lie in the immediate aftermath of World War II and the onset of the Cold War. Viewing the Soviet Union as the paramount threat, the United States pursued postwar foreign policy objectives intended to buttress the devastated economies of its allies. If western European nations and Japan could recover economically, they would provide a bulwark against Soviet expansion—or so the thinking went. In 1947, the United States agreed to the General Agreement on Tariffs and Trade, an international accord that knocked down domestic barriers to global free trade. Specifically, GATT brought about the elimination of tariffs that previously had protected American industries from foreign competition. Government leaders framed GATT as a double win for Americans. Increased free trade would prove beneficial to the American economy, they claimed, by spurring innovation. At the same time, it would grant manufacturers in Europe and Japan greater access to U.S. markets. By strengthening key allies, GATT would give the United States a strategic advantage in its global chess match with the Soviet Union.

Unfortunately, GATT's promised leveling of trade barriers turned out to be one-sided. According to historian Quentin Skrabec, the United States allowed foreign competitors into American markets, but the latter did not reciprocate. "Anything that distributed manufacturing away from the US was considered a positive," he writes, while "dumping low-priced goods on the American market was almost encouraged." In the end, GATT did what it was supposed to do, but at a tremendous cost. It unleashed a "remarkable amount of trade liberalization between nations," Skrabec concludes, as "American jobs were clearly being traded for peace and a united front against communism."[18] Competing on a playing field tilted against them, many American industries suffered.

None more than steel. In 1947, U.S. steel manufacturers exhibited global dominance, producing eighty-five million tons of steel and controlling an astounding 57 percent of the global market. Compared to the American colossus, Japan produced a minuscule amount that year: less than one million tons.[19] However, it did not take long for Cold War policies designed to bolster allies to effect a sea change. Between 1947 and 1960, American banks and American-controlled international agencies allocated over $2 billion to allies to help build up their steel industries. Eugene Grace, president of Bethlehem Steel, sounded the alarm in 1949. "We are industrializing the whole world," he ominously observed, and "deindustrializing the United States." Japan stood as a chief beneficiary of American generosity. Though lacking "abundant raw materials, capital, or engineering talent," writes historian Judith Stein, "the Japanese became the world's leading steel producer."[20] It was a remarkable reversal. By 1960, America's share of the world market had shrunk to 26 percent as Japan's remarkable ascendancy continued unabated.[21] That year, Japan manufactured 25 million tons of steel; by 1973, Japanese output had more than quintupled to 129 million tons. Along with U.S. trade policy, other factors abetted Japan's rise. During the Korean War, the United States purchased steel from Japan for strategic reasons.[22] And when American steelworkers walked off the job in 1959, the strike compelled car manufacturers and other companies to purchase imported steel. Pleased with the product and the price, these companies assembled new supply chains to access foreign-made steel, rendering permanent what had been a temporary stopgap measure.[23] By the 1970s, the death knell for the American steel industry had begun to sound.

Deindustrialization hit Pennsylvania especially hard. Just ten miles from Hershey, the town of Steelton was home to one of Bethlehem Steel's largest factories. By the 1970s, it was clear that this once-proud plant had entered a prolonged and irreversible decline, slowly becoming a shell of its former self. "Fierce competition from overseas," write Michael Barton and Simon Bronner, had "cut the fat and the muscle out of American steelmaking."[24] Steel was not the only Pennsylvania industry to sustain a mortal blow. Just to the north of Hershey lies a five-hundred-square-mile region that possesses 95 percent of the nation's anthracite coal, which fueled much of the industrial revolution during the Gilded Age. However, starting in the 1920s, the nation increasingly turned to other fossil fuels that were easier to mine—oil, gas, and bituminous coal. Though anthracite's decline was gradual, the story had reached its dismal conclusion by 1970. Whereas coal mines had employed 175,000 Pennsylvanians in 1917, that number had plummeted to 3,000 in 1970. The industry was practically dead.[25]

Deindustrialization came at a terrible cost. Barry Bluestone and Bennett Harrison estimate that between thirty-two million and thirty-eight million jobs vanished in the 1970s as plants shut down. Though most workers found new employment, the new jobs often paid substantially less. "Virtually all studies of workers who lose their jobs as the result of a plant closing," the authors point out, "show that a large proportion . . . take years to recover their lost earnings and many never find comparable work at all."[26] Indeed, as blue-collar jobs disappeared, workers shifted to the service industry. Instead of manufacturing steel or assembling cars, Americans rang up cash registers or waited tables. "Stripped of industrial capacity and meaningful work," the United States was, the AFL-CIO warned, becoming "a nation of citizens busily buying and selling cheeseburgers and root beer floats." The United States, formerly a global power in heavy industry, had been reduced to a nation of "hamburger stands." Though this was an exaggeration, the AFL-CIO made a powerful point about the economy's new and, in its view, unsatisfying trajectory.[27]

The loss of jobs traumatized industrial cities and towns, pushing once-thriving communities into crisis. "What de-industrialization ignores," wrote the Social Welfare Institute of Boston College, is that "people want to improve their community." The loss of jobs overseas leaves behind an "industrial refuge" and "whole subcommunities without life space or work." According to Quentin Skrabec, anyone under the illusion that the postwar policies had not exacted a terrible price should visit one of the formerly prosperous industrial cities. A "simple ride through the downtowns of Detroit, Akron, Trenton, and others," he writes, "would eliminate any belief in . . . the wonders of the post-industrial age."[28] Bailey and Farber noted that, in the 1970s, formerly upbeat Americans described their future in a "language of loss, limits, and failure." Exacerbating their sense of gloom was the stark realization that deindustrialization was no temporary trend, easily reversed in the foreseeable future. Instead, the 1970s presented a new normal: people had to accept the harsh reality that those jobs were never coming back and that postwar prosperity, which had infused American life with optimism for over two decades, was over.[29] It was a hard pill to swallow.

In Pennsylvania and other states, the loss of industries ironically created fertile conditions for a new one to emerge: heritage tourism. "Out of these ashes have risen the kinds of heritage sites," writes Carolyn Kitch, "that are meant to restore local pride and create a new kind of revenue in struggling towns and cities." As industry declined, the state witnessed a concomitant rise in the number of museums, preservation sites, memorial parks, and heritage centers focused on industrial history. More than mere "tributes," these sites constituted "determined attempts to make the past useful in the present and future."[30] While Hersheypark did not offer anything as educationally extensive as these venues, it planned to highlight coal mining, at least initially.

Industrial-Themed Entertainment

Given the importance of coal in state history, Hershey executives and RDA agreed in 1971 to include mining in the master plan. This initiative bore its first fruit when the Coal Cracker, a flume ride, made its debut in 1973 (fig. 21). The next year, the park added the Sky Ride, which carried guests across and above the park in coal-themed cable cars. The plan was that these two rides would anchor an entire themed area, one designed to resemble a Pennsylvania mining town, which would open in 1974.[31] In other words, the rides would precede the themed area that would eventually envelop them. Unfortunately, budgetary setbacks, caused by the economic factors discussed above, prevented Hersheypark from fully actualizing this plan. That said, the mining initiative did enjoy an auspicious start with the Coal Cracker.

The Coal Cracker delighted riders by delivering an amalgam of old and new. The name of the ride itself was retrospective in that it honored the legacy of the coal industry. Before settling on this name, park officials considered other options that also invoked coal mining: "Anthraciter," "Minetown Rambler," "Shenandoah Limited," and "Shamokin Chute."[32] Mining also informed RDA's architectural design for the ride's appearance. Visually, the ride had an "unfinished" exterior, the park explained, "reminiscent of 19th century Pennsylvania mining towns." However, the

Fig. 21 Riders got soaked on the Coal Cracker. Courtesy of HCA.

veneer of rough-hewn wood belied what was truly a technological marvel. In communicating to the press, Bruce McKinney spoke less about coal mining and more about the ride's astounding engineering. The one hundred thousand gallons of water required for the ride, he explained, would come from a fourteen-thousand-square-foot artificial lake. Two pumping stations, which together generated a total of 650 horsepower, would inject twenty-five thousand gallons of water per minute into the flowing system. "To put the power of these pumps in perspective," McKinney explained, "they require more electrical power than we use for all other rides combined." In this way, the Coal Cracker's crude facade of logs and planks masked a technologically sophisticated thrill ride.[33]

The Coal Cracker did deliver thrills (and continues to do so). After passengers board a fiberglass boat in the loading station, the ride ferries them for three to four minutes along a winding water channel that can be quite pleasant on a hot summer day. Lulled into a state of relaxation by the gentle part of the ride, guests may falsely assume that they will escape the Coal Cracker without experiencing terror or even getting wet. Such riders are mistaken. The boat eventually reaches an elevation of fifty-five feet before it pauses, for a split second, prior to the final drop that is the ride's climax.

Riders scream as their boat hurtles down a steep decline, plunges into the water, and hydroplanes across its surface. As the ride returns the boat to the station, riders laugh, compare the wetness of their clothes, and perhaps plan to get in line again.[34] Children who wrote letters to the park cited the Coal Cracker more than any other attraction. "I liked the Coal Cracker because it's scarey [*sic*] when you go down the steep hill," wrote one fourth grader. "I liked all of the rides," said another, "but the one I liked the most was the Coal Cracker. When we went down the hill it felt like my stomach was in my throat . . . I got wet."[35]

The Sky Ride, which opened in 1974, also packaged a sensory experience in coal-mining theming. Resembling a ski lift in its operation, the Sky Ride allowed guests to board from Rhineland, cross much of the park in the air, and disembark near the Coal Cracker. Along the way, guests could enjoy an aerial view of park attractions.[36] To honor coal mining, RDA themed one loading station, which it called "Minetown Station," and the cars themselves. Each car bore the name of one of Pennsylvania's historic mining sites, such as Reading, Tamaqua, Kulpmont, and Scranton. In this way, a press release claimed, the park paid "tribute to the important industrial coal region of Pennsylvania."[37] On "Mine Workers' Day," Hersheypark celebrated the coal industry by welcoming workers and hosting representatives from the United Mine Workers of America.[38] Parkgoers who got hungry after the Sky Ride could head over to a restaurant also given a mining theme—Minetown Vittles.[39]

While promoting the Coal Cracker in 1973, Hersheypark hinted that this ride represented just the beginning. The flume would form a part of an elaborate themed area, the Pennsylvania Minetown, projected to open in 1976.[40] Since Minetown had originally been scheduled for 1974, the new date meant that the project had been pushed back two years. Unfortunately, the delay did not stop there; the park then held up Minetown a second time. "The proposal to finish theming the Minetown area per the original redevelopment was scheduled several years ago," read an internal document. "For various logistical reasons, it was postponed." In 1978, the park listed "complete Minetown Theme area" among its primary objectives for the year.[41] Though the park was prioritizing the project again, it decided to abandon RDA's ambitious vision from 1971. According to McKinney, the RDA plans were lovely but not practical. "A lot of the ideas from the plan," he said, "get brought down to reality because of space and cost."[42] To study the mining concept and recommend something realistic, the park contracted Berger/Spiers Associates, a Harrisburg-based architectural firm. With their precarious budget in mind, park executives instructed the firm not to imagine expensive new attractions but rather to suggest small additions and to theme what was already there.[43]

As the firm commenced work, it recognized that coal mining presented a problem for a theme park. Of course, coal mining was a moribund industry in Pennsylvania. What is more, the mines themselves, even during their profitable years, had subjected workers to grueling conditions. In short, they were not happy places. Thus, the challenge facing Berger/Spiers was to make something dismal appear uplifting and fun. In its refreshingly candid report, the firm highlighted this challenge. The "depressing building forms" and the "labor intensive life of the mining communities," the firm wrote, must somehow "be translated into pleasant experiences." Compounding the difficulty was mining's rather bleak aesthetic. Mining "conditions," the firm explained, did not offer the "dramatic, glamorous, or romantic shapes or colors" that theme park designers depend on to "stimulate . . . the imaginations . . . of the people who will attend the park." Mining was not just depressing—it was drab.[44]

In 1978, Berger/Spiers presented a plan that shared several concepts. The area would include murals depicting mining scenes, a few modest coal-themed rides, clusters of birch and pine trees, and fiberglass structures resembling piles of coal. Guests could also dine at the "Mine Shaft Restaurant" and have their photograph taken in period costume at the "Minetown Tintype."[45] These were interesting ideas, but they remained just that—ideas on paper. In 1979, park executives decided to "shelve" the Minetown project indefinitely.[46] Though company records do not present a clear rationale for the choice, the Berger/Spiers plan was probably not at fault. Minetown was almost surely the casualty of cutbacks during a larger retrenchment at HERCO in the late 1970s.

Hershey's Chocolate World

M. S. liked to recall fondly how a chocolate-making machine at the 1893 Chicago World's Fair had captivated him. Predicting that others shared his fascination, he started allowing visitors into the chocolate factory in 1910. His hunch proved correct: people loved observing chocolate production. Nobody paid admission because M. S. saw the factory tour as a way to promote his products without formally advertising. In 1927, he formalized the tour and had the factory keep official records. In those years, the daily visitor count rarely exceeded two hundred. However, the tour hit a milestone in 1935 when two thousand people showed up in a single day. That year, the factory processed more than fifty thousand guests. Though discontinued during the war, factory tours resumed later in the 1940s and enjoyed surging popularity in the 1950s. In 1951, the tour attracted over one hundred thousand people, a number that had doubled by 1959. The human traffic only increased from there. The year 1965 witnessed half a million tourists, and in 1971, the total approached one million. On a single summer day in 1972, the factory groaned under the collective weight of the 18,078 people who passed through.[47] Finally, on September 1, 1972, the factory tour reached another milestone when the ten-millionth person entered the plant.[48] The factory tour had become popular beyond M. S.'s wildest imagining—and that was a problem.

From the perspective of plant managers, the mass of humanity was affecting chocolate production and generating worrisome risks. Sam Tancredi noticed that the collective body heat of the tourists was altering the temperature in the facility and causing the air-conditioning to go "awry." He also feared that a guest would toss something foreign into one of the vats, contaminating the chocolate. But most worrisome of all was the possibility that someone would stick a hand into a machine and become maimed for life. That person, Tancredi knew, would "sue forever."[49] Richard Bacastow shared the same concerns, as did the Food and Drug Administration. Both Hershey Foods and the FDA, he recalled, were aware of the "sanitary problems" caused by people trooping through the factory with their dirty street shoes and uncovered hair. "What they're dragging into a food plant," he said, "we weren't sure."[50] The factory tour was a wonderful tradition that offered a tangible link to M. S. However, it was also placing safety and food purity in jeopardy. Something had to be done.

Ken Bowers, who worked in public relations, remembered Hershey officials weighing three options in the early 1970s. The easiest solution was simply to terminate the tour. However, everyone agreed that this option "didn't make a lot of sense" in a town that had promoted tourism for decades and was expanding Hershey Park. Managers also were not keen on the second option, which involved placing both distance and barriers between the tourists and production. In what would be an "extensive renovation," the company would install "glass-enclosed walkways" on the ceiling, allowing tourists to observe chocolate making from a lofty vantage point. Though intriguing, this promised to cost too much and presented a logistical nightmare. In the end, executives settled on option 3: Hershey would terminate factory tours but construct a new venue to teach tourists about chocolate production.[51]

That decision, though ending one debate, sparked another: how exactly should the new facility advance its educational mission? Hershey Foods had to decide, Bowers explained, whether to build a "mini plant" that would replicate the real factory's operations or construct something resembling a "world's fair ride." Unsure which concept to choose, Hershey brought in an outside firm to make a recommendation. That firm was RDA.[52] "John O. Hershey calls me on the phone," Ira West recalled, and "says too many people are taking the tour . . . and they may not meet code." "If a two-year-old potties in his pants," Hershey exclaimed to West, "you have a code violation!" By the end of the call, West had agreed to design a new visitor center and pitch the plan to the board of directors. West promptly got to work. After opting for the world's fair concept, he drew sketches, built three-dimensional models, and even shot a short film depicting a possible ride. He also collaborated with ERA, which Hershey had also commissioned. As West performed the design work, ERA crunched the numbers regarding square footage, projected attendance, and construction costs. West then put together a cohesive presentation, part of which he set to music from the film *Willy Wonka and the Chocolate Factory* (1971), and flew to Hershey. Before delivering his presentation, he learned of a problem. Someone had leaked to the board that the total cost was going to come in at $10 million—an exorbitant sum. As West pitched his proposal, the facial expressions of board members reflected their skepticism. However, the leak ended up helping rather than hurting West's case. "I gave a spirited presentation," he recalled, which included his excellent idea to locate the visitor center adjacent to Hersheypark's entrance. People would visit the center because it was free, West reasoned, "and then find themselves a one-minute walk from the park." As West approached his conclusion, he shared his estimate for the total cost:

$7 million. Delighted by a number that was $3 million less than expected, the board quickly "huddled" and rendered a verdict: "Sold!"[53]

Ira West had secured the contract to build Chocolate World. Too busy to handle the job himself, he assigned the detail work to Ralph Bowerman, who converted West's vision into an architectural plan.[54] The centerpiece of Chocolate World was an automated ride, educational but fun, that taught guests how chocolate was made and where the ingredients came from. The experience began when guests stepped onto a circular platform that revolved at the same speed as the approaching empty cars moved.[55] This well-engineered loading system made it easy for guests to board the cars. These cars were also technologically advanced, equipped with speakers in the headrests that transmitted narration in stereo sound. The futuristic cars, West boasted, represented a "new generation" of theme park vehicles that were "more sophisticated . . . than has ever been designed."[56] Over the next nine minutes, the ride conveyed visitors through a sequence of dioramas, each of which illustrated a stage of chocolate production. In this way, guests witnessed an overseas cocoa plantation, a ship transporting cocoa beans to the United States, a Pennsylvania dairy farm, and multiple units within the chocolate factory (fig. 22).

For each diorama, guests heard the voice of a character, such as a cocoa bean plantation owner, ship's captain, plant worker, and child. Along with sharing information, this character cracked jokes. "Psst! Over here—yeah, to your left," said the "sexy voice" accompanying the Hershey's Kiss exhibit. "That machine drops milk chocolate onto that conveyor belt and they cool in the familiar form of Kisses . . . at a rate of millions per day." Riders also heard the following from a Pennsylvania German farmer as they passed by a diorama featuring a cow pasture and milk tanks: "Welcome to my dairy farm. You know something? Hershey wouldn't be able to make milk chocolate without me—or maybe I should say without my cows . . . heh. Those 65-foot-high milk tanks over there at the chocolate plant hold 50,000 gallons each. And if you think that is a lot, you should hear how much milk is used yearly by the Hershey plant in Pennsylvania—nearly 200 million quarts!"[57] Ralph Bowerman, who presumably wrote the script, hired actors to read the lines. In October 1972, about eight months prior to Chocolate World's opening, RDA submitted a copy of the script and a film of the ride,

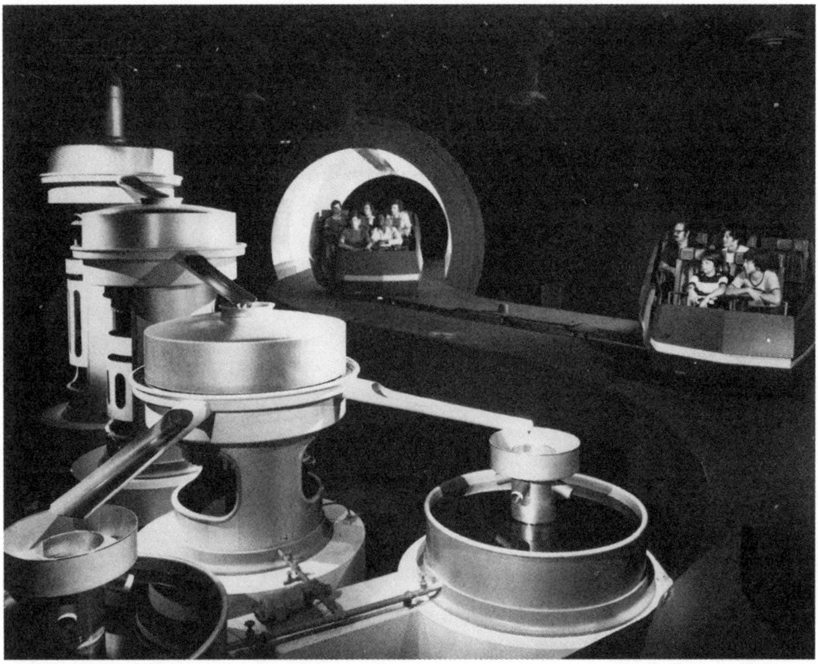

Fig. 22 The automated ride at Hershey's Chocolate World taught tourists about chocolate production. Courtesy of HCA.

including voice-overs, to Hershey executives and the board of directors for Hershey Foods for approval.

They hated it. "The job was very poorly done by Duell," responded William Schiller, the board's chairman. "The attempt at comedy didn't seem very successful" to Schiller, who also wished to see "more education" and less "entertaining." Jim Bobb, president of Hershey Estates, objected to the dairy farmer's voice, which he saw as "accented too much in the Dutch manner." On the whole, he was "very disappointed" in a ride that failed to meet the standard set by Disney World. As negative as these comments were, the most concerning feedback came from Richard Uhrich, vice president of Hershey Foods. He saw PR dynamite in the diorama depicting Brazil, where cocoa bean plantations hired entire families—including children—to pick cocoa pods. Concerned about how activists might react to implied child labor, Uhrich urged RDA to change the setting to West Africa, where "the picking of the pods is done by the farmer himself, or by hired laborers." RDA made this and other changes.[58]

The problematic Brazil diorama shed light on a potentially explosive issue that no one had anticipated when the company first decided to transition from the factory tour to Chocolate World. The former, which had taken place in the actual plant, demonstrated only the final phases of production: how workers and machines converted cocoa, sugar, and milk into chocolate bars. In contrast, Chocolate World had the capacity to showcase *all stages of production*, including the overseas origins of key ingredients like cocoa. The danger was that cocoa's association with child labor would damage the company's wholesome image, carefully crafted over the years to feature verdant cow pastures, a visionary founder, a happy town, and a state-of-the-art factory. After collecting feedback, Lou Santangelo in public relations shared the bad news with Ira West. "I know that you are involved in several projects other than Chocolate World," he began respectfully, but the "creative part of the project is not receiving the attention that it must be given." Dissatisfied, Santangelo requested that West give the ride his personal attention. Revisions, he insisted, would need to be made prior to Chocolate World's grand opening. In response, West and Bowerman adopted an accelerated schedule to complete the work and have the facility ready to greet visitors by June 1973.[59]

Chocolate World dazzled guests when it opened. West and Bowerman, rejecting the cold sterility of steel and concrete, designed a luxuriant green environment, enclosed in glass and including a skylight to allow in natural light. Themed to resemble a village in a cocoa-harvesting region, the facility housed a tropical garden filled with 1,350 exotic plants and 99 tree varieties, including authentic cocoa trees.[60] When visitors entered the botanically rich space, they found it enchanting (fig. 23). "Here larger than life palm trees . . . are interspersed with tall hibiscus plants, lovely with pink blossoms," wrote a reporter from Maryland, who called herself "entranced."[61] Though visually spectacular, Chocolate World appealed to other senses as well. Those who had toured the real chocolate factory always spoke fondly of the chocolate smell. To replicate that sensory experience, RDA had sweet-smelling ethyl vanillin vapors released into the building through the air-conditioning system. "One thing which fascinates the visitor," wrote a local newspaper, "is the pervading odor of chocolate" or, more accurately, "almost chocolate."[62]

Fig. 23 Visitors entered a botanically rich space themed to resemble a village in a cocoa harvesting region. Courtesy of HCA.

Of course, visitors wished not just to smell chocolate but to taste it. In its report, ERA had recommended that Chocolate World hand out free samples. Though that did not happen at first, West and Bowerman did create two ways for guests to consume chocolate. Ensconced in the tropical vegetation, a thatch-roofed snack stand served delectable chocolate treats. Guests could also visit a gift shop that sold Hershey's merchandise—both the standard candy that one could buy anywhere and novelty items that were exclusive to Chocolate World. Given that admission to Chocolate World was free, profits depended entirely on these specialty items. Citing the example of Disneyland, ERA predicted that the "majority of visitors will wish to purchase souvenirs that are unique to Hershey" and that such sales can "help to inflate average expenditure levels." At Chocolate World, visitors would open their wallets to purchase expensive tote bags, giant Kisses, replicas of chocolate molds, recipe books, and oversized Hershey bars. Ironically, consumers who had grumbled a few years earlier about the shrinking nickel bar could now purchase an absurd ten-pound version of it (fig. 24).[63]

After Chocolate World opened, it was local retailers who started to grumble. They noticed that sales of Hershey products abruptly dropped. Quite mysteriously, Chocolate World's presence was adversely affecting local

Fig. 24 Bill Dearden used an oversized Hershey bar to play pied piper with students from the Milton Hershey School. Photo: Harry Benson.

chocolate sales. Ira West got to the bottom of the mystery. Before Chocolate World, anyone wishing to buy a Hershey's product in town could do so only in a local store (even Hersheypark did not sell Hershey's chocolate in 1973). However, West found that Chocolate World sparked irrational behavior among some consumers. Fans of Hershey chocolate convinced themselves that the candy sold at Chocolate World was fresher, higher in quality, and somehow more genuine than what was found in stores. In other words, the ordinary Hershey bar acquired an aura of authenticity in its new setting. "It was in fact the same product," explained Ira West, but "perception matters." To steer customers back to local vendors, Chocolate World artificially hiked its prices. The move, though well-intentioned, only exacerbated the situation. Consumers saw the higher price not as a deterrent but as evidence of the superiority of Chocolate World's inventory. In this way, a measure intended to suppress demand succeeded only in exciting it.[64]

To improve the visitor's experience, Chocolate World gathered various forms of feedback from guests. During the venue's first twelve weeks, sixty-two people filed complaints, the majority of which addressed one of three problems: visitors could not smell the chocolate aroma, they desired a free sample, or they believed the ride paled in comparison to the old factory tour. Though these were valid criticisms, a different metric revealed that most visitors were satisfied with the experience. In late July 1973, the staff conducted two hundred interviews with visitors who had just completed the tour. Though 5 percent stated a preference for a factory tour, an impressive 95 percent reported having a good time (though many did request free samples). Commenting specifically on the ride, visitors likened it to a world's fair attraction, admired its mechanics ("a remarkable engineering feat"), and praised it for holding the attention of youngsters ("children were wide-eyed the whole way through it"). As for the lobby, guests were dazzled by the botanical splendor ("fascinated by tropical garden"), enjoyed the village theme ("huts in sales area are eye-catching"), and appreciated the venue's spaciousness ("lobby was comfortable; not congested").[65]

From the press, Chocolate World received mostly positive reviews, though some reporters pointed to the same flaws identified by guests. "The automated tour does not include free samples and cannot provide the almost overwhelming smell of chocolate," wrote one reporter before issuing her overall endorsement: Chocolate World is "bound to delight and inform visitors" by telling "the whole chocolate story, from Africa to the candy center, more effectively than the factory could."[66] Writing for a local paper, Betsy Rupe offered the community's perspective. Yes, the new facility impressed with its modern presentation. That said, Hershey residents had, for many decades, "thought of the inside of the plant as part of the scenery." Though the factory's interior, unlike the Bandshell or Cocoa Inn, had not technically disappeared, it was as good as gone because it was now hidden from public view. Instead of accessing the "real world that has made the Hershey bar famous," residents must now accept a tourist-friendly "simulated world" and, thus, cannot help being "a little nostalgic."[67]

Chocolate World occupied a pivotal position in Hersheypark's symbolic landscape. In the park's progression through time, it followed the Coal Cracker and Sky Ride, which paid tribute to the dying coal industry. Chocolate World, by portraying a vibrant industry that was sure to grow, represented Hershey's industrial present and its promising horizons. In this sense, Chocolate World marked the place where the guest's temporal gaze shifted from the past to the future.

Modernity at Hershey: The Giant Wheel, Kissing Tower, and Monorail

Carrousel Circle also encompassed two temporal orientations, capturing at once the park's retrospective gaze and its future-looking orientation. Though the Carrousel itself, a revolving antique, obviously symbolized the past, just off to its side rose a spectacular steel colossus that dominated the skyline—the Giant Wheel. With one representing the past and the other the future, the two attractions seemed like unlikely companions in their shared space. However, according to Bruce McKinney, their placement reflected the larger temporal philosophy animating Hersheypark. The park intentionally juxtaposed symbolic structures, he explained, to create a "heritage-modern contrast." Guests would see old and new side by side and grasp the concept of civilizational "evolution" over time. To inspire such comparisons in Carrousel Circle, designers themed the modern Giant Wheel to resemble the old-fashioned Carrousel in shape and color.[68] Even though the Giant Wheel constituted a new ride, one could also view it as a next-generation carousel, where a powerful mechanical arm lifted riders into the air and rotated them vertically in the sky (fig. 25). If the Carrousel elicited nostalgia in guests, the Giant Wheel inspired a different emotion: awe.

In this way, the Giant Wheel exemplified what cultural historian David Nye has called the "technological sublime." For centuries, humanity deployed the word *sublime* to capture their emotional state—wonder tinged with terror—when viewing a spectacular natural sight, such as a lightning storm, Niagara Falls, or the Grand Canyon. Nye noted that modern structures and events could evoke a similar emotion. For example, Americans who lit their homes with kerosene lamps and knew nothing of electricity experienced the technological sublime at the 1893 Chicago World's Fair. When they beheld the instantaneous illumination of thousands of electric lightbulbs, they felt an emotion akin to religious awe. In the twentieth century, technologically sublime structures and events included the Hoover Dam, the Empire State Building, and the fiery ignition of the Saturn V rocket that launched the Apollo 11 astronauts into space in 1969.[69]

Designed in Switzerland by Intamin AG, the Giant Wheel provided Hersheypark with a technologically sublime attraction. To promote the ride, the park scripted a detailed press release that used engineering to awe readers:

Fig. 25 The Giant Wheel looms over the Carousel as the coal-themed cars of the Sky Ride pass by. Courtesy of HCA.

> The Giant Wheel is actually twin rotating wheels mounted on a 116-foot cross arm and pivoted atop a steel pylon. Each of the twin wheels will have 12 enclosed gondolas with a capacity of 8 per car. Wheels will load in the horizontal position and then change plane continuously towards the vertical as the ride begins. Since the wheel is also spinning as the change of plane takes place, riders will enjoy several different sensations of movement simultaneously. The wheel makes 4 revolutions per minute, with the ride lasting approximately 3 minutes. It has a capacity of 2,000 people per hour. . . . Because of the structure's tremendous weight—over 135 tons—a special foundation is being installed utilizing more than 200 cubic yards of concrete in a slab 25 feet square and 10 feet thick. . . . The ride will be powered by motors with 250 horsepower located in an air-cooled housing unit at the base of the pylon.

The description accurately conveyed the basics of the experience: after riders board a gondola, an arm lifts them high into the air, where they revolve for three minutes. While the experience sounded fun, the press release intensified its appeal by focusing on the ride's mechanics. The Giant Wheel came across as a marvel of engineering that epitomized the technological sublime. To increase the spectacle, the park shined a spotlight on the Giant Wheel—literally. "Floodlighting will be used" at night, the press release added, "to enhance the spectacular impression created by the twin rotating wheels in flight." In the same piece, Ralph Bowerman revealed that the ride was a prototype, a comment designed to excite thrill seekers who gravitated toward rides that could be found nowhere else. However, not everyone embraced the allure of a prototype. Cautious parkgoers viewed prototypes as scary because they lacked established safety records. To reassure such people, Bowerman explained that the Giant Wheel possesses "a remarkable simplicity of mechanics" that "relies upon proven and well-tested engineering systems."[70]

Unfortunately, the Giant Wheel behaved like the prototype that it was. Its technology may have been sublime, but it was prone to malfunction. Bruce McKinney must have winced when across his desk slid a memo from a construction manager concerning the Giant Wheel's "present, past, and future problems." The memo listed all the flaws plaguing the ride.[71] Harold Sitler, the park's electrician, described the trouble caused by the frequent breakdowns. The mechanical arm had a habit of lifting a gondola-bearing wheel into the air before triggering electrical failure. At this point, the entire ride would shut down, leaving close to one hundred passengers stranded 130 feet off the ground. Since there was no auxiliary system to control the arm, Sitler and his team had to "pull it down" manually using force, an exhausting effort that required an hour. Though such episodes left riders annoyed (and perhaps petrified), they at least walked away unharmed. However, what if electrical failure were to happen during a storm? This was the question that haunted Sitler, who realized that the consequences would be disastrous: the inert Giant Wheel, with passengers on it, would become a giant lightning rod. To prevent this tragedy, Sitler installed a hydraulic system to back up the electrical system. In an emergency, the park could quickly lower people and transport them to shelter. Despite the headaches that the Giant Wheel caused, Sitler still insisted it was a "good ride."[72]

Two years later, Hersheypark prepared to unveil a second symbol of modernity. In February 1975, curious residents looked on as seventy-five trucks poured over three million tons of cement into a gaping chasm in the earth.[73] "It was neat to watch them build it," remembered Jack Silar, a park manager. "The amazing part was the hole in the ground."[74] After the cement for the foundation dried, a colossal crane ascending 350 feet began to lower into place the enormous cylindrical sections of the latest attraction—the Kissing Tower.[75] The Kissing Tower was the first major attraction to receive a candy theme; in both name and appearance, it invoked the iconic chocolate drop wrapped in silver foil. Guests entered a chocolate-colored cabin and peered out through bubbled observation windows shaped like Hershey's Kisses.

Despite the allusion to candy, the Kissing Tower really stood for modernity. Custom-made by Intamin AG, the Kissing Tower did not resemble rides at other theme parks. Its closest antecedent was probably Seattle's Space Needle, built to symbolize progress at the 1962 World's Fair. Like the Space Needle, the Kissing Tower has a modern design—clean, lean, and spare. Also like Seattle's landmark, it elevates visitors to a spectacular height before providing them with a panoramic view of their surroundings. Specifically, it can lift 1,200 people per hour to a zenith of 330 feet. During the ride, the cabin undergoes three slow revolutions: while ascending, at the apex, and during the descent.[76] "The view from atop the 330-foot Kissing Tower," wrote a reporter, "shows a well-ordered kingdom" where all "falls neatly into a master blueprint" (fig. 26).[77] An awe-inspiring piece of engineering, the Kissing Tower occupied the park's new "contemporary area" named "Tower Plaza." Unlike the other themed areas, which all honored history, the Tower Plaza showcased modern attractions. For example, it was the home for the Turnpike, an attraction that, similar to Autopia in Disneyland's Tomorrowland, allowed guests to drive gasoline-fueled cars on a miniature highway.[78]

In Hershey, the Kissing Tower commanded the skyline. As visitors approached in their cars, they could see the striking landmark from a distance. By including a horizon-shattering structure in its plans, RDA borrowed a theme park strategy that Walt Disney, a hot dog lover, had playfully called a "wienie." A wienie, according to Imagineer John Hench, is an "archetypal" structure, monumental in size, that guests notice from far away. After seizing their attention, the wienie tacitly invites them to enter the park. An "intriguing distant view" of a wienie, Hench explained, "tells

Fig. 26 The Kissing Tower gave visitors a 360-degree aerial view of Hersheypark. Courtesy of HCA.

guests where they can go from where they are, promising an adventure." Inside Disneyland, Sleeping Beauty Castle magnetically pulled parkgoers, as did the lofty Matterhorn Bobsleds and the Moonliner rocket.[79] Similarly, the Kissing Tower, a monarch of modernity, presided majestically over Hersheypark, beckoning people toward it from all locations.

One final modern attraction actually predated the park's redevelopment: the Monorail. Monorails first appeared in the United States in the 1950s. Wishing to excite guests with a futuristic mode of travel, Walt Disney placed his streamlined monorail in Tomorrowland in 1959.[80] In 1964, tourists at New York's World's Fair could traverse the extensive fairgrounds in a sleek monorail.[81] Though inspired by these uses of the technology, Hershey officials were thinking mainly in practical terms when they decided to construct a monorail in 1968. A monorail, they reasoned, would reduce traffic by linking Hershey Park to downtown. Starting in 1969, tourists wishing to visit the park and observe chocolate production could board the conveyance at the Hershey Arena station, positioned just outside the park, and disembark at a downtown location near the chocolate factory. During the scenic mile-long loop, they traveled noiselessly along an elevated track in comfortable fiberglass cars.[82]

In the early 1970s, the park's redevelopment prompted Hershey executives to rethink the Monorail's role. Originally intended to facilitate sightseeing, the Monorail unexpectedly undermined Hersheypark in a fashion no one had anticipated. It turned out that lots of people were eager to see the new park but wished to avoid paying admission. Such people could simply board the Monorail at the Arena and peer down at the park while gliding over it. Recognizing the problem, John Hart assigned a barker to stand at the Arena station and redirect people to the park. Ultimately, the solution was to close the two external stations and open a new one inside the park. This single change transformed the Monorail's mission: what had been a practical means of transportation became a theme park ride.[83]

Though the Monorail truly was a new technology in transportation, Hersheypark accentuated its modernity by juxtaposing it with the Dry Gulch Railroad (fig. 27). Built in 1961, the Dry Gulch Railroad preceded the renovation and had been partly inspired by Disneyland. Since everyone had seen Walt Disney circle Disneyland in his classic locomotive on television, Hershey officials decided to add a steam-powered railway to Hershey Park.[84] The two rides, one symbolizing the past and the other the future, presented guests with another iteration of McKinney's guiding concept, the "heritage-modern contrast." In its new role, the Monorail contributed to Hersheypark's larger narrative of civilizational progress. Possessing a futuristic sheen with its elevated track and computerized systems, the Monorail joined the Kissing Tower and Giant Wheel as an avatar of modernity in Hersheypark's symbolic landscape.

The Monorail presented one additional benefit. The ride's duration of several minutes allowed Hersheypark to provide passengers with an audio tour of the park. The script for the 1976 audio tour reveals that the park aspired, in Disneyland fashion, to convey a narrative. It portrayed the Hersheypark experience as a progression through "six themed areas" that was simultaneously a journey across time. Guests started time traveling in Tudor Square, "Hersheypark's 17th century English village," before advancing to Rhineland, where "all the buildings are replicas of those constructed during this

Fig. 27 The Monorail and Dry Gulch Railroad contributed to the park's deliberate contrasting of modernity and history. Courtesy of HCA.

time period." Next up was Carrousel Circle, "a nostalgic theme area featuring one of the oldest carrousels still in use in America." Monorail riders heard Der Deitsch Platz described as a "19th century Pennsylvania Dutch Village" where visitors observe the blacksmith "demonstrating the ancient and dying art of blacksmithing." The Monorail introduced riders to Minetown, which "pays tribute to the Pennsylvania Coal Regions" and includes the Sky Ride with its "specially designed cabins that resemble coal cars." Civilization's inexorable march toward progress culminated with attractions symbolizing modernity. "We are now approaching Tower Plaza," the voice announced, "Hersheypark's contemporary theme area, featuring the famous 330-foot-high Kissing Tower." In 1976, the Kissing Tower represented the height of modernity. However, it would not wear the crown for long. To build anticipatory excitement for the coming summer, the audio tour announced that Hersheypark planned to unveil something far more spectacular in 1977: a high-speed roller coaster with a 360-degree vertical loop.[85]

The sooperdooperLooper

Fastest! Highest! Scariest!

In 1976, an unusual-looking man toured Hersheypark. To anyone paying attention, his lederhosen and Austrian hat signaled his outsider status. An observer could also assume—based on the private escort the man received from Hershey's top brass—that he was someone of high importance. As the stranger surveyed the landscape, the Hershey people filled his ear with their grandiose wish. They wanted something sensational, they exclaimed, a "one-of-a-kind ride." Hearing their desires, the man nodded approvingly and responded, "I can build anything for the money."[86] The mystery man was Anton Schwarzkopf, and Hershey executives were counting on him to deliver a transformative new ride. In seeking Schwarzkopf's expertise, Hersheypark was not alone. In the mid-1970s, a thrill ride craze gripped the theme park industry. As the world's authority on modern roller coasters, Schwarzkopf found himself in demand.

Not merely benefiting from this vogue, Schwarzkopf was responsible for creating it. That said, when Schwarzkopf first started out, he seemed like a better fit for the Craft Barn than for high-tech coaster design. A cartwright hailing from the Bavarian town of Münsterhausen, Schwarzkopf at first built wooden wagons, not thrill rides. His career trajectory changed in 1955 when he visited an amusement park exposition in Munich. After studying a carousel, he challenged himself to build a better one. After mastering carousel mechanics, he moved next to bumper cars and then finally to roller coasters, where he was instrumental in pushing the industry from wooden to steel coasters. But his greatest contribution was to resurrect a design feature that had been discarded seven decades earlier: the vertical loop. "We didn't invent it," Schwarzkopf insisted, citing as progenitors both a Russian coaster and one from turn-of-the-century Coney Island. He did, however, bring the looping roller coaster back to life after it had disappeared.[87]

Why had it vanished? Simply put, the laws of physics render looping prohibitively precarious and unpleasant. This was a lesson that the hardy souls who ventured onto Coney Island's infamous Flip Flap learned, even if they did not grasp the mathematics (fig. 28). As riders hurtling forward at a high speed hit the loop's daunting curve, they curled upward along the steep incline, causing gravitational forces to instantly spike. Riders

Fig. 28 The Flip Flap, Coney Island, circa 1900. The ride thrilled (and sickened) parkgoers. Photo: A. Loeffler, Tompkinsville, NY, no. 662. Lot 5941-5. Library of Congress Prints and Photographs Division, Washington, DC.

abruptly felt many times heavier than they were, and some also became nauseatingly sick as blood rushed away from their heads. This was not fun. This was torture. Schwarzkopf, who studied the physics of this loop, estimated that it subjected people to an astounding 12 Gs (in comparison, the Apollo astronauts experienced 3 or 4 Gs during liftoff). Expensive to build and hazardous to ride, the early looping coasters like the Flip Flap failed to establish themselves in the amusement park industry and disappeared after just a few years in operation. The concept laid dormant until 1973, the year that Schwarzkopf revived it. His main innovation was geometric. By pressing the circular loop into a teardrop shape, he reduced the gravitational forces to a safe level while still delivering plenty of exhilaration. In the United States, theme parks responded to the news with anticipatory excitement.[88]

That is, until the insurance companies balked. For them, a looping coaster with inherent safety risks exposed them to an intolerable amount of liability. While expressing many doubts about Schwarzkopf's coaster, insurance companies zeroed in on its restraining bar. Centrifugal force would keep riders securely in place as long as the cars remained in motion on the loop. But what if a coaster train slowed or stopped at precisely the wrong time—when riders were in the loop? Would upside-down riders fall to certain injury and possible death? To convince his skeptics, Schwarzkopf took a gamble. He flew representatives from the major insurance companies to Münsterhausen to demonstrate the safety of his prototype. After loading guests into the cars and sending them on their way, he did something daring: he braked the coaster train so that it came to a full stop at the peak of the loop. Riders screamed out of sheer terror, but none of them fell out because the restraining bar worked. With his naysayers convinced (though traumatized), Schwarzkopf prepared for the avalanche of business that was sure to come.[89]

He did not have long to wait. Schwarzkopf's first client, Magic Mountain in California, commissioned him to design and build the coaster that became the Great American Revolution. Though the historical name was in keeping with the coming bicentennial, the coaster truly was revolutionary in terms of its design: it was the first vertical looping coaster of the modern era.[90] After Magic Mountain unveiled this steel behemoth in 1976, it caused an immediate sensation. "The loop coaster is living up to its advance billing," said the park's manager, and "is generating more conversation" than any other ride in years. In August, the park reported that attendance had risen 27 percent from that time the previous year.[91] Impressive numbers like these in an adverse economy not only attracted attention but also triggered a wave of copycatting. Theme parks looking to install gaudy new looping and corkscrew roller coasters entered into multimillion-dollar contracts with either Schwarzkopf, who worked under the umbrella of Intamin AG, or Arrow Dynamics, a California company.[92] One of the first parks to join the craze was Hersheypark.

Bruce McKinney remembered the exact moment that inspiration struck. In 1976, he traveled to New Orleans to attend the annual convention of the International Association of Amusement Parks and Attractions. At the event, he happened upon an issue of *Amusement Business*, the industry's trade journal, and flipped right to a story on Magic Mountain's new attraction. And there it was! McKinney beheld a photograph, taken in West

Germany, of Schwarzkopf's people running tests on the Revolution. McKinney marveled at the terrifying yet elegant geometry of the majestic loop. The article detailed how the supercoaster had been dismantled in Germany and all 650 pieces shipped to California, where engineers had reassembled it like a "jigsaw puzzle."[93] However, McKinney was not concerned with the logistics—he had started to dream. "I harbored all of these feelings of what it would be like to have that thing in Hershey," McKinney recalled. After the convention, McKinney pitched his idea to the HERCO board. Though a Schwarzkopf-designed coaster would cost $3 million (a staggering sum at the time), McKinney guaranteed that it would "put us on the map." The board, though leery about the price tag, decided to place its trust in McKinney. Shortly thereafter, Schwarzkopf visited Hershey to scout out sites for the new attraction.[94]

Upon first glance, the decision to sink millions of dollars into a single ride appears like pure folly. In an unfavorable economic climate, prudence would seem to dictate a different course, such as the addition of several budget-friendly rides. However, Hersheypark and other theme parks applied a different logic. As stagflation created a drag on attendance, parks recognized the pressing need for a countervailing force, a ride with so much attractive power that it could overcome the consumers' frugality and pull them into the park. In this high-stakes poker game, parks bet on the new generation of roller coasters. In doing so, they were following a simple motto: "You've got to spend it to make it."[95]

Across the country, roller coasters started exploding in popularity. This point was made forcibly to John O. Hershey when an issue of *Popular Mechanics* appeared on his desk. Turning to the article titled "Super Thrill Rides," Hershey beheld a picture of the Revolution and read about the dawning era of the megacoaster: "Hurtling through space at breathtaking speeds upside down is a stunt you'd expect an aerobatic pilot to do, but now you can experience such wild sensations yourself . . . in a new generation of super thrill rides springing up at amusement parks all over the country. In them, you plunge down precipitous drops, do rolls and loops, pull Gs like a dive bomber pilot, even experience periods of weightlessness like astronauts."[96] Though we do not know how Hershey reacted to the article, he probably found it heartening. After all, the article, by describing the public's fascination with "super thrill rides," reassured him that Hersheypark had acted wisely by eschewing conservatism and wagering $3 million on a Schwarzkopf-designed coaster.

Fear also motivated Hersheypark's bold move. Though acquiring a supercoaster was a gamble, so, too, was passing on the latest theme park trend. Executives understood the consequences of not having a headlining coaster to promote: the overly cautious park risked being left behind by rivals. "Competitive forces were everywhere and we were in an arms race," recalled McKinney, metaphorically likening theme park rivalries to the Cold War. "Who could bring in the fastest, the highest, the scariest ride?"[97] A later issue of *Popular Mechanics* underscored this notion of an arms race. In an era characterized by intense competition, a theme park "is only as good as its hottest thrill ride," declared the magazine, which estimated that "there are probably 20 or more parks in the country today claiming superlative—tallest, fastest, scariest—thrill rides."[98] Thanks to a calculated bet, Hersheypark could join in the boasting. The costly new addition would be only the second looping coaster in America and the first in the Northeast.

In December 1976, the supercoaster arrived from West Germany, ready to be assembled.[99] During a frigid winter, the work crew poured 8.3 million pounds of cement to form the foundation and welded together the steel components—all five hundred tons of them.[100] "When the construction was going on," McKinney recalled, "people would line the fences" just to catch a glimpse of the technological wonder slowly taking shape.[101] The job of naming the coaster fell to McKinney, who generated two possibilities: "Super Duper Looper" and "Merry Derry Dip." McKinney favored the latter as a nod to the local community (Hershey is located in Derry Township). This preference aligned with his larger philosophy, which was that new attractions should always be incorporated into established theming. If chosen, Merry Derry Dip would allow the new coaster to join other attractions that honored the area's history. As we have seen, the park themed its flume ride to pay tribute to coal mining and the Giant Wheel to harmonize with Carrousel Circle. Unfortunately for McKinney, he would not have his way. When he sought the input of his wife and two daughters, they did not hesitate in choosing the Super Duper Looper, outvoting him three to one. After a few playful tweaks, the official name became the "sooperdooperLooper."[102]

On the surface, the debate regarding the name seems trivial. However, both the name and the coaster itself point to a major shift in Hersheypark's overall trajectory. Until this juncture, Hersheypark had largely adhered to RDA's design strategy, which favored historically themed environments over exhilarating roller coasters. However, the park had parted ways with RDA following the construction of the Kissing Tower.[103] Paul Serff, the park's general manager, cited two reasons for the change in direction. First, the fact that the earlier phases of redevelopment, all overseen by RDA, had gone over budget prompted a "reality check" among executives. Second, the Hershey people were rapidly becoming experts in the theme park business. By 1976, they trusted themselves enough to deviate from RDA's plans.[104]

The Looper epitomized the break from RDA. Recall that Ira West recommended historical theming and admonished the Hershey people not to fall under the spell of thrill rides. Whereas all generations of parkgoers could enjoy historical reconstructions, terrifying coasters appealed mainly to teenagers. It therefore did not make sense, in RDA's opinion, to cater to a single demographic. The Looper clearly violated both major tenets of RDA's philosophy. First, as a marvel of modern engineering, the Looper did not lend itself to historical theming, and the park chose not to force historicity onto it. Second, with its intimidating fifty-seven-foot vertical loop, the coaster was sure to scare away entire categories of park guests and entice mainly teenagers and daredevils (fig. 29). Hersheypark, in sum, was deviating from a strategy it had followed faithfully since 1971. Would the risky gambit work?[105]

Better Than Sex

To increase the chances that it would, Hersheypark unleashed an unprecedented torrent of advertising. The park invested $1 million in ads placed in newspapers, magazines, travel brochures, television, radio, billboards, bumper stickers, and milk cartons. Many ads featured an artist's rendering of the Looper and promised that "Hersheypark will turn your world upside down!" The park also worked with a local radio station to hold a contest, granting the winner the privilege of being the Looper's inaugural rider from the general public. That individual would receive the first commemorative "button of courage," awarded to the Looper's initial five thousand riders. Finally, the Furry Tales visited area malls and shopping centers to perform their show, generate enthusiasm, and hand out coupons and promotional materials. Noting the cost and scope of the advertising,

Fig. 29 The sooperdooperLooper, though repelling some, attracted large numbers of brave visitors. Courtesy of HCA.

a trade journal quipped that only "hermits" will be unaware of the Looper when it opens.[106]

Just before opening day, Hersheypark welcomed 250 members of the media to the "Sooper Skybreaking." At this press preview, journalists could ride a coaster that their invitation called "perfectly safe but positively insane." That is, if they dared. Understanding people's hesitation, the park commenced the evening with an hour of "Attitude Adjustment," during which reporters sipped cocktails, presumably to work up their courage, and placed bets on "who will and who won't have the nerve." After a brief ceremony, a park official turned carnival barker hollered, "Step right up so you can be our first looper riders." For the inaugural ride, Bruce McKinney persuaded his reluctant wife, Sally, to join him. He was vice president, he soberly explained to her, and thus it was their duty to ride the Looper first. Unfortunately, the Looper, as if on cue, chose this inopportune moment to misbehave. As a throng of reporters looked on, the train left the station carrying the McKinneys, ascended the initial incline, and stopped. Harold Sitler, the electrician, performed a rescue operation to return the McKinneys and other stranded riders to the platform. "We had to walk him and his wife down," remembered Sitler, who called the incident "embarrassing." The $3 million Looper was off to an inauspicious start. Thankfully, Hersheypark's fortunes changed. Sitler fixed the electrical problem, and members of the media—perhaps with some trepidation—started taking rides. Radio disc jockeys boarded the Looper, holding tape recorders to capture their impressions before, during, and after the breathtaking loop. They later played these recordings on their shows. Dean Wise, a local reporter, captured the reactions of his peer journalists as they disembarked: "Wow, what a ride!" "It surely was wild." "What a way to get a byline!" "That's even better than sex!"[107]

In the days that followed, many of these reporters published stories sharing their experience. Charles Shaw expressed shock that his editor had picked him to attend the Skybreaking. "I am a coward when it comes to heights, drops, fast speeds, and sharp turns," he confessed before asking, "What am I doing here?" As the ride started, the tense Shaw noticed that his knuckles were "white" and his "palms moist," as if he were seated in a dentist's chair. During one steep drop, he described himself as "too nervous to close my eyes, too scared to yell." Yet as the ordeal ended, it occurred to him that it had not been an ordeal at all: "You realize it was rather fun."[108] In her account, Sue Smith characterized her younger self as the "kid who hung out at the merry-go-round and occasionally dared a ride on the Ferris Wheel." She did not go near roller coasters. As for the Looper, she "dreaded" it and prayed that the preview event would get rained out. When Smith's turn came, the operator, unaware of her angst, placed her in the scariest position—the front seat. Over the next ninety seconds, the coaster delivered "hair-raising thrills," enough "to keep its passengers' knees a little bit wobbly" and "their stomachs a touch queasy." At the conclusion, she "crawled" out of the car, collected a well-earned souvenir button proclaiming her achievement, and headed to the Carrousel ("where I belong," Smith wrote). Though not a convert to roller coasters, Smith nevertheless found the Looper exhilarating and described the adventure as "Ninety Seconds You'll Never Forget."[109] Unlike Shaw and Smith, Lorrie Brown yearned to try the Looper—at least, she thought she did. "Ever since I've known about those centrifugal-force, really-and-truly upside-down roller coasters, I've had the urge to do it," she informed readers. However, when her editor assigned her to the Skybreaking, her nerves got the better of her ("Oh, no!"). Though apprehensive, she went ahead with the ride, describing the "frightening" experience as a "whirlwind of motion, thrills and screams." When the train pulled into the station, she felt pure ecstasy: "What a trip! The sooperdooperLooper delivers!" Her final message to readers conveyed her unqualified enthusiasm: "Would I hang upside down six stories high and ride the sooperdooperLooper again? You bet!"[110]

If park officials even skimmed these articles, they probably breathed a sigh of relief. The articles all spoke to the Looper's ability to generate thrills. However, if they read more deeply, they may have discerned a pattern: the rider's initial fear *prior to the ride* was followed by exhilaration *during the ride* and, finally, by a cathartic sense of relief and even accomplishment *after the ride*. In short, the Looper elicited a visceral reaction in riders before ultimately delivering a psychological reward. Something was going on in the brains of riders. But what? In 1976, Chaytor Mason, a psychology professor at the University of Southern California, used the tools of his field to elucidate the massive appeal of next-generation coasters. "A thrill ride permits one to test himself," he wrote. "You experience a sensation, realize it's not so bad and achieve the satisfaction of knowing you gained control over yourself." Why do so many people "yell their heads off"? "A scream is a release of a fear response," Mason explained, "but on a roller coaster it's all right."[111]

Theme park designers corroborated this psychological explanation. According to designer John Wardley, human beings are attracted to "exhilarating pursuits" such as skydiving, white water rafting, or drag racing, but they lack the resources to do them and, ultimately, "haven't got the guts." Yet the desire lingers, a fact that allows the roller coaster to become a proxy for truly dangerous activity. "With a roller coaster, you can get the sensation of an exhilarating pursuit," he observes, without incurring any actual risk. In other words, it provides "the adrenaline buzz in a completely safe and conveniently packaged way." Eddie Sotto, a former Disney Imagineer, conveys the appeal of coasters in similar fashion. "We create things that look ominous and terrifying," Sotto writes, so that riders "subconsciously have that anxiety." When the ride is over, "it's very pleasurable because you survived," and "people reward themselves." Sotto boils down his theory into a simple mathematical equation: *fear – death = fun*.[112] Park managers not only grasped the Looper's psychological appeal but capitalized on it. After exiting the Looper complex, riders were handed a coupon for a T-shirt bearing the proud message "I survived the sooperdooperLooper" (fig. 30).[113] Both the ride and the souvenir shirts proved to be wildly popular. "We sold out," McKinney recalled. "I can't tell you how many times we reordered T-shirts."[114]

As stagflation depressed tourism nearly everywhere, the Looper propelled Hersheypark to a breakout year. It did so by magnetizing the park, transforming it into an irresistibly attractive venue of fun and adventure. All summer long, Hersheypark enjoyed robust attendance. One day in July, the park had to turn people away at the gate; the "problem" was that the park had already reached its maximum capacity of twenty-five thousand people.[115] For the entire season, 1.7 million people came, giving the park its best year and the third-largest attendance increase in the nation among theme parks.[116] "It was one huge success in 1977," remarked McKinney, as the people "poured in." Of course, more people meant greater profit. One day, the financial officer informed McKinney that the vault was filling up with money well before the armored truck arrived to transport it to the bank. As a consequence, the park would have to arrange for a second pickup. As McKinney listened, he probably smiled. This was a very good problem to have.[117]

Fig. 30 Riders rushed to purchase souvenir T-shirts after surviving the Looper. Author's collection.

The Problems of a Prototype

Though people came in droves to "survive" the Looper, some never had the opportunity to test their mettle. That was because the electrical failure that had nearly ruined the press event was no anomaly. The Looper was a prototype, and as such, it bedeviled park managers with its tendency to break down. During their weekly meetings, they discussed the faltering brakes, compressor issues, air valve malfunctions, and broken springs, which frequently caused temporary shutdowns. Problem-free days were the exception, not the rule. "The Looper was run 500 times last night," a pleasantly surprised manager reported at a meeting, "and it did not stop once!"[118] All the closures caused another problem: angry guests. In 1977, Hersheypark was inundated with complaint letters written by exasperated guests who had come specifically to ride the Looper.[119] John Zerbe, the operations manager, conceded that, as far as the Looper was concerned, there was "a lot of downtime." "It was a prototype" with "electronics [that] are very, very sophisticated," he explained. "It just had some bugs."[120] Robert Payne, the park's operations manager, was less charitable and more blunt: "The Looper and I were enemies."[121]

On one occasion, a bug caused something far worse than a closure. During the summer of 1977, William Harter, a senior at Lebanon High School, worked as a trainee in Hersheypark's school-career program.[122] On August 25, Harter was removing bolts from one of the Looper's magnetic switches, an action that usually cuts the power to the coaster. On this occasion, however, it didn't. The switch remained live, and the train, still receiving electrical current, lurched toward the unsuspecting boy and struck him.[123] After reaching the site, the park's medical team determined that Harter's injuries were life-threatening. Unfortunately, since the accident had occurred high off the ground, the park had to summon the local fire company to lower the boy down from a platform. Harter was rushed to the HMC, where he was pronounced dead. Hersheypark immediately closed the Looper and launched an investigation into the cause of the accident.[124] One week later, the park disclosed in a press release that Harter had been "moving a control device when he accidentally set the train in motion behind him." Unsatisfied by this explanation, Thomas Ehrgood, the lawyer retained by Harter's parents, denounced as "insensitive" the implication that Harter had caused his own death. "I don't understand how such a dangerous occurrence could be tripped by a simple motion," he told the press. "This does not say much for their safety measures."[125] He was right. The safety measures did not meet an acceptable standard. That was the conclusion of the federal government, which investigated on its own through the Occupational Safety and Health Administration. In September, OSHA determined that Hersheypark had committed two violations, the most serious of which concerned the main electrical disconnect for the ride, which was "not locked out to attain zero mechanical state during maintenance." The park accepted OSHA's findings, paid the $2,000 fine, and released a statement indicating that Harter "was not negligent and [in] no way was at fault."[126]

The tragedy taught park officials an important lesson. Supercoasters like the Looper possessed the seductive power to attract multitudes and, in doing so, turn red ink black. However, their mechanical and electrical complexity meant that they required more than the usual precautionary measures. They demanded a fail-safe system. It was a tragic and painful way to learn a lesson, but Hersheypark did learn it. In the wake of Harter's death, the park instituted a new lockout system to ensure the safety of workers making repairs or performing maintenance on rides. Mechanics were issued keys, Harold Sitler explained, that they used to physically "lock" a ride, rendering it completely inactive. "When you're working on a ride," Sitler explained, "you lock the ride so that nobody can turn it on." These new measures increased safety not just on the Looper but on all rides.[127]

Conclusion

The summer of 1977 proved to be pivotal. As the sensational Looper drew 1.7 million people to the park, local residents took notice. "It was a highly successful year," recalled Bruce McKinney, one that he likened to 1973 from the standpoint of community acceptance. The park was changing people's minds. "It's beautiful and it's great and we're proud of it," formerly skeptical residents repeatedly told McKinney. "This is a good thing for us."[128] As the park flourished, so, too, did its profits. Financially, Hersheypark bucked the national trend by fending off the ill effects of stagflation—but only for a year. At a meeting of park managers in August 1977, someone cited an ominous statistic. Magic Mountain, which had enjoyed surging attendance in 1976 with the debut of the Revolution, was reporting a drop-off of 6.5 percent for the current year. Since Magic Mountain was one year ahead of Hersheypark in its experiment with a supercoaster, executives should have taken notice.[129]

It is not clear that they did. For 1978, Hersheypark predicted a modest uptick in attendance to 1.8 million visitors. Unfortunately, attendance actually declined in 1978 as the poor fundamentals of the economy reasserted themselves. Given stagflation and a continuing gasoline crisis, many families that might have planned a trip to Hersheypark saw it as a luxury they could not afford. As the 1978 summer season neared its end, park managers discussed the dismal attendance figures. "The future does not look fantastic for us," stated one executive. "We are now looking towards 1.5 million people in 1978 which is a far cry from our projection of 1.8." Hersheypark was not the only theme park to suffer. Busch Gardens, a comparable park in Virginia, reported an attendance figure that, according to one section manager, was a "carbon copy of ours." That same year, park officials received the

Hersheypark forecast report, an internal document that predicted the park's short-term economic outlook. "We have a very real and severe problem," the report warned, that "is to be kept extremely confidential and is not for general discussion." As adverse economic forces continued to undermine tourism, park executives braced for lean times ahead. "We are not going to run scared," announced one executive. That said, the group entered what they called "super saver" mode, which meant all departments must practice extreme cost-consciousness.[130] Happy days, at least for now, were over.

Conclusion

The Eighties and Beyond

After the 1978 season disappointed, Hersheypark experienced additional setbacks. In 1979, stagflation and the gasoline crisis continued to depress tourism at theme parks everywhere. At Hersheypark, a polio scare in nearby Lancaster and an unusually rainy summer further hurt attendance.[1] Worst of all, the park was rocked by a local disaster that seized the nation's attention for weeks. About twelve miles south of Hershey, the utility company Metropolitan Edison operated two nuclear power plants on Three Mile Island (TMI), a skinny sliver of land on the Susquehanna River. Before constructing the plants, Metropolitan Edison had engaged in a largely successful public relations campaign designed to convince people not to associate nuclear power with the atomic bomb.[2] The first plant, TMI-1, started generating commercial electricity in 1974, and TMI-2 followed in 1978. The cooling towers—eerily white, hyperbolic in shape, and taller than the Kissing Tower—dominated the landscape, inspiring some and unsettling others.[3] Indeed, David Nye notes that the technological sublime taps into society's "hopes and fears,"[4] and TMI provoked both emotions. The hope was that modern science could miraculously deliver cheap and clean power during an energy crisis. The fear was that something might go horribly wrong.

It did. In the predawn hours of March 28, 1979, instrumentation at TMI-2 failed to detect that a valve had accidentally been left open. It was a small error that carried large consequences. As water that was supposed to cool the reactor flowed out of the system, the temperature rose, and radiation started to leak from the core into the surrounding air and water. Two days after the initial incident, Walter Cronkite, the anchor of *CBS Evening*

News, referred to it as the "worst nuclear power plant accident of the atomic age," adding ominously that "the horror tonight is that it could get much worse." The reactor, many feared, might explode. Fortunately, this cataclysmic scenario did not transpire, though the core did partially melt down.[5] In response to the accident, Governor Dick Thornburgh urged all pregnant women and preschool-age children living within a five-mile radius of TMI to evacuate. Thousands of people from the affected area drove off to stay with relatives. Those with nowhere to go were directed to the Hersheypark Arena, just outside the theme park.[6]

When Paul Serff, the park's general manager, received a call from local police inquiring about the arena's availability for evacuees, he did not hesitate to cooperate. "They can come over here," he said before heading to the arena to kick the Hershey Bears off the ice and start preparing.[7] Serff was joined by Bruce McKinney, John Zerbe, and other HERCO officials. Working with the Red Cross, they arranged for evacuees to have cots, plenty of food, and Hershey staff available around the clock to help. "It was scary," Zerbe recalled. "We were there night and day and took in all these people," without knowing "how severe this thing was."[8] For several days, between 150 and 200 displaced men, women, and children found temporary shelter in the arena (fig. 31). To entertain the children, Hershey employees passed out coloring books, balloons, and toys.[9] They also opened boxes of Hershey bars and passed out the candy. Despite HERCO's effort to provide comfort, evacuees nevertheless found the experience unnerving. "I'm mainly confused," said one woman, cradling an infant. "We just don't know how much danger there is."[10]

The large media presence—about seventy-five journalists from newspapers, radio, and television—only agitated people further.[11] "They were rude" and "obnoxious" to the evacuees, Zerbe said with disgust, "and I'll never forget it." He described how reporters would thrust microphones into the faces of women unaccompanied by men and ask, "Where is your husband?"[12] The Reverend Howard Kishpaugh, who volunteered to help, was also appalled by the media's behavior. "I was very angry," he recalled, and "I said so." Kishpaugh strongly disapproved of the unethical way reporters conducted interviews with evacuees. "They told them what to say," feeding a vulnerable people lies about nuclear power so that they could use the interviews for their own "self-aggrandizement."[13] If the crisis brought out

Fig. 31 Hershey and Red Cross employees entertained children in the Hersheypark Arena during the Three Mile Island crisis. Historical Society of Dauphin County, Harrisburg, PA / Allied Pix Collection.

the worst in the media, it had the opposite effect on the Hershey employees. After the crisis had passed, the Red Cross extended its gratitude,[14] as did Governor Thornburgh, who publicly thanked the company for "responding without hesitation" to an emergency.[15]

Not everyone believed that the Hershey people had acted in good faith. An area resident named Anne Miller sent an explosive letter to the *Hummelstown Sun* accusing Hershey of dishonest, artful, and self-serving behavior. Shortly after the incident, Miller asserted, a PR scheme began "emanating" out of HERCO in "direct proportion to the radioactive emissions" seeping out at TMI. At the center of the scheme lay the evacuation center, which was not, she contended, as selfless as it appeared. Beneath the "cloak of civic-mindedness" lurked a "purely venal motive." The incident had terrified Hershey executives, who instantly recognized its potential to doom the company. If dramatic action were not taken, tourists would cancel their vacations, and consumers would stop buying chocolate that they perceived as tainted by radioactivity. Staring into the "financial abyss," the Hershey people concocted a "slick" public relations stunt that deployed the evacuation center as an act of misdirection: it would keep the public's attention on Hershey's humanitarian "image" instead of TMI's disastrous effect on its park and products. Though the scheme was "deviously conceived," in her opinion, it was nevertheless a "veritable stroke of PR genius" from a company that answers only to the "profit motive," "our chocolate-guzzling children be damned." To punish the company, she was leading a boycott against HERCO.[16]

If Hershey executives harbored concern that the community had turned against them, they did not have to worry for long. The provocative letter triggered a fierce reaction, as one resident after another wrote the newspaper to chastise Miller and back the company. One man began by observing that many corporations hesitated to offer aid during crises. "And do you know why, Ms. Miller?" he asked, before supplying the answer: "Because they get all kinds of trouble and slaps in the face from people like you." One woman was incredulous as to "why anyone would criticize the one group who tried to help." Though HERCO could have chosen to distance itself from TMI, it instead "went out on a limb . . . to help those who had nowhere else to go." Another woman applauded the dedicated HERCO employees whom she witnessed emerging from the arena after "long hours volunteering" with "expecting mothers and families with young children." A cancer patient expressed his gratitude to the Hershey people for building the HMC; his lifesaving radiation treatments were "made possible by HERCO and TMI." The Reverend Kishpaugh shared that he was privy to the private meetings of Hershey officials in the arena. These "compassionate" people cared only for the "welfare of the evacuees" and "gave little thought to the material advantages of the Hershey interests." An activist who staunchly opposed nuclear power wrote to repudiate Miller and make certain that readers did not confuse Miller's agenda with her movement. Finally, a couple informed Miller that while she was busy boycotting, they would "be sure to ride the Sooperdooperlooper once for you and eat an extra chocolate bar for your children."[17]

Over the course of three weeks, Hershey executives watched the drama in the *Hummelstown Sun* unfold. "Many rebuttals were received," commented a park manager at a meeting, "defending HERCO" and indicating "very good public support."[18] The outpouring of pro-Hershey sentiment suggested that even in the postcompact era, the community maintained faith in the company. That being said, the TMI incident did inflict damage on park attendance, which was already reeling thanks to rainy weather, high gas prices, stagflation, and the Lancaster polio scare. So much adversity at once, Paul Serff said, had a "devastating effect on the park."[19] "We really suffered that year," remembered Kenneth Hatt, a HERCO executive, "because of the loss of revenue, the loss of tourists," and "people afraid to come into the area."[20] "I would venture to guess Hershey lost one half their attendance," said a fan of the park, "because I can remember it being empty."[21] Though the park may have seemed empty, attendance only dropped 5 percent.[22] Nevertheless, it had been a horrendous year. If 1977 had, in McKinney's estimation, represented the park's "zenith," then 1979 brought the "nadir."[23]

The late 1970s also marked the end of Hersheypark's redevelopment. For a ten-year span starting with the Looper's completion in 1977, the park did not add a single major attraction, which was astounding. To answer the obvious question—*why not?*—we must examine HERCO's larger philosophy. Ever since the start of the redevelopment in 1971, the park had sponged up much of HERCO's available capital. That money was mostly well spent. Delivering profits even during down years, Hersheypark amounted to, in McKinney's words, a "cash cow."[24] Though McKinney wished to continue installing new rides, Ned Book had other ideas when he became HERCO's CEO in 1980.[25] To McKinney's chagrin, Book, a former hotelier, diverted capital from Hersheypark and into hotels and other properties located outside Hershey. HERCO bought an amusement park in Connecticut (Lake Compounce) and hotels in Philadelphia, the Poconos region, and even Corpus Christi, Texas. The fact that many disagreed with Book's strategy prompted McKinney to refer to this juncture as the start of "contentiousness."[26]

Though Book's strategy ultimately failed, he did follow a defensible rationale. He viewed the TMI incident and the other local disasters as cautionary tales. "We had a whole series of bad years in the seventies that were just horrendous," Book explained. The problem, in his view, was that all of HERCO's assets were concentrated in one place—Hershey. When disaster struck, all assets suffered. With the board's approval, Book endeavored to reduce the company's vulnerability by diversifying assets and spreading them out geographically—hence, the faraway investments in places like Texas. Though sound in theory, the dispersal strategy faltered in reality. "What happened," Book recalled, "is that each of the markets we chose had its own difficulties." Book expected the Hershey Philadelphia Hotel to thrive given its proximity to a new convention center, which was scheduled to open the same year. Unfortunately, the convention center was delayed, and the hotel lost money. In Texas, Book identified a shortage of hotels in secondary cities like Corpus Christi, Austin, San Antonio, and El Paso. The plan was to build a "prototype" in Corpus and then "cookie-cutter it" in the other cities. Sadly, other developers had the same idea. As multiple hotels opened in Corpus, the city experienced excessive capacity, a glut that caused both the occupancy rate and the room rate to plummet. In Connecticut, a strong economy created a labor shortage that prevented Hershey from fully staffing its amusement park. To describe these projects, Book repeatedly used the same word: *disaster*. Though many of these assets became profitable years later, Hershey had long since divested and moved on. "Timing," Book noted, is "critical."[27] Paul Serff agreed. Almost "everything that we tried outside of Derry Township . . . was wrong or bad timed."[28]

Lacking capital, Hersheypark made the best of lean times. Jack Silar, who became general manager in 1983, believed that it was impossible to overstate the invigorating influence of a new ride. "Getting a new ride," he said, "puts new life into everybody." In the absence of new rides, Silar and his staff had to get creative to attract guests. For example, they would hold birthday parties to mark the anniversaries of popular rides.[29] However, the greatest innovation from this period was Christmas Candylane. Kenneth Hatt, HERCO's president, wanted the park to do something to celebrate Christmas. He came up with Candylane, a holiday event that turned Hersheypark into a generator of revenue in December, previously a dormant month.[30] Starting in 1983, the maintenance crew decorated the entire park for Christmas. They installed Santa in a workshop, placed small choirs at strategic spots, converted Tudor Square into a Christmas village, stuck curved pipes into the ground and painted red and white stripes on them to resemble candy canes, deployed product characters to spread holiday cheer, strung up thousands of lights, and even mounted and illuminated a Christmas tree on top of the Kissing Tower.[31] "Oh, all the lights," said Ruth Troutman, who had started going to Hershey Park in the 1930s. "It was magical."[32] Through ingenious ideas like this one, Hersheypark was able to bear fruit even in a fallow period.

The park entered a new era in 1986 when Bruce McKinney took the helm at HERCO. McKinney was determined to invest in Hersheypark again. He stopped the "arterial bleed," recalled Paul Serff, which for years had drained money from Hersheypark and redirected it to far-flung hotel ventures.[33] After generating capital by selling these assets, McKinney jump-started the new era by ordering a sensational ride.[34] For the 1987 season, the park introduced Canyon River Rapids, a $4 million water ride that delighted patrons (and soaked them) by simulating white water rafting. With this attraction, Hersheypark surpassed the 1.7 million in attendance attained in 1977, the Looper's inaugural year. For McKinney, the record-breaking attendance vindicated his Hershey-centric vision. "Look what happened," he said, "Hersheypark achieved its greatest attendance and level of profitability in years." McKinney was only getting started. In 1991, the park unveiled Sidewinder, a thrilling "boomerang" coaster that subjected riders twice (once while hurtling forward and once in reverse) to high speeds, corkscrew inversions, and a 360-degree loop. In 1994, attendance rose to 1.85 million as people flocked to Hersheypark to experience TIDAL FORCE, the world's tallest splashdown ride. The very next year, the park opened the Wildcat, a modern wooden coaster with a name that honored the past (the earlier Wild Cat dated back to 1923). This exhilarating ride helped the park surpass two million in attendance in 1996.[35]

As the new thrill rides opened, the chocolate theming also intensified. After the 1979 season, HERCO commissioned a marketing study to determine people's main impressions of Hersheypark in the major cities of the Northeast. Unsurprisingly, the answer was not British history or preindustrial crafts—it was chocolate. As a result, the park moved to capitalize further on this association, creating a new logo modeled off the iconic Hershey bar and developing a slogan, "Go for the Chocolate. Stay for the Fun!"[36] The chocolatizing of the park continued unabated in the 1980s and 1990s, with strolling product characters assuming larger roles. "The Chocolate characters became more important," said one executive, an expected part of the experience. If families do not see one, "they will write me and call me."[37] In 1995, HERCO hoped to attract people to a job fair by posing a silly question in a newspaper: "Anyone interested in dressing up as a 7-foot chocolate bar?"[38]

It was a sign of the times. Hersheypark, without any formal declaration, was turning away from the vision that had defined the 1970s redevelopment and embarking on a new path. Jack Silar claimed that a reckoning took hold among executives. "They realized that we needed to establish our own identity," he said, and that "we couldn't be a Disney of the Northeast." From its inception, Disneyland has excelled at themed environments, leaving breathtaking thrill rides to lesser venues. Trying to emulate the Disney model, Hersheypark had hired RDA to build not roller coasters, but themed areas catering to local and regional audiences. Following this vision, the park had installed historical attractions, agricultural entertainment, and exhibitions featuring Pennsylvania German culture. According to Silar, the problem was that this "folksiness wasn't selling tickets" the way a thrill ride could. "You put in a roller coaster and we're going to knock their socks off," he said. "It took us a while . . . to realize that."[39] Realize it, they did. Reflecting on the 1970s, McKinney characterized himself and others as depending too heavily on RDA, and he described RDA as being "too beholden to Walt Disney's model." "If you have five million in budget, you can't spend four million on costuming and architecture and leave only one million for rides." The industry was also evolving, McKinney stressed, and was no longer about having "the best reproduction of an English village." It was about who had "the best roller coaster or water ride."[40]

As HERCO poured its capital and creativity into chocolate theming and thrill rides in the late 1980s and 1990s, the vision that had shaped the redevelopment faded. This fundamental shift in approach raises a question: what happened to the attractions from the 1970s? The answer is that most of the engineered rides—like the Coal Cracker, Kissing Tower, and sooperdooperLooper—continued to thrive (and still do today). As for the other attractions, Hersheypark quietly closed some down and repurposed others.

Dutch Days was the first to go. In 1975, the event moved from the arena, which got hot in the summer, to a cluster of tents erected in a nearby field. The big crowds did not follow. "That's when it just fizzled," recalled Cy Little.[41] Ned Book described the outdoor festival as a "fiasco." "There were the same people doing the same old thing and it was indicated by the crowd," he wrote of the lackluster event, "or I should say, the lack of a crowd."[42] Rufus Hollinger, the organizer, called ticket sales a "disaster area" and morosely joked that "we should apply for Federal Funds." He attributed the event's demise to several mishaps. The program highlighted quilting, but no quilters were present. The pungent odor of sauerkraut permeated the air, diminishing the appeal of maple sugar products.[43] Worst of all, there was the "inclement weather." Dutch Days in the rain "wasn't exactly popular," Hollinger said, adding that the craft people's tools and materials got soggy. By the late 1970s, the energy and sense of mission that had powered Dutch Days for three decades had dissipated. The final blow came in 1978 when Hollinger, always the driving force behind the event, informed HERCO of his wish to retire the following year. "To be perfectly blunt," he later said, "we could not find anybody who was willing to do what I did."[44] After the 1979 festival, Book informed Hollinger that it would be the last. "You certainly handled the sad aspect of the meeting very well," Book wrote Hollinger, "and left feelings on a high and optimistic note."[45]

A year later, the park eliminated the Animal Garden. The problem here was not the popularity of the attraction—kids loved petting animals—but the possibility of legal ramifications following an animal-related injury. Managers found it worrisome that the donkey was frequently biting guests, sending them to first aid. After consulting with the HMC, the park decided that the risks outweighed the benefits. "Yeah, we shut down the Animal Garden," McKinney said, "because we . . . did not like the idea of kids potentially getting infected."[46] The closure of the Animal Garden did not mean that animal lovers were out of luck. In 1978, ZooAmerica, which specialized in the wildlife of North America, opened on land adjacent to the park. Since admission to Hersheypark included the zoo, it became a de facto attraction.[47]

Vitality also drained out of the Craft Barn, Tudor Square, and Rhineland. The Craft Barn's fate was not to vanish all at once, but to face incremental erasure. The process got underway in 1980 when the park converted part of the barn into a restaurant (the Craft Barn Kitchen), shrinking the space available for craft exhibitions.[48] By 1990, a crafts shop and photography studio had also moved in, taking the last of the exhibition space. "The Craft Barn kind of slipped a little each year," Hollinger remarked at the time, "until now there is very little in what you would call legitimate craft."[49] It was also in 1990 that Der Deitsch Platz vanished from the park map.[50] Tudor Square and Rhineland experienced slow deaths also. "The theming and costuming were just too expensive," said McKinney, "and weren't having enough impact to lure people back to the park."[51] In 1983, the park converted part of Tudor Square into a restaurant.[52] Two years later, the park's promotional brochure depicted the two areas as places one could

"Shoppe Around!" In a photograph, a park attendant wearing lederhosen helps an old couple select a balloon.[53] The inclusion of elderly people was probably not accidental. Kids, the park tacitly admitted, did not see much fun in European architecture. Though Tudor Square and Rhineland survived as structures, they did little more than provide two clusters of shops and restaurants with charming Old World atmosphere. The historical cores that had been so central to the redevelopment were gone.

That Hersheypark mostly abandoned its 1970s vision prompts a question: what did the redevelopment accomplish? According to Bruce McKinney, it succeeded in winning over the community. Looking purely at the economic benefits, many residents "woke up" to the fact that every admission ticket brought tax revenue to the township.[54] The year 1974, for example, netted $800,000 in tax revenues, and later years boasting even higher attendance would bring in over $1 million. This annual influx of money revealed an irony that few in the community had anticipated. Funds flowing into Derry Township's budget through the amusement tax helped to pay for the sorts of services and amenities previously covered in the compact. So, while M. S.'s compact was gone, the high quality of life it had delivered endured. The park also generated 1,200 jobs for local residents and their children in 1974, a number that would continue to climb over the years.[55] When teenagers in spiffy uniforms came home with paychecks, this accelerated the community's acceptance of the park. Adults worked there, too; schoolteachers in particular seized the opportunity to earn income in the summer. As an employer of thousands of young people, Hersheypark also sparked many romances. To this day, married couples frequently tell McKinney that they met while working at the park.[56]

Finally, local restaurants, stores, and hotels saw the park as a magnet for business. Joseph Spinner, a hotelier and restaurateur, had fond memories of Hershey Park from the golden age. "I remember my parents giving me a dollar," he recalled in 1991, "and that was good for a whole day's entertainment." Nostalgic for the park of his youth, Spinner understood those residents who opposed the redevelopment and yearned to turn back the clock. "If we could only go back to when [the town] was very intimate," they would tell him. Yet, as a business owner, Spinner profited from the tourists who flooded the town in the summer. He appreciated not only that the park had been renovated but also that the work had been done so well. "I always thought it was a grand thing, the improvements they did," he shared. "I think it's a beautiful park. It's well run, it's clean."[57] Spinner was one of many who had benefited financially from the redevelopment—a fact not lost on McKinney. Stringing together adjectives, he called the park a "positive dynamic economic generator" that forced the community to reverse its assessment: residents came to see it as a blessing, not a betrayal. To demonstrate the park's advantages, McKinney described an exchange with a county official from the economically depressed western part of the state. Hoping to create jobs and bring Hershey-level prosperity to his community, the man inquired if Hershey would build a theme park in his area. "There was envy," McKinney said with a smile.[58]

Economics aside, Hersheypark also pursued a social objective in the 1970s. As this book has shown, residents who had adored their town during the era of the compact reacted with resentment to the changes of the late 1960s and early 1970s. To placate the community, executives had collaborated with RDA to create a sensitive design for the new park that celebrated local and regional heritage. Along with honoring the past, Hersheypark, like Disneyland, presented a landscape of reassurance. As guests progressed through the park, the sequence of historically themed areas was supposed to influence them. They would observe civilizational evolution in the park's architecture and accept change in Hershey. Did residents actually undergo this psychological transformation?

When asked this question in 2022, Bruce McKinney responded emphatically, "Definitely."[59] McKinney is surely correct, given that he has spoken to hundreds of community members over the last five decades. That being said, the emotional attachment of parkgoers to 1970s attractions is, from a historian's perspective, hard to document. People's feelings about places tend to surface when they lose them and are forced to cope. For example, we know that residents cherished the Bandshell because they expressed anger and nostalgia in the years following its destruction. Since the redevelopment's major attractions either remain in operation (think of the Coal Cracker, Kissing Tower, and sooperdooperLooper) or continue to exist as hollowed-out structures (the Craft Barn and Rhineland), it is hard to gauge just how meaningful they are to people.

What we can state for certain is that the community largely accepted Hersheypark. While many residents came to appreciate the aforementioned economic benefits, Bruce McKinney also found that children played an unexpected role in winning over their parents. "The local community was won over," he explained, partly because "kids were positive right away." They were not familiar with Hershey Park, and so they saw Hersheypark, with its "new rides and entertainment," as "the place to be." Once children embraced the park, they broke down the resistance in their reluctant parents. "Acceptance," McKinney discovered, "worked its way up generations." But there were holdouts. A few residents rejected Hersheypark when it was new and refused to soften their stance as the years passed. "Even today," McKinney remarked in 2010, some people howl, "They took the park away from us!"[60]

In each case, people in this category had an attachment to the past too strong to overcome. Aimee Rex fits this profile. Born in 1917, Rex had become a veritable human time capsule of Hershey history when, in 2008, she volunteered to give an oral history at the age of ninety-one. As a child, Rex enjoyed many iterations of something readers of this book may be tired of contemplating—the Perfect Hershey Day. "We could go over to the park, and I heard [John Philip] Sousa play one Sunday" she recalled. Rex also harbored fond memories of the swimming pool, Carrousel, Miniature Railway, picnicking, and ballroom ("I remember the first time I was in the ballroom. . . . It was Rudy Vallée."). Rex loved the free-and-open park, which crucially had "no fences." That, she insisted, had been M. S.'s vision. "Everything he did," she declared, "he did for the workers."[61] Rex did not just revere M. S.; she knew him. Her father was D. Paul Witmer, the town's foremost builder. M. S. hired Witmer to construct many of the town's famous structures: the Community Building, multiple buildings at the Milton Hershey School, and Hotel Hershey. For the latter, M. S. handed Witmer a postcard showing a small hotel on the Mediterranean and requested something similar but larger. Witmer also built some of the structures inside Hershey Park.[62]

How did Aimee Rex respond to the sweeping changes of the 1960s and the jarring demolitions of the 1970s? Given her adoration of M. S. and her affection for the town, she unsurprisingly mourned the loss of old Hershey: "Nothing's there. Nothing is the same." Apart from the Cocoa Inn's destruction (which she accepted after her father confirmed the sinkhole), she largely disapproved of Hershey's transformation, associating it with the modern values she disliked. "I've lived in two different worlds," she said. "This generation is just speed and greed. It's terrible. I lived in a better time." As for Hersheypark, she did visit the park twice since the redevelopment but expressed "no interest in going anymore." Rex's passionate feelings about old Hershey could not be overcome by any theme park design, not even one that honored the past.

Though Rex remained unconverted, Hersheypark did steal a victory of sorts even from her. Recall McKinney's observation that acceptance "worked its way up generations." Something like that happened in Rex's family. Her unyielding opposition softened ever so slightly when she saw her grandchildren take advantage of the employment opportunities Hersheypark afforded them. The park hired her granddaughter to train new staff in proper customer relations. "She is Director of Learning and Leadership Development," a beaming Rex stated with satisfaction, adding that the young woman's great-grandfather (D. Paul Witmer) "would be very proud of her." Rex also shared that her grandson, when in high school, took a job as a strolling Hershey bar. During one of Rex's rare and grudging visits to the park, he lunged at her in his costume: "That's the first time I was hugged by a Hershey bar."[63]

Aimee Rex stands for a certain kind of person, one who was too invested in the past to accept the changes (though even she conceded that young people benefited from Hersheypark). Others preferred the past but showed a willingness to adjust. As a child in the 1940s and 1950s, Dina Willard often visited Hershey Park, where she relished riding the Carrousel. As an adult, she married twice, first to a teacher at the Milton Hershey School. As the wife of a faculty member, she "became part of a family" and learned the rich traditions of the town's most revered institution. When he abruptly died in the early 1970s, she found herself without a steady income and five children to feed. To pay the bills, she took a position as a nurse at a local school, which is where she met her second husband. A physician at the HMC, he appeared one day to register his son for kindergarten. Together, the couple raised their eight children.

Hersheypark was a godsend. On a typical summer day, Willard would supervise household chores in the morning before taking the brood to the park in the afternoon. Since each child had a season pass, the family could afford this routine. "We spent a lot of time in the park," she said. While finding the park "wonderful," the family did notice the paucity of rides resulting from RDA's prioritizing of theming over thrills. "There were very few rides," the perceptive Willard noted. "The attraction was just going there and being entertained." When the children reached their teenage years, they all got summer jobs at the park. The park, she recognized, had played a central role in her children's lives. "Hersheypark," she remarked, is "in their blood."

As Willard reviewed her life in Hershey, she realized that her experience straddled two eras. To comprehend the town's transformation, she deployed her two husbands' employers as symbols: the tradition-based Milton Hershey School and the modern HMC. At the "old school," she observed, "I had the ability to see . . . the traditions," and then the HMC exposed her to the "new development" of the town. That exposure clearly changed her mode of thinking. During the TMI incident, she planted peas and onions in her garden while others evacuated. How did she manage to remain so calm? She accepted her scientific husband's assurances that there was no need to panic. "When the radiologists leave town," he said, "we'll leave town." Having a perspective shaped by two eras, Willard reflected on the town's evolution: "We've seen a lot of changes in Hershey." Willard classified Hershey as a "small town" before the "development and tourism" changed the "whole climate" of the place. Did she *embrace* the transformation? Not exactly. It is more accurate to say that she *understood* and *accepted* it but preferred the "small-town atmosphere" of a "simpler time." In comparison with Aimee Rex's strong dislike of change, Dina Willard represents a moderate position.[64]

Dena Thomas epitomizes a third point of view. Though hailing from nearby Lancaster, Thomas harbored affection for Hershey that rivaled that of any resident. With memories of the town dating back to the 1960s, she experienced both old and new Hershey. Before the redevelopment, her family would spend magical days in Hershey taking the factory tour and enjoying Hershey Park. "We always had family picnics here," she recalled in her oral history, "and we were given one dollar." With that dollar, the kids would go on rides while the adults congregated at the Bandshell. She would always ride the Comet twice ("I like anything fast"), but the Fun House was "where you got your money's worth." That is because one could behave in a way that people today "consider dangerous" (because of the possibility of injury) but "back then was just really a lot of fun." In the evening, the family would listen to the "big stars" play at the Starlight Ballroom. Though M. S. died before Thomas was born, her deep connection to Hershey Park, consummated through many Perfect Hershey Days, allowed her to intuit his vision. "Milton Hershey thought of everybody as like one big family," she observed, explaining further that the park's purpose was "keeping that family happy."[65] M. S. might have chosen different words, but she got the gist of it.

When asked about the redevelopment, Thomas expressed ambivalence. She had experienced enough of old Hershey to respect M. S.'s legacy, view park structures as meaningful symbols, and sympathize with the distraught community. Concerning the latter, she started to mention that she understood why "there were a lot of people that might have—" before stopping mid-sentence. She was most likely about to say, "been upset by the changes." However, rather than complete her thought, she blurted out the single change that hurt the most: "They stopped the picnicking inside the park!" Thomas felt the sting from this loss because she, like so many others, had engaged in symbol formation. For her, picnics stood for the intangible things that mattered most in her life—childhood happiness, family togetherness, and M. S.'s vision. Though she missed the old park, her mind never calcified into rigid resistance. "I mean, I can see why they did it," she said of the redevelopment. While feeling nostalgia for the old park, Thomas was willing to give the new park a try.[66]

She loved the new park too. Though appreciating the Comet as a transitional object, she caught Looper fever in 1977. After hearing that the first riders would receive commemorative buttons, she arrived early on opening day to secure her place in line. While waiting, she beheld the terrifying loop and wondered what it was going to feel like. Of course, Thomas "survived" and collected her reward. Two decades later, she recalled thinking that it was "the greatest thing in the world" to have been among the first to experience the Looper: "So, yeah, it's a neat memory." And when Thomas filed this memory away, it joined a growing collection of others that drew—and this is critical—from *both* iterations of the park. In other words, Hersheypark had become as meaningful to Thomas as Hershey Park once was. As she grew older and aged out of thrill rides, her love for the place never waned. "Hersheypark, to me, isn't just a place to go for entertainment," she shared, "it's a place that I embrace." It could even be therapeutic. When she encountered difficulty becoming pregnant, the park gave her a "happy place" where she could forget her troubles. Though she finally conceived in 1980, the pregnancy resulted in a stillborn. Severely depressed but refusing to take pills, Thomas visited the park often, enjoyed the company of the friends she made there, and recovered from her loss.

As the summers rolled by, Thomas realized that she had become profoundly bonded to the park—both versions of it. This recognition inspired her to take an extraordinary action, one so unorthodox that she hesitated to share it in her oral history. "Okay, I'm going to tell you guys this," she declared, deciding to risk embarrassment by revealing her secret. Since the park had played a central role in her life, it was only fitting that the relationship endure after her death. Thomas divulged that she had left instructions for an undertaker to scatter her ashes in the park: "It's in my will. Yeah, it is, honest to God."[67]

Of course, it is impossible for a theme park to manufacture strong emotional attachments like this. They have to happen organically. That said, Hersheypark clearly wishes to help today's visitors form a connection to the park's rich history while simultaneously remaining on the cutting edge of theme park technology. In 2020, Hersheypark unveiled Chocolatetown, a themed area located at the park's entrance that cost $150 million to build. As it had done in the 1970s, Hershey collaborated on the project with an external design firm (PGAV Destinations) to theme the area and install state-of-the-art attractions. Chocolatetown offers a virtual reality experience called Hyperdeck that places guests in imaginary worlds. More importantly, it is home to Candymonium, one of the park's newest and most sensational roller coasters. Candymonium is technically a *hypercoaster*, a term reserved for coasters that ascend to greater heights (210 feet) and thrill riders with greater drops than their predecessors. With chocolate-brown tracks and trains colored to signify candy brands (Reese's, Twizzlers, and Kisses), Candymonium perfectly embodies the park's winning formula: *chocolate theming + thrill rides = success.*

These modern attractions notwithstanding, Chocolatetown is also remarkable for its retrospective gaze. Hersheypark clearly intends for there to be a "heritage-modern contrast," words that Bruce McKinney used to describe the design principle guiding the 1970s redevelopment. Just as

Hersheypark back then had preserved old rides and built new attractions to honor local heritage, so, too, does Chocolatetown encourage guests to engage the past. "A foundational element of the project was to connect the development to Hershey's history and the legacy of our founder," explained John Lawn, CEO of Hershey Entertainment and Resorts Company (formerly HERCO). He noted that Chocolatetown makes "both subtle and obvious nods to the legacy of Milton S. Hershey." The most "obvious nods" include the large cement nickel bars near the entrance, a panoramic mural depicting an aerial view of Hershey from 1906, and Milton's Ice Cream Parlor. In addition, the park enshrined the Carrousel in a pavilion at Chocolatetown's center that harks back to Hershey's golden era. In this way, the Carrousel has reprised its role as transitional object on a new stage. The park also recovered one of the original rides, one that had been absent for decades. When you walk into Chocolatetown's merchandise shop, you encounter a car from the Miniature Railway, purchased by M. S. in 1910. Finally, Chocolatetown offers guests an intriguing way to orient themselves historically: the Compass Rose.[68] Consisting of more than twenty bronze medallions set in concrete, the Compass Rose directs guests to important landmarks in Hershey history: the Milton Hershey School, Hotel Hershey, the old chocolate factory, and Hershey's Chocolate World, to name a few. One medallion even points guests toward Cuba, the site of Central Hershey, M. S.'s sugar operation.[69]

John Lawn also noted that some "nods" to history were "subtle" and easy to miss. Only the most observant guests will notice that three bricks embedded in Chocolatetown's Starbucks have a slightly different color. These are no ordinary bricks. The coffeeshop rests on the exact location previously occupied by the old front gate. Designed by RDA in the early 1970s, that gate featured distinctive parapets that harmonized with Tudor Square's castle tower. Though the park demolished both the front gate and Tudor Square in 2019 to create space for Chocolatetown, it preserved three bricks. "We salvaged bricks from the old gate," explained Lawn, inserting "three of them into the building to pay homage to the historic threshold of that era of our history."[70] If this act of preservation sounds familiar, it should: history is repeating itself. When Hershey Estates demolished landmarks from Hershey Park in the 1970s, it chose to save two, the Comet and Carrousel, to maintain a vital link to the past. Hershey Entertainment and Resorts Company has now torn down structures from the 1970s redevelopment but has found a way to perpetuate their memory.

Are these memories that anyone wants to save? Readers will remember that, in the 1970s, the front gate was where the despised fences converged and the much-maligned admissions policy was enacted. For many residents, the front gate symbolized something awful—the abandonment of M. S.'s vision. Given the ferocity of the community's response, one might have expected the front gate's 2019 demise to have elicited applause. But times have changed. The people who protested vociferously fifty years ago have either aged or left us. They have been succeeded by new generations of Hersheypark fans, who have had five decades to create symbols of their own. Did these people form emotional attachments to the front gate and Tudor Square? Did they care when these structures were razed?

I confessed above that I lacked hard evidence proving that guests had found meaning in the attractions from the 1970s redevelopment. That statement is not entirely accurate. The recent demolitions did open a small window into the psyches of local residents and park fans. While writing this book, I worked closely with Tesa Burns, archivist at Hershey Community Archives. One day, while discussing Tudor Square and the old entrance, she shared that although she loved the new Chocolatetown entrance, the loss of those structures had saddened her. She followed up our conversation with an email in which she expanded on her comment. Describing childhood excursions to the park, she wrote that she had "such distinct memories of walking in through the old entrance." Those memories included the "tree-lined path," the stately iron gates, and the "quaint shops" of Tudor Square and Rhineland. After returning to Hershey later in life for professional reasons, she started visiting the park again. As an adult, she felt pangs of "nostalgia" for the entrance and the European architecture. "I was definitely sad to see it go," she said of the demolished entrance area, "because of its historical significance—but also because of the memories."[71] Tesa's reaction got me thinking: surely, she could not be alone in feeling this way. Might others have expressed their emotions somewhere online? Playing this hunch, I turned to the internet.

I discovered that in 2019, a Hersheypark enthusiast uploaded to YouTube a sentimental video capturing Tudor Square and the front entrance one last time before their destruction. Below the video, you will find the responses of viewers who chime in to express their feelings. One viewer shares that, for whatever reason, he decided to take a photograph of the gate the very first time he passed through it. He now vows "never [to] delete that photo." For another viewer, the sign on the gate had come to symbolize childhood—and now it is gone. "NOOOOO NOT MY CHILDHOOD SIGN!!!!" this distraught fan exclaims. "I don't know how I'm gonna look at Hershey the same way. Farewell buddy." One viewer, who adores "the Tudor look," now misses the "old design and buildings," which are "more charming" than the new entrance. Another adds that he wishes the park had found a way to expand the entrance "without destroying the old buildings." One man expresses his emotions this way: "Damn. I really miss that gate. I have no idea why but just seeing it [in the video] got me so excited. It's not the same." One concise commenter captures his nostalgia in four simple words: "The good old days." Finally, a viewer imparts that he will "miss the old entrance" because the new one "seems too commercialized and disneylike."[72]

Disneylike? That comment carries a rich irony. Back in the early 1970s, the objective of Hershey Estates had been to convert a rusting amusement park into a Disney-style theme park. To achieve this goal, Hershey had hired the top firm in the industry, RDA, to handle the theming. Ira West even said of Tudor Square that "Disney would not have done a better job."[73] In short, the very structures that the YouTube respondent appreciated because they were *not* "disneylike" were intended to be exactly that. However, as time passed, Hershey executives experienced an epiphany. Jack Silar articulated the revelation well when he said, "We couldn't be a Disney of the Northeast" and "needed to establish our own identity."[74] Hersheypark had finally discovered what it was good at—*being Hersheypark*. And though Chocolatetown's theming may inspire comparisons to Disney, Chocolatetown could exist only in Hershey and nowhere else. Its many "nods" to history render it distinct. In fact, these nods even suggest that we should revise the park's formula, shared on this book's very first page, to reflect the crucial role played by the past at present-day Hersheypark: *chocolate theming + thrill rides + **heritage** = success.*

The park signaled its enthusiastic embrace of this formula at the groundbreaking for Chocolatetown in 2019. On a windy January day, John Lawn presided over a ceremony where he and invited guests delivered short speeches to a gathering. One by one, the presenters would deploy the past, often speaking reverentially about M. S., before pivoting to the present and future. "We are now living on the legacy of . . . Milton Hershey," remarked Suzanne Jones, a Hershey vice president. "It is on that legacy that this investment will continue so that many more generations . . . can make more memories in Hershey." Similarly, Susan Cort of the Derry Township Board of Supervisors invoked the "legacy" of M. S., credited him with creating Hershey's "vibrant community," and heralded Chocolatetown as "the next chapter." State Representative Tom Mehaffie briefly reminisced about the indelible impression the park's entrance had made on him in the late 1970s. He then described Hersheypark as an "economic driver" that has generated $1.2 billion in tax revenue for the community, attracts millions of people every year, and promises to thrive in the future with the addition of Chocolatetown.

At first, the speeches seem conventional. Upbeat and optimistic, they are exactly what one expects to hear at a groundbreaking ceremony. However, when we place them in the context of history—specifically, the 1970s redevelopment—their conventionality takes on new meaning. Recall that, in 1971, John Hart and Bruce McKinney had to work up their nerve before facing hostile crowds at information sessions. In contrast, John Lawn can describe a massive demolition and costly construction project without a hint of trepidation in his voice. He does not have to tiptoe around the subject of change for fear of stoking the ire of a sensitive community. In Hershey, change is no longer controversial. Indeed, the opposite is true: Hershey Entertainment and Resorts has earned the trust of the community and can embark on major projects assured of its support.

The groundbreaking also reflects the fact that the past has ceased being problematic. We are struck by how the speakers can link M. S.'s legacy to the present and the future with ease. John Lawn does not feel any obligation to justify Chocolatetown as the answer to the familiar question, "What would Milton Hershey do?" Seeing the past not as a *burden* but as a *blessing,* Lawn believes it confers identity on the park, inspires innovation, motivates employees, evokes community pride, fascinates out-of-town visitors, and attracts new residents. Of course, this positive view of the past was never inevitable. It was the 1970s redevelopment that broke local resistance to change and helped the company and community emerge from the patriarch's shadow. In fact, we might conceive of this conversion of the past

Fig. 32 The groundbreaking ceremony for Chocolatetown. Courtesy of HCA.

into an asset as a gift handed across the chasm of time—it is how seventies Hersheypark quietly empowers present-day Hersheypark.

Of course, a groundbreaking ceremony is ultimately about the future, and this one was no exception. After the speeches, John Lawn nodded one final time to the past, stating that "this development leans . . . heavily on Mr. Hershey's history." He then directed the invited speakers, two students from the Milton Hershey School, and three product characters to pick up candy-themed shovels and stick them into the ceremonial dirt (fig. 32). The Chocolatetown project was officially underway.[75] It was a hopeful moment that captured the spirit of M. S., who never seemed preoccupied with the past. It certainly was not the past that fired his imagination 120 years earlier when he first beheld the green expanses of Derry Church. On that fateful day, he gazed out on the rolling hills and rich pastures, all pregnant with possibility, and conjured up his vision.

notes

Introduction

1. Tim Stuhldreher, "Hersheypark 2020 Plan Includes Tearing Down Iconic Tudor Village Entrance as Part of $150M Expansion," *LancasterOnline*, January 4, 2019, https://lancasteronline.com/news/local/hersheypark-2020-plan-includes-tearing-down-iconic-tudor-village-entrance-as-part-of-150m-expansion/article_a90c2384-0edb-11e9-b9f6-0be887aab076.html.
2. D'Antonio, *Hershey*, 131–32, 169, 186; Green, *Company Town*, 35–38.
3. Bongartz, "Chocolate Camelot," 93.
4. Kurie, *In Chocolate We Trust*, 51–52.
5. Ned Book Oral History, 1996, 96OH15, Hershey Community Archives (hereafter HCA).
6. Watts discusses Disneyland's pro-American message in *Magic Kingdom*, 392–93. Similarly, Steiner describes Disneyland as providing the "key symbolic landscapes" for America. Steiner, "Frontierland as Tomorrowland," 3. In the same fashion, Marling locates Disneyland's "power" in its ability to provide America with a "cultural metaphor." Marling, *Designing Disney's Theme Parks*, 9.
7. Author's interview with Bruce McKinney, July 22, 2010.
8. "Global Theme Park Market Poised for Remarkable Growth," *Yahoo! Finance*, September 11, 2024, https://finance.yahoo.com/news/global-theme-park-market-poised-003000408.html.

Chapter 1

1. Austin Geiling Jr. Oral History, 1991, 91OH30, HCA.
2. Koehn and Helms, "Candy Land," 23.
3. Geiling Oral History.
4. Geiling Oral History.
5. Geiling Oral History.
6. Yoder and Graves see the terms Pennsylvania German and Pennsylvania Dutch as "interchangeable." Yoder and Graves, *Hex Signs*, 1. For a discussion of the two terms and scholarly preferences, see Bronner and Brown, *Pennsylvania Germans*, x.
7. McMahon, "Milton Hershey's World," 553.
8. D'Antonio, *Hershey*, 41–54.
9. Cadbury, *Chocolate Wars*, 142–43; Bongartz, "Chocolate Camelot," 91.
10. D'Antonio, *Hershey*, 95; Brenner, *Emperors of Chocolate*, 84–85.
11. Dubofsky, *Industrialism and the American Worker*, 35–82.
12. Baxter, "Paradox of a Capitalist Utopia," 651–56.
13. Baxter, "Paradox of a Capitalist Utopia," 656, 659–63.
14. Schneirov, "'To the Ragged Edge of Anarchy,'" 27–28.
15. Bassett, "Pullman Strike of 1894," 34.
16. Crawford, *Workingman's Paradise*, 42.
17. "The Burning of the World's Fair Buildings," *Harper's Weekly*, July 21, 1894, 687.
18. Crawford, *Workingman's Paradise*, 42.
19. Crawford, *Workingman's Paradise*, 42–43.
20. Crawford, *Workingman's Paradise*, 45, 83–84, 95, 101.
21. Green, *Company Town*, 36.
22. Though scholars lack incontrovertible proof that Hershey toured Bournville, most believe such a visit took place. McMahon, "Milton Hershey's World," 572; Green, *Company Town*, 36; D'Antonio, *Hershey*, 85–86; Cadbury, *Chocolate Wars*, 146–47.
23. Crawford, *Workingman's Paradise*, 71.
24. Harvey, *Model Village*, 9–14.
25. Bradley, *Cadbury's Purple Reign*, 90.
26. Cadbury, *Chocolate Wars*, 132–33.
27. Bradley, *Cadbury's Purple Reign*, 63.
28. D'Antonio, *Hershey*, 90, 100–102; Bongartz, "Chocolate Camelot," 91–92.
29. Green, *Company Town*, 36.
30. "A New Town Near Derry Church to Cost a Million," *Harrisburg (PA) Independent*, February 19, 1903. Article is quoted in McMahon, "Milton Hershey's World," 567.

31. Koehn and Helms, "Candy Land," 16.
32. McMahon, "Milton Hershey's World," 552–53, 556; D'Antonio, *Hershey*, 116.
33. Green, *Company Town*, 38.
34. For impressions of the junior college, see Howard B. Kishpaugh Oral History, 1990, 90OH17, HCA.
35. Richard Seiverling Oral History, 1991, 91OH19, HCA.
36. Brenner, *Emperors of Chocolate*, 117.
37. McMahon, "Milton Hershey's World," 552–53, 556; D'Antonio, *Hershey*, 116.
38. Brenner, *Emperors of Chocolate*, 114.
39. D'Antonio, *Hershey*, 120.
40. Edward Mott Woolley, "How Hershey Pays Back His Chocolate Millions," *McClure's*, April 1924, 78, 86–87.
41. James Young, "Hershey, Unique Philanthropist," *New York Times*, November 18, 1923.
42. McMahon, *Milton Hershey School*, 10, 19; Fernandez, *Chocolate Trust*, 1–3.
43. Young, "Hershey." In wishing to care for orphaned children, Milton and Kitty Hershey were not outliers. In 1917, Father Edward Flanagan founded his school for homeless boys in Omaha, Nebraska. Shortly thereafter, he established Boys Town, a community with the same mission, outside the city. Dunne, "Father Flanagan of Boys Town," 373.
44. Gene Sajeski Oral History, 1996, OH38, Hershey-Derry Township Historical Society (hereafter HDTHS).
45. McMahon, *Milton Hershey School*, 19–20, 47.
46. Cadbury, *Chocolate Wars*, 184–85, 194, 235, 246.
47. Ohmann described this phenomenon in *Selling Culture*.
48. Young, "Hershey."
49. Bongartz "Chocolate Camelot," 99.
50. Hotchkiss and Franken, *Leadership of Advertised Brands*, 141–44, 159, 166, 186, 216. This study is cited in D'Antonio, *Hershey*, 177.
51. Lamme and Mullikin Parcell, "Promoting Hershey," 204.
52. Lamme and Mullikin Parcell, "Promoting Hershey," 204.
53. Winpenny, "Milton S. Hershey Ventures into Cuban Sugar," 491–96; D'Antonio, *Hershey*, 161, 222–23.
54. D'Antonio, *Hershey*, 190, 222.
55. Kasson, *Amusing the Million*, 23, 26, 34.
56. Lindsay, *Madness in the Making*, 271.
57. Snavely, *Hershey Story*, 76, 84.
58. A larger band shell was built in 1914. Jacques, *Hersheypark*, 7–9, 15, 19, 21–27, 34.
59. Snavely, *Hershey Story*, 84.
60. Jacques, *Hersheypark*, 19.
61. Whitenack, *Hersheypark*, 38.
62. Jacques, *Hersheypark*, 43, 49–55.
63. Jacques, *Hersheypark*, 59, 67, 74.
64. Whitenack, *Hersheypark*, 41.
65. Jacques, *Hersheypark*, 66, 74.
66. Bongartz "Chocolate Camelot," 93.
67. D'Antonio, *Hershey*, 102.
68. Koehn and Helms, "Candy Land," 28–29.
69. Gilbert Nurick Oral History, 1989, 89OH04, HCA.
70. Richard Bacastow Oral History, 1990, 90OH11, HCA.
71. Edwin Zechman Oral History, 1991, 91OH13, HCA.
72. Kishpaugh Oral History.
73. John Shuey Oral History, 1991, 91OH22, HCA.
74. Aimee Rex Oral History, 2008, 2008OH03, HCA.
75. Kurie, *In Chocolate We Trust*, 10.
76. Dekle, *Building a New Life*, 6.
77. Foschetti, "Nativization of an Immigrant Community," 66.
78. Dekle, *Building a New Life*, 7, 13.
79. Foschetti, "Nativization of an Immigrant Community," 14.
80. Foschetti, "Nativization of an Immigrant Community," 14.
81. James Stover Oral History, 2006, 2006OH31, HCA.
82. Nita Deaner Oral History, 1989, 89OH36, HCA.
83. D'Antonio, *Hershey*, 211.
84. Dekle, *Building a New Life*, 7.
85. Samuel Tancredi Oral History, 1990, 90OH18, HCA.
86. Foschetti, "Nativization of an Immigrant Community," 22–23.
87. Tancredi Oral History.
88. Foschetti, "Nativization of an Immigrant Community," 22–26.
89. Dekle, *Building a New Life*, 15.

90. Millie Pichini Landis Oral History, 1989, OH9, HDTHS.
91. Foschetti, "Nativization of an Immigrant Community," 22–26.
92. Jean Ranerio Oral History, 1993, 92OH37, HCA.
93. Margo, "Employment and Unemployment," 43.
94. Stover Oral History.
95. June Herr Oral History, 1993, 93OH10, HCA.
96. Koehn and Helms, "Candy Land," 26.
97. D'Antonio, *Hershey*, 198–200, 209–10.
98. Robert Bird, "Benefited Labor, Hershey Asserts," *New York Times*, April 12, 1937.
99. Samuel Hinkle, unpublished manuscript, 348, HCA.
100. Bacastow Oral History.
101. Tancredi Oral History.
102. Ranerio Oral History.
103. Foschetti, "Nativization of an Immigrant Community," 61.
104. John Elting, "Trouble in Paradise: Why Hershey Workers Want a Union," *Forbes*, May 1, 1937, 14–15.
105. Tancredi Oral History.
106. Ignazio Romanucci Oral History, undated, 2003OH18, HCA.
107. Tancredi Oral History.
108. William Dearden Oral History, 1989, 89OH06, HCA.
109. D'Antonio, *Hershey*, 213–15.
110. Weir, "Dark Chocolate," 42–43.
111. Weir, "Dark Chocolate," 42–43.
112. Capita, "Strike in Utopia," 19.
113. Weir, "Dark Chocolate," 42–43, 46–47.
114. D'Antonio, *Hershey*, 215.
115. Capita, "Strike in Utopia," 31.
116. "Score Hurt in Riot," *New York Times*, April 9, 1937.
117. Dekle, *Building a New Life*, 16.
118. Weir, "Dark Chocolate," 45, 51.
119. Bird, "Benefited Labor, Hershey Asserts."
120. Koehn and Helms, "Candy Land," 27.
121. Samuel Hinkle Oral History, 1975, 91OH01, HCA.
122. D'Antonio, *Hershey*, 213, 219.
123. Capita, "Strike in Utopia," 17.
124. Dekle, *Building a New Life*, 15.
125. Tancredi Oral History.
126. Foschetti, "Nativization of an Immigrant Community," 62–63.
127. Foschetti, "Nativization of an Immigrant Community," 63.
128. Dekle, *Building a New Life*, 48.
129. Foschetti, "Nativization of an Immigrant Community," 33, 64.
130. Kurie, *In Chocolate We Trust*, 44.
131. Though "new" to Hershey Park in 1944, the Carrousel was constructed in 1919. Jacques, *Hersheypark*, 86, 93; Mary Hubler Oral History, 1982, OH 89OH43, HCA.
132. Seiverling Oral History.
133. Henry Stump Oral History, 1982, 89OH64, HCA.
134. Zechman Oral History.
135. Dekle, *Building a New Life*, 42.
136. Kurie, *In Chocolate We Trust*, 45.
137. Anna Reider Oral History, 1995, 95OH02, HCA.
138. George Lafferty Oral History, 1996, OH51, HDTHS.
139. Mr. and Mrs. Nelson A. Wagner Oral History, 1995, OH40, HDTHS.
140. Mary Shenk Oral History, 1998, OH91, HDTHS. Emphasis in the original.
141. Robert Rath Oral History, 2007, OH/2008OH09, HCA.
142. Cyril Little Oral History, 1990, 90OH25, HCA.
143. Helen Jane Whiteman Oral History, 1990, 90OH15, HCA.
144. Herr Oral History.
145. Stover Oral History.
146. Ruth Troutman Oral History, 2006, OH/2006OH08, HCA.
147. Carol Lucas Oral History, 2007, OH/2008OH10, HCA.
148. Harvey Deitrich Oral History, 1998, OH80, HDTHS.
149. Kurie, *In Chocolate We Trust*, 51–52.
150. Hinkle, unpublished manuscript, 458.

Chapter 2

1. Snavely, *Hershey Story*, 372–73.
2. Lawrence Hughes, "'Never Felt Need to Advertise': Hershey," *Advertising Age*, December 27, 1948, 31–33.
3. Author's interview with Bruce McKinney, December 16, 2022.
4. Richard Zimmerman Oral History, 1995, 95OH04, HCA.
5. Cadbury, *Chocolate Wars*, 235.
6. Cadbury, *Chocolate Wars*, 233–37.
7. Brenner, *Emperors of Chocolate*, 47.

8. Richard Bacastow Oral History, 1990, 90OH11, HCA; Earl Houser Oral History, 1989, 89OH18, HCA.
9. Cadbury, *Chocolate Wars*, 258.
10. Brenner, *Emperors of Chocolate*, 179–82.
11. Brenner, *Emperors of Chocolate*, 183–87.
12. Kawash, *Candy*, 164–65.
13. Levenstein, *Paradox of Plenty*, 115.
14. Hughes, "'Never Felt Need to Advertise,'" 31–33.
15. Pottker, *Crisis in Candyland*, 77.
16. Kawash, *Candy*, 283–84.
17. Brenner, *Emperors of Chocolate*, 183–87.
18. Larry Johns Oral History, 1991, 91OH21, HCA.
19. William Suhring Oral History, 1990, 90OH29, HCA.
20. Brenner, *Emperors of Chocolate*, 223.
21. Hughes, "Never Felt Need to Advertise," 33.
22. Suhring Oral History.
23. Samuel Hinkle, unpublished manuscript, 455, HCA.
24. Hinkle, unpublished manuscript, 453–54, 469, 471, 478.
25. Gilbert Nurick Oral History, 1989, 89OH04, HCA.
26. Samuel Hinkle Oral History, 1975, 91OH01, HCA.
27. See two pamphlets, "Hershey Foods" and "A Brief History," printed by the Hershey Foods Corporation, box 37, folder: Chocolate World 1973, accession 92004, HCA.
28. "Record '60 Profit Indicated for Hershey Chocolate," *Wall Street Journal*, December 28, 1960.
29. Zimmerman Oral History.
30. Zimmerman Oral History.
31. Zimmerman Oral History.
32. Hinkle, unpublished manuscript, 455.
33. Brenner, *Emperors of Chocolate*, 182.
34. "Harold S. Mohler, 1919–1988," online encyclopedia, HCA, posted September 7, 2018, https://hersheyarchives.org/encyclopedia/mohler-harold-s-1919-1988.
35. Zimmerman Oral History.
36. Bruce McKinney Oral History, 2002, 2002OH01, HCA.
37. John Dowd Oral History, 1991, 91OH32, HCA.
38. William Dearden Oral History, 1989, 89OH06, HCA; Rich Rein, "Bill Dearden Takes over Hershey and Becomes a Sugar Daddy to Some Young Orphans," *People*, June 21, 1976, 64.
39. Though technically hired under Hinkle, Rawley stated that he "did not know Sam Hinkle" and worked under Mohler, Dearden, and Zimmerman. John Rawley Oral History, 1991, 91OH17, HCA.
40. Brenner, *Emperors of Chocolate*, 217, 219, 221.
41. Johns Oral History.
42. Zimmerman Oral History.
43. Austin Geiling Jr. Oral History, 1991, 91OH30, HCA.
44. Brenner, *Emperors of Chocolate*, 196, 221–22.
45. Suhring Oral History.
46. Dowd Oral History.
47. Hinkle, unpublished manuscript, 766.
48. Suhring Oral History.
49. Brenner, *Emperors of Chocolate*, 223.
50. Reese's Peanut Butter Cup commercial, YouTube, uploaded December 10, 2021, https://youtu.be/uOWzrwxj35A.
51. Dowd Oral History.
52. Dearden Oral History.
53. Suhring Oral History.
54. Ken Bowers Oral History, 1993, 93OH13, HCA.
55. Samuel Tancredi Oral History, 1990, 90OH18, HCA.
56. Bacastow Oral History; Houser Oral History.
57. Ned Book Oral History, 1996, 96OH15, HCA.
58. Ehud Yonay, "It's Not All Sweetness in Hershey, PA," *Newsday* (Melville, NY), May 11, 1972.
59. Kenneth Wolfe Oral History, 2009, 2009OH11, HCA.
60. Wolfe Oral History.
61. Zimmerman Oral History.
62. Book Oral History. Book's recollection about the town's feeling of entitlement is corroborated by Robert Raffensberger, chief of the Hershey fire department, who stated that the prevalent attitude about these services was that "they owe it to us." Robert Raffensberger Oral History, 1995, 95OH03, HCA.

63. Bill Hawkins, "Era of Benevolence to End," *Patriot News* (Harrisburg, PA), March 22, 1970, box 3, scrapbook 2 (1969–82), accession 86001, HCA.
64. Yonay, "It's Not All Sweetness." See also Kurie, *In Chocolate We Trust*, 57.
65. Nurick Oral History.
66. Zimmerman Oral History.
67. Hinkle Oral History.
68. Hinkle Oral History. C. Max Lang says the actual figure was $25 million. Lang, *Impossible Dream*, 46.
69. Lang, *Impossible Dream*, 41, 49, 100, 105.
70. Eugene Jacques Oral History, 1990, 90OH09, HCA.
71. Kurie, *In Chocolate We Trust*, 55.
72. McKinney Oral History.
73. Lang, *Impossible Dream*, 41, 119–21.
74. Howard Phillippy Oral History, 1991, 91OH03, HCA.
75. Raffensberger Oral History.
76. The Reverend Thomas Guinivan recalled Mrs. Harrell's comments. Thomas Guinivan Oral History, 1990, 90OH10, HCA.
77. Jacques Oral History.
78. Zimmerman Oral History.
79. Brenner, *Emperors of Chocolate*, 265.
80. Author's interview with Bruce McKinney, July 22, 2010.
81. McKinney Oral History.
82. Robert Payne Oral History, 1998, OH82, HDTHS.
83. Kurie, *In Chocolate We Trust*, 56, 58.
84. Yonay, "It's Not All Sweetness."
85. Jacques Oral History.
86. Margaret Clark Oral History, 1975, 2001OH02, HCA.
87. McKinney Oral History.
88. Author's interview with McKinney, 2010.
89. Kurie, *In Chocolate We Trust*, 47–48.
90. Edward Tancredi Oral History, 1991, 91OH31, HCA.
91. Book Oral History.

Chapter 3

1. Jacques, *Hersheypark*, 120–21.
2. Author's interview with Bruce McKinney, December 16, 2022.
3. Bruce McKinney Oral History, 2006, 2006OH14, HCA.
4. Jacques, *Hersheypark*, 123.
5. Hersheypark News, December 13, 1971, box 37, folder 5, accession 92004, HCA.
6. "Hershey Plans a 'Theme Park,'" *Harrisburg (PA) Evening News*, December 13, 1971, box 3, scrapbook 2 (1969–82), accession 86001, HCA.
7. "Hershey Plans a 'Theme Park'"; Jacques, *Hersheypark*, 121.
8. Ned Book Oral History, 1996, 96OH15, HCA.
9. Jacques, *Hersheypark*, 112–17.
10. Book Oral History.
11. McKinney Oral History, 2006.
12. John O. Hershey Oral History, 1990, 90OH24, HCA. Italics added. For details on the integration of the Milton Hershey School, see also Gilbert Nurick Oral History, 1989, 89OH04, HCA.
13. Price, *Walt's Revolution!*, 19–20, 32–33, 60.
14. ERA, "Analysis of Redevelopment Potentials at Hershey Park," March 14, 1971, box 44, folder 24, accession 92004, HCA.
15. McKinney Oral History, 2006.
16. Bruce McKinney Oral History, 2002, 2002OH01, HCA.
17. Author's interview with Bruce McKinney, July 22, 2010.
18. Hershey Oral History.
19. McKinney Oral History, 2002.
20. Richard Zimmerman Oral History, 1995, 95OH04, HCA.
21. Price, *Walt's Revolution!*, 19, 26.
22. Younger, *Theme Park Design*, 10. The *Wall Street Journal* was still referring to Disneyland as a "unique amusement park" in 1958. Mitchell Gordon, "Disney's Land: Walt's Profit Formula," *Wall Street Journal*, February 4, 1958.
23. Price, *Walt's Revolution*, 19, 26.
24. Price, *Walt's Revolution*, 19–20, 26–27.
25. Price, *Walt's Revolution*, 29–31.
26. Sorkin, "See You in Disneyland," 6.
27. Schickel, *Disney Version*, 313.
28. Sorkin, "See You in Disneyland," 6.
29. "The Disneyland Story," episode 1 of *Walt Disney's Disneyland*, aired October 27, 1954, on ABC, YouTube, uploaded June 20, 2017, https://youtu.be/k_1xsPytKJw.
30. Price, *Walt's Revolution*, 31, 129.

31. Price, *Walt's Revolution*, 129.
32. Snow, *Disney's Land*, 257.
33. Cross and Walton, *Playful Crowd*, 168.
34. Younger, *Theme Park Design*, 1.
35. Marling, "Disneyland, 1955," 175.
36. Younger, *Theme Park Design*, 6, 12–13, 84.
37. Chytry, "Disney's Design," 38–39.
38. King and O'Boyle, "Theme Park," 6–7.
39. Charlie Haas, "Disneyland Is Good for You," *New West*, December 4, 1978, 16.
40. Watts, *Magic Kingdom*, 287. For the pro-America stance of historians and intellectuals, see Pells, *Liberal Mind*, 96–107, 130–47.
41. Watts, *Magic Kingdom*, 392–93.
42. Watts, *Magic Kingdom*, 392–93.
43. Younger, *Theme Park Design*, 8, 143.
44. Marling, "Disneyland, 1955," 194.
45. For Disney's mission to teach Americans about science, see Mechling and Mechling, "Atom According to Disney."
46. Cross and Walton, *Playful Crowd*, 169.
47. Hench quoted in Haas, "Disneyland," 18.
48. Watts, *Magic Kingdom*, 28.
49. Haas, "Disneyland," 18.
50. Schickel, *Disney Version*, 314.
51. Watts, *Magic Kingdom*, 387.
52. Watts, *Magic Kingdom*, 394–95.
53. Gordon, "Disney's Land."
54. Watts, *Magic Kingdom*, 383–84, 391.
55. Virgintino, *Freedomland U.S.A.*, 11–12.
56. Hill, *Imagineering*, 24.
57. Price, *Walt's Revolution*, 128–31.
58. Virgintino, *Freedomland U.S.A.*, 14.
59. Hill, *Imagineering*, 24.
60. Hill, *Imagineering*, xvi, 24.
61. Price, *Walt's Revolution*, 83–84, 129.
62. Watts, *Magic Kingdom*, 7–8.
63. Obituary for Randall Duell, *Los Angeles Times*, December 3, 1992.
64. Bureau of the Census, *Historical Statistics*, 11.
65. Obituary for Randall Duell, *Los Angeles Times*, December 3, 1992.
66. Hill, *Imagineering*, 24.
67. Hill, *Imagineering*, 27–29.
68. Virgintino, *Freedomland U.S.A.*, 57–58.
69. Hill, *Imagineering*, 29–35.
70. Hill, *Imagineering*, 37–38, 40–43.
71. Price, *Walt's Revolution*, 109.
72. Wilson, *Six Flags*, 7–8; Hill, *Imagineering*, 65, 94; obituary for Rachel Coleman Duell, *Los Angeles Times*, June 28, 2001.
73. Gail Bronson, "A Merry Go-Round: Companies See Profits in Amusement Parks," *Wall Street Journal*, August 2, 1972.
74. Author's interview with Ira West, July 20, 2010.
75. Author's interview with West.
76. Hersheypark News, December 13, 1971.
77. Hill, *Imagineering*, 219.
78. Author's interview with West.
79. Notes on trips to theme parks, box 30, file: Hersheypark—1972, accession 92004, HCA; author's interview with West.
80. Author's interview with West.
81. Author's interview with West.
82. Author's interview with West.
83. Hill, *Imagineering*, 224.
84. Author's interview with West.
85. McKinney Oral History, 2006.
86. Book Oral History.
87. Author's interview with McKinney, 2010.
88. Hersheypark News, December 13, 1971.
89. RDA also recommended, and Hershey executives tentatively approved, themed areas that had nothing to do with Pennsylvania: a New England fishing village, frontier area, and Indian village. Hersheypark News, December 13, 1971. However, these themed areas never escaped the idea phase. According to Bruce McKinney, RDA initially imagined the entire East Coast as Hersheypark's region—hence a New England village. RDA had also built western-themed areas for other parks and wished to replicate the model in Hershey. However, John O. Hershey, John Hart, and Bruce McKinney did not believe these areas fit in Hershey; they crafted a different direction for the park that did not include them. "As the park evolved, everyone realized that it wasn't about Indians or the West or New England," McKinney explained, "it was about Pennsylvania Germans and barns and coal." RDA, he added, "had to be schooled" on the needs of Hershey. Author's interview with McKinney, 2022.

90. Author's interview with McKinney, 2010.
91. King, "Disneyland and Walt Disney World," 119.
92. Author's interview with McKinney, 2022.
93. McKinney Oral History, 2006.
94. "Mixed Emotions: Hershey People Rap on Expansion of Hershey Park," *Lebanon (PA) Daily News*, March 14, 1972, box 30, file: Hersheypark—1972, HCA.
95. Cyril Little Oral History, 1990, 90OH25, HCA.
96. Book Oral History.
97. McKinney Oral History, 2006.
98. Author's interview with McKinney, 2010.
99. Author's interview with McKinney, 2022.
100. McKinney Oral History, 2006.
101. Jacques, *Hersheypark*, 127.
102. "Growth of Hershey Complex Will Affect Us," *Elizabethtown (PA) Chronicle*, February 8, 1973.
103. "Mixed Emotions."
104. Book Oral History.
105. Author's interview with McKinney, 2010.

Chapter 4

1. Bruce McKinney Oral History, 2006, 2006OH14, HCA.
2. Hersheypark report, box 37, folder: Flood of '72 Affects Hersheypark, accession 92004, HCA; McKinney Oral History; Jack Silar Oral History, February 11, 2009, 2009OH04, HCA; Harold Sitler Oral History, May 15, 2006, 2006OH18, HCA; Cyril Little Oral History, 1990, 90OH25, HCA; Rufus Hollinger Oral History, 1990, 90OH22, HCA; Jacques, *Hersheypark*, 52, 109, 131–32; "Hersheypark Noted as Major Tourist Attraction," *Lebanon (PA) Daily News*, April 1, 1974.
3. Mary Levens Oral History, 1989, 89OH39, HCA.
4. Sampson, *Hogan*, 65–67.
5. Ned Book Oral History, 1996, 96OH15, HCA.
6. Confidential memo from W. R. Mayer, Hershey Estates, August 3, 1970, box 2, folder: Cocoa Inn, Demolition, 1970–71, accession 200124, HCA.
7. Helen Jane Whiteman Oral History, 1990, 90OH15, HCA.
8. Davidoff Houts and Whitenack, *Images of America*, 118.
9. Book Oral History.
10. Stella Cake, "Cocoa Inn and Hershey Lumber Mill; Two Historic Sites in Hershey," *Hummelstown (PA) Sun* November 11, 1970, box 2, folder 1: Cocoa Inn, Demolition, 1970–71, accession 200124, HCA.
11. Handwritten note sent to James Bobb, October 6, 1970, box 2, folder 1: Cocoa Inn, Demolition, 1970–71, accession 200124, HCA.
12. "Cocoa Inn Tumbles Down," *Patriot-News* (Harrisburg, PA), December 30, 1970, box 2, folder 1: Cocoa Inn, Demolition, 1970–71, accession 200124, HCA. See also "Implosion of the Cocoa Inn," YouTube, uploaded November 23, 2021, https://www.youtube.com/watch?v=manrJSr24Qg.
13. Roger Conner, "Cocoa Inn Turned into Rubble," *Harrisburg (PA) Evening News*, December 29, 1970, box 2, folder 1: Cocoa Inn, Demolition, 1970–71, accession 200124, HCA. In 1973, Hershey hired Roger Conner to direct its public relations and advertising office. "Roger Conner Named Ad, PR Head," *Hummelstown (PA) Sun*, January 17, 1973, box 3, scrapbook 2 (1969–82), accession 86001, HCA.
14. Robert Raffensberger Oral History, 1995, 95OH03, HCA.
15. Robert Rath Oral History, 2007, OH/2008OH09, HCA.
16. Warren Foley Oral History, 2000, 2000OH05, HCA.
17. Dionisio Castelli Oral History, 1989, 89OH27, HCA.
18. John Shuey Oral History, 1991, 91OH22, HCA.
19. Rath Oral History.
20. Raffensberger Oral History.
21. Dick McCrone, "Doomed Hershey Ballroom Heard Best Bands," *Harrisburg (PA) Evening News*, October 4, 1972, box 37, folder 16, accession 92004, HCA.
22. Terence Faul Oral History, 1991, 91OH20, HCA.

23. "Bandshell in Hersheypark Demolished," *Lebanon (PA) Daily News,* October 24, 1972.
24. Roger Conner, "Era Comes to an End with Bandshell Demolition," *Dauphin (PA) Historian,* November 8, 1972, box 37, folder 16, accession 92004, HCA.
25. Dick McCrone, "Site of Sunday Band Concerts Enjoyed by Thousands Is Razed," *Harrisburg (PA) Evening News,* October 25, 1972, box 37, folder 15, accession 92004, HCA.
26. Edwin Zechman Oral History, 1991, 91OH13, HCA.
27. Lewis, *Divided Highways,* ix, 282.
28. Klapp, *Collective Search for Identity,* vii–viii, 4, 24–29.
29. Philomena Castelli Oral History, 1992, 92OH39, HCA.
30. Levens Oral History.
31. Mary Hubler Oral History, 1982, OH 89OH43, HCA. Italics added.
32. Hubler Oral History.
33. June Herr Oral History, 1993, 93OH10, HCA.
34. Herr Oral History.
35. Author's interview with Bruce McKinney, December 16, 2022.
36. Author's interview with Bruce McKinney, July 22, 2010.
37. Bruce McKinney Oral History, 2006, 2006OH14, HCA.
38. Author's interview with Ira West, July 20, 2010.
39. Author's interview with McKinney, 2010.
40. Winnicott, *Playing and Reality* 1–15, 51; Herdt, "Transitional Objects."
41. Curry, "Reality of Make-Believe," 54.
42. Winnicott, *Playing and Reality,* xi, 1–15, 106–9; Herdt, "Transitional Objects."
43. Winnicott, *Playing and Reality,* 106–8; Herdt, "Transitional Objects."
44. "Walking Distance," season 1, episode 5, of *The Twilight Zone,* aired October 30, 1959, on CBS. For an overview of the episode, see Presnell and McGee, *Critical History of Television's "The Twilight Zone,"* 36–37.
45. Hersheypark News, December 13, 1971, box 37, folder 5, accession 92004, HCA.
46. Press release for 1975 season, box 80, folder 1, accession 92004, HCA.
47. Author's interview with West.
48. Letter from Dr. and Mrs. Kremkau, September 28, 1974, box 49, folder: Paul Serff . . . complimentary letters, accession 92004, HCA.
49. Rath Oral History.
50. James Stover Oral History, 2006, 2006OH31, HCA.
51. Samuel Hinkle Oral History, 1975, 91OH01, HCA. Kenneth Hatt, who was executive vice president of Hershey Estates in the 1970s, described his role as a collector in the increasingly vibrant market for Hershey memorabilia. Hatt Oral History, 1989, 89OH17, HCA.
52. Cross, *Consumed Nostalgia,* 12.
53. Ed Welch, "The Complete History of the Antiques Trade, Abridged," *Journal of Antiques and Collectibles,* August 3, 2006, https://journalofantiques.com/misc/a-complete-history-of-the-antiques-trade-abridged. The *New York Times* and the publishers of *American Heritage* released guides for new antique collectors in the 1970s. See Schwartz and Wade, *"New York Times" Book of Antiques,* and Durant, *American Heritage Guide to Antiques.*
54. Rich Mueller, "Sports Collecting's Real 'Boom' Was in the 1970s," *Sports Collectors Daily,* January 6, 2017, https://www.sportscollectorsdaily.com/sports-collectings-real-boom-1970s.
55. Ryan Ellett, "History of a Hobby: The Perfect Storm, 1971–1975," *Radio Recall,* October 2009, https://www.mwotrc.com/rr2009_10/historyotr.htm.
56. Gerald Clarke, "The Meaning of Nostalgia," *Time,* May 3, 1971, 77.
57. Kompare, *Rerun Nation,* 104–5, 116–18.
58. Reinehr and Swartz, *A to Z of Old Time Radio,* 293.
59. *Liberty: The Nostalgia Magazine,* Summer 1971.
60. Matty Simmons, editorial, *Liberty: The Nostalgia Magazine,* Summer 1971, 9.
61. Clarke, "Meaning of Nostalgia," 77.
62. Richard Lingeman, "Proms and Liking Ike," *New York Times,* June 17, 1973.
63. Miller and Nowak, *Fifties,* 5.

64. Davis, *Yearning for Yesterday*, 18, 49, 103.
65. Davis, *Yearning for Yesterday*, 6, 105–6.
66. Davis, *Yearning for Yesterday*, 6, 106.
67. Davis, *Yearning for Yesterday*, 6, 105–7.
68. John Hubley, dir., *Everybody Rides the Carousel* (Hubley Studios, 1975).
69. Bradbury, *Something Wicked*.
70. Author's interview with McKinney, 2022.
71. Dina Willard Oral History, 2007, 2007OH15, HCA. Italics added.
72. Willard Oral History.
73. Keith Dittenhauer to John Hart, March 31, 1972, box 30, folder: Files of John T. Hart, accession 92004, HCA.
74. Press release for 1975 season.
75. "Hersheypark Opens Sunday with Many New Attractions," *Lebanon (PA) Daily News*, May 8, 1972, box 3, scrapbook 2 (1969–82), accession 86001, HCA.
76. Doraine Mitchell Oral History, 2006, 2006OHS23, HCA.
77. Hubler Oral History.
78. Ehud Yonay, "It's Not All Sweetness in Hershey, PA," *Newsday* (Melville, NY), May 11, 1972
79. Economics Research Associates, box 30, folder: Hersheypark—1973, accession 92004, HCA.

Chapter 5

1. "Welcome to Hersheypark '73," *Patriot-News* (Harrisburg, PA), May 27, 1973, box 30, folder: Hersheypark—1973, accession 92004, HCA.
2. Bofinger-Kaplan Public Relations, Hersheypark preview, box 30, folder: Hersheypark—1973, accession 92004, HCA.
3. "How Sweet It Is . . . at Hersheypark," *Messenger Press* (Allentown, PA), July 5, 1973. During the summer months of 1973, the same article appeared in newspapers from cities across the country: Louisville, Kentucky; Sierra Madre, California; Chicago, Illinois; Lancaster, Pennsylvania; Elgin, North Dakota; Debring, Ohio; Washington, DC; Crowley Ridge, Arkansas; Woburn, Massachusetts; Cameron, Missouri; Henderson, Nevada; and Arden, North Carolina. See box 25, folder 6, accession 92004, HCA.
4. Murray Dubin, "Chocolate Town in Midst of a Bittersweet Change," *Philadelphia Inquirer*, May 11, 1973.
5. Hill, *Imagineering*, 228.
6. Trash memo, March 2, 1973, box 30, folder: Hersheypark—1973, accession 92004, HCA.
7. Author's interview with Ira West, July 20, 2010.
8. Author's interview with West; Robert Coker's 1982 interview with Randall Duell and Ira West, Thrillride.com, accessed September 14, 2022, https://thrillride.com/RDuellinterview/RDuellInt1.html. See also Doug Barnes, "The Ira West Interview 1/24/17," episode 339 of *The Season Pass* (podcast), posted January 24, 2017, https://seasonpasspodcast.libsyn.com/tspp-339-the-ira-west-interview-12417.
9. "Hershey Seeks Helpers for Summer," *Lancaster (PA) Farming*, December 30, 1972.
10. "The Walt Disney Look," box 2, folder 1, accession 200706, HCA.
11. *Hospitality Handbook*, 1973, box 1, folder 23, accession 200124, HCA.
12. The same article appears in two places in the archives because two executives viewed it as worth saving. "Racial Balance Poses No Deterrent to Carowinds," *Amusement Business*, July 28, 1973, box 25, folder 6, accession 92004, HCA. See also Hershey Entertainment and Resorts Collection, box 30, folder: Hersheypark—1973, accession 92004, HCA.
13. Bofinger-Kaplan Public Relations, Hersheypark preview.
14. Richard Quinn, Walt Disney World, to Norman Hetrick, Hershey Estates, April 24, 1973, box 30, folder: Marketing Division, accession 92004, HCA.
15. Bruce McKinney Oral History, 2006, 2006OH14, HCA.
16. Rufus Hollinger Oral History, 1990, 90OH22, HCA.
17. McKinney Oral History.
18. For an account of preview day, see "Of This and That," *Mount Joy (PA) Bulletin*, May 23, 1973, and McKinney Oral History.

19. "Hersheypark Tops 22,000 at Opener," *Amusement Business*, June 2, 1973, box 30, folder: Hersheypark—1973, accession 92004, HCA.
20. McKinney Oral History.
21. Author's interview with Bruce McKinney, December 16, 2022.
22. Mike Barnes, "Mark Wilson, Magician . . . Dies at 91," *Hollywood Reporter*, March 8, 2021.
23. Hersheypark entertainment proposal, box 30, folder Hersheypark—1973, accession 92004, HCA.
24. Letter from Bill McDonald, July 1974, box 49, folder: Paul Serff . . . complimentary letters, accession 92004, HCA.
25. "TV Roundup," *Philadelphia Inquirer*, May 11, 1973.
26. Cyril Little Oral History, 1990, 90OH25, HCA.
27. "Big Opener for Hershey Despite Threatening Weather," *Amusement Business*, June 14, 1975.
28. Joe Sharkey, "Hershey Park: A Fun Place for Everyone in the Family," *Philadelphia Inquirer*, July 28, 1972, box 30, File: Hersheypark—1972, accession 92004, HCA.
29. Press release for 1975 season, box 80, folder 1, accession 92004, HCA.
30. "Hersheypark Noted as Major Tourist Attraction," *Lebanon (PA) Daily News*, April 1,1974.
31. Hersheypark entertainment proposal. For the dolphin trainer, see Little Oral History.
32. *The Snapper* (student publication, Millersville University), July 3, 1974.
33. Hersheypark News, 1974, box 37, folder 9, accession 92004, HCA.
34. Klapp, *Collective Search for Identity*, 28, 316.
35. Guy, *Tudor England*, 116–53, 212–49, 339–43, 427–29.
36. Gilbert, *Picture of the Pennsylvania Germans*, 2–3.
37. "Tudor Square Recreates Bygone English Lifestyle," *Patriot-News* (Harrisburg, PA), May 27, 1973, box 10, folder 1, accession 90016, HCA.
38. Audio tape for Tudor Square and for Rhineland, 1974, box 64, folder 4, accession 92004, HCA.
39. Press release for the 1974 season, box 80, folder 1, accession 92004, HCA; "Tudor Square Recreates Bygone English Lifestyle."
40. Author's interview with West.
41. Press release for 1974 season.
42. Author's interview with West.
43. Postcard, 1974 promotional materials, box 80, folder 1, accession 92004, HCA; "Tudor Square Recreates Bygone English Lifestyle"; "How Sweet It Is . . . at Hersheypark."
44. "Hersheypark New Face, Same Fun," *Lebanon (PA) Daily News*, March 12, 1973; "Rhineland Features German Delights" (newspaper clipping), box 10, folder 1, accession 90016, HCA; "How Sweet It Is . . . at Hersheypark." As a comical note, employees joked about the quality of the food in Rhineland by singing the following lyrics to the tune of "My Favorite Things" from *The Sound of Music* (1965): "Rolls that are broken / And Sour Kraut that's soggy. / Butter that's melted / And pickle juice that's boggy / Baked beans that are covered with scum that clings / These are a few of my favorite things." *Park Life* (employee newsletter), September 3, 1976, box 63, folder 4, accession 92004, HCA.
45. Murphy, *William Penn*, 124–27, 142.
46. Gilbert, *Picture of the Pennsylvania Germans*, 1, 12, 55.
47. Looking back, we can fault Hersheypark for limiting itself to English and Germanic cultures. Today, most history-oriented venues would make different choices and likely include the African American experience. However, in the early 1970s, the nation had yet to fully absorb the impact of the civil rights movement. It would take a few more years for popular culture to reflect and integrate these lessons. For example, Alex Haley's best-selling novel *Roots: The Saga of an American Family* (1976) was still a few years away. That novel and the sensational television miniseries that followed popularized African American history and convinced millions to see it as an important part of the larger American story.

48. Author's interview with West.
49. McKinney Oral History.
50. Letters to sponsors, box 30, folder: Marketing Division, accession 92004, HCA.
51. Letters from a fourth-grade class, box 49, folder: Paul Serff . . . complimentary letters, accession 92004, HCA.
52. Michael Strauss, "We've Got a Ticket to Rise," *Holiday* 55, no. 4 (June–August 1974): 75.
53. McKinney Oral History.
54. Hersheypark News, 1975, box 37, folder 15, accession 92004, HCA.
55. "Hersheypark Opens 69th Season," *Hanover (PA) Evening Sun*, May 9, 1976. Italics added. See also *Lititz (PA) Record-Express*, June 19, 1975; *Lebanon (PA) Daily News*, March 30, 1976; *Altoona (PA) Mirror*, August 27, 1977; *Delaware County (PA) Daily Times*, September 29, 1977.
56. "Hersheypark Among Top 15," *Lebanon (PA) Daily News*, March 30, 1976.
57. *Recreation Management* 17, no. 8 (October 1974): 15.
58. Gordon Greer, "Super Colossal Amusement Parks: America's 15 Best," *Better Homes and Gardens*, August 1974, 95–100.
59. Hersheypark News, 1975; *Lebanon (PA) Daily News*, March 30, 1976; *Hanover (PA) Evening Sun*, October 24, 1974; *Waynesboro (PA) Record Herald*, May 10, 1974; *Huntingdon (PA) Daily News*, May 16, 1975; *Lititz (PA) Record-Express*, February 27, 1975.
60. "Good-Bye, Hershey," undated, box 58, folder 17, accession 92004, HCA.
61. Curtis Demmy, "Rain Checks and Peanut Shells," *Paxton (PA) Herald*, June 27, 1973, box 30, folder: Hersheypark—1973, accession 92004, HCA.
62. Margaret Clark Oral History, 1975, 2001OH02, HCA.
63. William Houck letter, *Paxton (PA) Herald*, July 11, 1973, box 30, folder: Hersheypark—1973, accession 92004, HCA.
64. Letters to sponsors, box 30, folder: Marketing Division, accession 92004, HCA.
65. "Hersheypark Opens 69th Season."
66. McKinney Oral History.
67. McKinney Oral History.
68. Hench, *Designing Disney*, 86–96.
69. "Furry Tales Growth and Development," public relations and advertising annual report, 1977, box 54, folder 4, accession 92004, HCA.
70. Hersheypark News, 1973, box 30, folder: Hersheypark—1973, accession 92004, HCA.
71. "The Furry Tales," *Susquehanna Magazine*, box 54, folder 4, accession 92004, HCA.
72. Charles Bofinger, 1976 brochure with revisions for 1977, box 58, folder 18, accession 92004, HCA.
73. "Original Pennsylvania Dutch Days," 1976, Bruce McKinney Files, box 1, folder 24, accession 200124, HCA.
74. "A Furry Santa?," *Lebanon (PA) Daily News*, December 18, 1975.
75. "Garnering the Facts," *Sunday Times* (Scranton, PA), June 23, 1974, box 30, folder: Hersheypark—1973, accession 92004, HCA.
76. Hersheypark News, 1974, box 37, folder 15, accession 92004, HCA.
77. Author's interview with McKinney.
78. Author's interview with McKinney.
79. McKinney Oral History.
80. The author could not find coverage of the Furry Tales in local newspapers after 1984.

Chapter 6

1. Snow, *Disney's Land*, 257, 267.
2. Rufus Hollinger Oral History, 1990, 90OH22, HCA.
3. Conkin, *Revolution Down on the Farm*, 99.
4. Conkin, *Revolution Down on the Farm*, 99–112.
5. Conkin, *Revolution Down on the Farm*, 100.
6. Hightower, *Hard Tomatoes, Hard Times*, vi.
7. Gardner, *American Agriculture*, 51, 98.
8. Danbom, *Born in the Country*, 248.
9. Klein and Hoogenboom, *History of Pennsylvania*, 481–82.
10. Cupper, *75th Farm Show*, 48.
11. Bernard Bailyn is quoted in Durnbaugh, "Pennsylvania's Crazy Quilt," 9–10.

12. Louden, *Pennsylvania Dutch*, 6–9.
13. Klein and Hoogenboom, *History of Pennsylvania*, 484; Hostetler, *Amish Society* (1968 ed.), vii.
14. Updike, *Of the Farm*.
15. Turner, "Significance of the Frontier," 47.
16. Walbert, *Garden Spot*, 32.
17. Dutch Days program guide, July 20–25, 1976, box 1, folder 24, accession 200124, HCA.
18. Hollinger Oral History.
19. Walbert, *Garden Spot*, 3–9, 17, 33, 36.
20. Hostetler, *Amish Society*, xi–xii, 310.
21. Hostetler, *Amish Society* (1968 ed.), vii–viii; Hostetler, *Amish Society* (1980 ed.), xii.
22. Author's interview with Simon Bronner, July 5, 2010.
23. Walbert, *Garden Spot*, 3–9, 36.
24. Press release for the 1975 season, box 80, folder 1, accession 92004, HCA.
25. Reports on other theme parks, box 30, File: Hersheypark—1972, accession 92004, HCA. See also John O. Hershey's memorandum to James Bobb, box 30, file: Hershey, accession 92004, HCA.
26. John Zerbe Oral History, 1996, 96OH04, HCA.
27. Hersheypark News, December 13, 1971, box 37, folder 5, accession 92004, HCA. See also Glass, *Pennsylvania Culture Region*, and Ensminger, *Pennsylvania Barn*.
28. Hollinger Oral History.
29. "Lebanon Woman Makes Porcelain, Wooden Dolls at Hersheypark," *Lebanon (PA) Daily News*, July 21, 1973.
30. "Park Visitors Discover Candlemaking Artistry," *Elizabethtown (PA) Chronicle*, June 28, 1973.
31. "Ephrata Non-Smokers Roll Others' Smokes," *Sunday News* (Lancaster, PA), August 19, 1973.
32. "Mahoney Native One of 4 Coal Jewelers Still Working," *Standard-Speaker* (Hazleton, PA), June 28, 1973.
33. Hollinger Oral History.
34. Hostetler, *Amish Society* (1980 ed.), xi, 372. This trend has continued. In 2001, Donald Kraybill reported that the Amish population was doubling roughly every twenty years. Kraybill, *Riddle of Amish Culture*, xi.
35. Betsy Rupe, "Artisans Preserve Craft Tradition," *Elizabethtown (PA) Chronicle*, August 16, 1973.
36. Bruce McKinney Oral History, 2006, 2006OH14, HCA.
37. Rupe, "Artisans Preserve." Italics added.
38. Mark Jury, "The Young Bring Back Old Crafts," *Parade*, October 15, 1972, box 37, folder: Pennsylvania Dutch Craft Barn, accession 92004, HCA.
39. Marquis, *Art Lessons*, 93, 98, 101, 125–26.
40. Straight, *Nancy Hanks*, 273–78.
41. Marquis, *Art Lessons*, 125–26; Straight, *Nancy Hanks*, 273–78. Though Congress never did create a third endowment, it did establish the American Folklife Center in the Library of Congress in 1976.
42. Jury, "Young Bring Back Old Crafts."
43. Jury, "Young Bring Back Old Crafts."
44. Gordon Greer, "Arts and Crafts Fairs: A Wealth of America," *Better Homes and Gardens*, May 1974, box 37, folder: Dutch Days 1973, accession 92004, HCA. For information on TV dinners, see Gitelson, "Populox," 76.
45. Greer, "Arts and Crafts Fairs."
46. Hollinger Oral History.
47. "17th Annual Pennsylvania Dutch Days," *Lebanon (PA) Daily News*, August 27, 1965.
48. Hollinger Oral History.
49. "Penna. Dutch Days," *Lebanon (PA) Daily News*, July 24, 1973.
50. Dutch Days program guide.
51. Rupe, "Artisans Preserve."
52. "Pennsylvania Dutch Days Adds New Craft," *Elizabethtown (PA) Chronicle*, August 1, 1974.
53. Rupe, "Artisans Preserve."
54. Dutch Days program guide.
55. Hollinger Oral History.
56. Hersheypark News, December 13, 1971.
57. Dutch Days program guide.
58. Dutch Days program guide.
59. Dutch Days program guide.
60. Walbert, *Garden Spot*, 33–34.
61. Dutch Days program guide.
62. Hostetler, *Amish Society* (1980 ed.), 310.

Chapter 7

1. Joanne Green, "Gay 90s Show Brightens Day for Hersheypark Visitors" *Lebanon (PA) Daily News*, July 2, 1977.
2. Fred Smedley, "She's Having a Heyday at Hershey," *Intelligencer Journal* (Lancaster, PA), June 24, 1977.
3. Green, "Gay 90s Show."
4. "Hersheypark Attendance High," *Lebanon (PA) Daily News*, October 18, 1974.
5. Construction ended up costing $8.2 million, whereas the budget had allotted $6.7 million. Hersheypark 1973 construction cost report, July 5, 1973, box 30, file: Hersheypark Redevelopment, accession 92004, HCA.
6. Bruce McKinney Oral History, 2006, 2006OH14, HCA.
7. Bailey and Farber, introduction to *America in the Seventies*, 1–4.
8. "Cocoa's Bittersweet Bounty—200 Years in Charts," *Winton*, July 11, 2017, https://www.winton.com/news/cocoas-bittersweet-bounty-200-years-in-charts.
9. Brenner, *Emperors of Chocolate*, 227, 242.
10. Brenner, *Emperors of Chocolate*, 227–29, 242.
11. "Cocoa's Bittersweet Bounty."
12. Brenner, *Emperors of Chocolate*, 206. Hershey Foods no longer controlled a sugar supply from Cuba, the company having sold its holdings in 1946. Chavez et al., "Hershey Sugar Mill," 431.
13. Rona Cherry, "Prices Rising 5c on Some Chocolate Bars," *New York Times*, October 28, 1976.
14. Rich Rein, "Bill Dearden Takes over Hershey and Becomes a Sugar Daddy to Some Young Orphans," *People*, June 21, 1976, 64; Brenner, *Emperors of Chocolate*, 229–30.
15. William Suhring Oral History, 1990, 90OH29, HCA.
16. Brenner, *Emperors of Chocolate*, 229–30.
17. 1973 annual report, Hershey Food Corporation, box 37, folder: Chocolate World 1973, accession 92004, HCA.
18. Skrabec, *Fall of an American Rome*, 47–48.
19. Tiffany, "Roots of Decline," 410; Skrabec, *Fall of an American Rome*, 45, 47–48.
20. Stein, *Running Steel*, 205–7.
21. Skrabec, *Fall of an American Rome*, 45.
22. Stein, *Running Steel*, 205–7.
23. Skrabec, *Fall of an American Rome*, 70.
24. Barton and Bronner, *Steelton*, 8.
25. Dublin and Licht, *Face of Decline*, 1–10, 114.
26. Bluestone and Harrison, *Deindustrialization of America*, 10, 26.
27. Carroll, *It Seemed Like Nothing Happened*, 129.
28. Skrabec, *Fall of an American Rome*, 46–47.
29. Bailey and Farber, *America in the Seventies*, 2–4.
30. Kitch, *Pennsylvania in Public Memory*, 3.
31. Hersheypark News, December 13, 1971, box 37, folder 5, accession 92004, HCA. See also RDA's 1971 sketch of Hersheypark for 1974, identifier: SOV 016.2, accession 85001.3, HCA.
32. Name suggestions, box 30, file: Hersheypark—1972, accession 92004, HCA.
33. "Hersheypark to Offer Double-Chute Flume Ride," *Bucks County (PA) Courier Times*, May 6, 1973. See also "Two New Rides Offer Up, Down Thrills," article from special advertising supplement, "Welcome to Hersheypark '73," *Patriot-News* (Harrisburg, PA), May 27, 1973, box 30, folder: Hersheypark—1973, accession 92004, HCA.
34. "Hersheypark to Offer Double-Chute Flume Ride."
35. Letters from a fourth-grade class, box 49, folder: Paul Serff . . . complimentary letters, accession 92004, HCA.
36. Jacques, *Hersheypark*, 136.
37. Sky Ride, coal cars, box 10, folder 26, accession 90016, HCA.
38. *Times Tribune* (Scranton, PA), September 26, 1976.
39. "Big Opener for Hershey Despite Threatening Weather," *Amusement Business*, June 14, 1975.
40. "New Amusement Ride to Open at Hershey," *Lebanon (PA) Daily News*, May 15, 1973.

41. Planning books, box 74, folder 3, accession 92004, HCA.
42. Author's interview with Bruce McKinney, December 16, 2022.
43. Planning books.
44. "Concept Design—Theming of Minetown Area," July 1978, box 74 folder 3, accession 92004, HCA.
45. "Concept Design—Theming of Minetown Area."
46. Section managers meeting minutes, August 17, 1979, box 49, file: Minutes 1978–79, accession 92004, HCA.
47. For statistics, see Josephine Novak, "45 Years of Hershey Plant Tours End with New Chocolate World," *Evening Sun* (Baltimore), June 25, 1973; Hershey Foods press release, June 27, 1973, box 2, folder 1, accession 200706, HCA; visitor statistics, box 37, folder: Chocolate World 1973, accession 92004, HCA.
48. Ken Bowers Oral History, 1993, 93OH13, HCA.
49. Samuel Tancredi Oral History, 1990, 90OH18, HCA.
50. Richard Bacastow Oral History, 1990, 90OH11, HCA.
51. Bowers Oral History.
52. Bowers Oral History.
53. The precise figure was $7,645,082. ERA, "Economic Potentials of Proposed Hershey Tour Facility," March 14, 1971, box 1, folder 1, accession 200706, HCA. See also author's interview with Ira West, July 20, 2010.
54. Author's interview with West.
55. "Hershey's Chocolate World Features Automated Ride," box 37, folder: Chocolate World 1973, accession 92004, HCA.
56. "Guests Get Impressions of Week-Old Cocoa World," *Elizabethtown (PA) Chronicle*, July 5, 1973.
57. Hershey's Chocolate World ride script, box 1, folder 6, accession 200706, HCA.
58. Feedback given to L. F. Santangelo, box 1, folder 6, accession 200706, HCA.
59. Correspondence from L. F. Santangelo to Ira West, box 1, folder 6, accession 200706, HCA.
60. Hershey Foods press release for winter 1973–74, box 37, folder: Chocolate World, accession 92004, HCA.
61. Libbie Powell, "Of People and Places," *Daily Mail* (Hagerstown, MD), August 8, 1975.
62. "Guests Get Impressions of Week-Old Cocoa World."
63. ERA, "Economic Potentials of Proposed Hershey Tour Facility."
64. Author's interview with West.
65. Breakdown of Hershey Chocolate World's complaints received, box 1, folder 12, accession 200706, HCA.
66. Mary Lou Corlett, "Hershey's Will Open New Visitors Center," *Patriot-News* (Harrisburg, PA), June 28, 1973, box 10, folder 16, accession 85006, HCA.
67. Betsy Rupe, "Hershey—Kiss It Good-Bye," *Elizabethtown (PA) Chronicle*, June 28, 1973.
68. Author's interview with Bruce McKinney, July 22, 2010.
69. Nye, *American Technological Sublime*.
70. "Giant Wheel Highlights Phase II," Hersheypark News, box 34, folder 75, accession 92004, HCA.
71. Memo on the Giant Wheel from E. K. Houser to Bruce McKinney, box 44, folder 1, accession 92004, HCA.
72. Harold Sitler Oral History, May 15, 2006, 2006OH18, HCA.
73. "Hersheypark Building New Kissing Tower," *Lititz (PA) Record Express*, February 27, 1975.
74. Jack Silar Oral History, February 11, 2009, 2009OH04, HCA.
75. "Hersheypark Building New Kissing Tower."
76. Charles Bofinger, "Hershey Park Expands Facilities," press release sent to business editors and trade publications, October 23, 1974, box 58, folder 17, accession 92004, HCA.
77. "It's When the Crowds Go That the Real Work Begins," *Doylestown (PA) Intelligencer*, August 26, 1976.
78. 1975 press releases, box 34, folder 77, accession 92004, HCA.
79. Hench, *Designing Disney*, 50–53.
80. Kurtti and Hunt, *Disney Monorail*.

81. Joseph Lelyveld, "Monorail at Fair Almost Gets Car," *New York Times*, February 12, 1964.
82. "Hershey Monorail Opening," *Sentinel* (Carlisle, PA), April 11, 1970.
83. Jacques, *Hersheypark*, 129–30, 134.
84. Jacques, *Hersheypark*, 107.
85. "Trip to Kissing Tower," 1976, box 67, folder 10, accession 92004, HCA.
86. Silar Oral History.
87. John Dornberg, "Anton Schwarzkopf—Just a Simple 'Pretzel' Merchant," *Popular Mechanics*, August 1980, 73. Schwarzkopf did not provide a name for the Coney Island coaster, but he did note that it opened in 1901, a fact that implies he was referring to the Loop the Loop. However, his description of the coaster—specifically its circular loop—suggests that he really meant the Flip Flap, an earlier and even less safe coaster. Samuelson, *American Amusement Park*, 25.
88. Dornberg, "Anton Schwarzkopf," 73; Samuelson, *American Amusement Park*, 25; Maher, *Apollo*, 153.
89. Dornberg, "Anton Schwarzkopf," 73.
90. Samuelson, *American Amusement Park*, 105, 108.
91. Steve Rogers, "Thanks to New Coaster Magic Mt. Crowds Up by 27 per Cent," *Amusement Business*, August 14, 1976.
92. Norman Sklarewitz, "Super Thrill Rides," *Popular Mechanics*, November 1976, 80–81, 154, box 58, folder 18, accession 92004, HCA.
93. "Spring Debut Eyed for Loop Coaster at Magic Mountain," *Amusement Business*, January 24, 1976.
94. Author's interview with Bruce McKinney, December 16, 2022.
95. Alvin Rosensweet, "Amusement Parks vs. Theme Parks," *Pittsburgh Post-Gazette*, January 10, 1978.
96. Sklarewitz, "Super Thrill Rides," 80–81, 154.
97. Author's interview with McKinney, 2010.
98. Robin Nelson, "Terror on Wheels—by Design," *Popular Mechanics*, August 1980, 70–72.
99. "New Ride, Zoo," *Hanover (PA) Evening Sun*, December 13, 1976.
100. "Hersheypark Construction Continuing," *Lebanon (PA) Daily News*, February 12, 1977.
101. McKinney Oral History.
102. Author's interview with McKinney, 2010.
103. Author's interview with McKinney, 2022.
104. Paul Serff Oral History, 1996, 96OH01, HCA.
105. Jacques, *Hersheypark*, 148.
106. Sally Holder, "Sooperdooperlooper Gets Gigantic Intro," *Amusement Business*, March 12, 1977.
107. Dean Wise, "Sooperdooperlooper," *York (PA) Daily Record*, May 9, 1977; Sue Smith, "The Sooper Looper: Ninety Seconds You'll Never Forget," *Lancaster (PA) New Era*, May 7, 1977; "Sooper Skybreaking," sooperdooperLooper press preview, May 6, 1977, box 62, folder 1, accession 92004, HCA; Sitler Oral History; Jacques, *Hersheypark*, 149; "Superdooperlooper Unveiling Draws 28,000 to Hersheypark," *Amusement Business*, May 28, 1977.
108. Charles Shaw, "SooperdooperLooper: Upside Down at 55 mph," *Intelligencer Journal* (Lancaster, PA), May 7, 1977.
109. Smith, "Sooper Looper."
110. Lorrie Brown, "Riding the Loop . . . with Eyes Wide Open," *Public Opinion* (Chambersburg, PA), May 10, 1977.
111. Sklarewitz, "Super Thrill Rides," 80–81, 154.
112. Younger, *Theme Park Design*, 1.
113. Jo McMeen, "SooperDooperLooper," *Daily News* (Huntingdon, PA), September 20, 1978.
114. McKinney Oral History.
115. "Hersheypark Crowds Force Gate Closure," *Amusement Business*, August 20, 1977.
116. "Hersheypark to Reopen May 7," *Sentinel* (Carlisle, PA), April 28, 1978.
117. Author's interview with McKinney, 2022.
118. Section managers meeting minutes, May 19, 1978.
119. See section managers meeting minutes, June 24, July 1, July 22, and August 12, 1977.

120. John Zerbe Oral History, 1996, 96OH04, HCA.
121. Robert Payne Oral History, 1998, OH82, HDTHS.
122. "HERCO Reopens Ride," *Lebanon (PA) Daily News*, September 2, 1977.
123. *Tyrone (PA) Daily Herald*, September 14, 1977.
124. "Youth Killed Working on Park Ride," *Lebanon (PA) Daily News*, August 26, 1977.
125. "HERCO Reopens Ride."
126. *Tyrone (PA) Daily Herald*, September 14, 1977.
127. Sitler Oral History.
128. McKinney Oral History.
129. Section managers meeting minutes, August 12, 1977.
130. Section managers meeting minutes, June 9, July 21, and August 2, 1978.

Conclusion

1. Barbara Elliott, "HERCO Regrouping After Disaster Tourism Year," *Lebanon (PA) Daily News*, January 27, 1980.
2. Zaretsky, *Radiation Nation*, 24–25.
3. Fasick, *Three Mile Island*, 12, 18–19.
4. Nye, *Technological Sublime*, xiii.
5. Zaretsky, *Radiation Nation*, 1.
6. Jim Kershner, "Scene at Hersheypark," *Sentinel* (Carlisle, PA), March 31, 1979.
7. Paul Serff Oral History, 1996, 96OH01, HCA.
8. John Zerbe Oral History, 1996, 96OH04, HCA.
9. "Hersheypark's Experience in Handling Crowds Helped," *Lebanon (PA) Daily News*, April 3, 1979.
10. Jim Kershner, "Scene at Hersheypark," *Sentinel* (Carlisle, PA), March 31, 1979.
11. Kershner, "Scene at Hersheypark."
12. Zerbe Oral History.
13. Howard B. Kishpaugh Oral History, 1990, 90OH17, HCA. Others also recalled the poor behavior of the media. See Ken Bowers Oral History, 1993, 93OH13, HCA; and Zerbe Oral History.
14. Kershner, "Scene at Hersheypark."
15. *Lebanon (PA) Daily News*, September 6, 1979.
16. Letters to the editor, *Hummelstown (PA) Sun*, box 4, folder 35: Bruce McKinney, Three Mile Island, News Clippings, accession 200124, HCA.
17. Letters to the editor, *Hummelstown (PA) Sun*.
18. Section managers meeting minutes, August 3, 1979, box 49, file: Minutes 1978–79, accession 92004, HCA.
19. Serff Oral History.
20. Kenneth Hatt Oral History, 1989, 89OH17, HCA.
21. Dena Thomas Oral History, 2006, 2006OH06, HCA.
22. Tina Veiders, "Despite Negatives, Hersheypark Season Off Only Five Percent," *Amusement Business*, October 13, 1979.
23. Bruce McKinney Oral History, 2006, 2006OH14, HCA.
24. McKinney Oral History.
25. Ned Book was named president of Hershey Estates in 1974 and CEO of HERCO in 1980. Chronology on HCA's website, accessed December 15, 2022, https://hersheyarchives.org/?s=edward+book.
26. McKinney Oral History.
27. Ned Book Oral History, 1996, 96OH15, HCA.
28. Serff Oral History.
29. Jack Silar Oral History, February 11, 2009, 2009OH04, HCA.
30. Author's interview with Bruce McKinney, December 16, 2022.
31. Candylane operating plans, box 36, file: Christmas in Hershey—1983, accession 92004, HCA; Jacques, *Hersheypark*, 165–66.
32. Ruth Troutman Oral History, 2006, OH/2006OH08, HCA.
33. Serff Oral History.
34. Author's interview with McKinney.
35. Jacques, *Hersheypark*, 42, 172–79, 185–87, 192–95, 200–201, 209.
36. Veiders, "Despite Negatives."
37. Jacques, *Hersheypark*, 192.
38. "HERCO Sponsors Annual Job Fair," *Lebanon (PA) Daily News*, December 12, 1995.
39. Silar Oral History.
40. Author's interviews with Bruce McKinney, December 16, 2022, and February 15, 2024.
41. Cyril Little Oral History, 1990, 90OH25, HCA.

42. Ned Book to Charles Bofinger, August 4, 1976, box 1, folder 24, accession 200124, HCA.
43. Report on 1975 Pennsylvania Dutch Days, box 1, folder 24, accession 200124, HCA.
44. Rufus Hollinger Oral History, 1990, 90OH22, HCA.
45. Ned Book to Rufus Hollinger, October 25, 1979, box 1, folder 24, accession 200124, HCA.
46. Section managers meeting minutes, July 7, 1978, box 49, file: Minutes, 1978–79, accession 92004, HCA; McKinney Oral History.
47. Jacques, *Hersheypark*, 152.
48. Craft Barn restaurant, 2003RP252.1-.2, HCA.
49. Hollinger Oral History.
50. Hersheypark map for 1990, *Amusement Parkives*, accessed November 21, 2022, https://amusementparkives.com/the-library/hersheypark/maps/1990-map.
51. Author's interview with McKinney, 2022.
52. Tudor restaurant conversion, 2003RP127.1, HCA.
53. Hersheypark brochure for 1985, eBay, last modified September 5, 2023, https://www.ebay.com/itm/285281833378.
54. Author's interview with Bruce McKinney, July 22, 2010.
55. "Hersheypark Opens 69th Season," *Hanover (PA) Evening Sun*, May 9, 1976.
56. Author's interview with McKinney, 2022.
57. Joseph Spinner Oral History, 1991, OH25, HDTHS.
58. Author's interview with McKinney, 2010.
59. Author's interview with McKinney, 2022.
60. Author's interview with McKinney, 2010.
61. Aimee Rex Oral History, 2008, 2008OH03, HCA.
62. D. Paul Witmer Oral History, 1975, 2001OH10, HCA.
63. Rex Oral History.
64. Dina Willard Oral History, 2007, 2007OH15, HCA.
65. Thomas Oral History.
66. Thomas Oral History.
67. Thomas Oral History.
68. Charlotte Coates, "Hershey's Chocolatetown: Inside the Sweet New Expansion at Hersheypark," *Blooloop*, September 9, 2020, https://blooloop.com/theme-park/in-depth/hersheys-chocolatetown.
69. "The Compass Rose at Hersheypark Honors Legacy of Founder," HersheyPA.com, July 16, 2020, https://stories.hersheypa.com/the-compass-rose-at-hersheypark-honors-legacy-of-founder.
70. Coates, "Hershey's Chocolatetown."
71. Email message from Tesa Burns to the author. January 17, 2023.
72. "Final Farewell to Hersheypark's Old Entrance," YouTube, uploaded January 1, 2019, https://youtu.be/eHsIkyZLk8k.
73. Author's interview with Ira West, July 20, 2010.
74. Silar Oral History.
75. "Hershey's Chocolatetown Groundbreaking Ceremony," YouTube, uploaded January 9, 2019, https://www.youtube.com/watch?v=A3SYuRCVL_U.

bibliography

Bailey, Beth, and David Farber, eds. *America in the Seventies*. Lawrence: University Press of Kansas, 2004.

Barton, Michael, and Simon Bronner. *Steelton*. Charleston, SC: Arcadia, 2008.

Bassett, Jonathan. "The Pullman Strike of 1894." *OAH Magazine of History* 11, no. 2 (Winter 1997): 34–41.

Baxter, Jane Eva. "The Paradox of a Capitalist Utopia: Visionary Ideals and Lived Experience in the Pullman Community 1880–1900." *International Journal of Historical Archaeology* 16, no. 4 (December 2012): 651–65.

Bluestone, Barry, and Bennett Harrison. *The Deindustrialization of America: Plant Closings, Community Abandonment, and the Dismantling of Basic Industry*. New York: Basic Books, 1982.

Bongartz, Roy. "The Chocolate Camelot." *American Heritage* 24, no. 4 (June 1973): 4–11, 91–99.

Bradbury, Ray. *Something Wicked This Way Comes*. New York: Simon and Schuster, 1962.

Bradley, John. *Cadbury's Purple Reign: The Story Behind Chocolate's Best-Loved Brand*. West Sussex: John Wiley and Sons, 2008.

Brenner, Joël Glenn. *The Emperors of Chocolate: Inside the Secret World of Hershey and Mars*. New York: Random House, 1999.

Bronner, Simon, and Joshua Brown, eds. *Pennsylvania Germans: An Interpretive Encyclopedia*. Baltimore: Johns Hopkins University Press, 2017.

Bureau of the Census. *Historical Statistics of the United States, Colonial Times to 1970*. Washington, DC: Government Printing Office, 1974.

Cadbury, Deborah. *Chocolate Wars: The 150-Year Rivalry Between the World's Greatest Chocolate Makers*. New York: PublicAffairs, 2021.

Capita, Joseph M. "Strike in Utopia: C.I.O. Versus the Hershey Chocolate Company, 1937." Master's thesis, Penn State Harrisburg, 1976.

Carroll, Peter. *It Seemed Like Nothing Happened: The Tragedy and Promise of America in the 1970s*. New York: Holt, Rinehart and Winston, 1982.

Chavez, Eros Salinas, Frank A. Delgado Mesa, Tony L. Henthorne, and Mark M. Miller. "The Hershey Sugar Mill in Cuba: From Global Industrial Heritage to Local Sustainable Tourism Development." *Journal of Heritage Tourism* 13, no. 5 (2018): 426–39.

Chytry, Josef. "Disney's Design: Imagineering Main Street." *Boom: A Journal of California* 2, no. 1 (Spring 2012): 33–44.

Conkin, Paul. *A Revolution Down on the Farm: The Transformation of American Agriculture Since 1929*. Lexington: University Press of Kentucky, 2008.

Crawford, Margaret. *Building the Workingman's Paradise: The Design of American Company Towns*. New York: Verso Books, 1995.

Cross, Gary. *Consumed Nostalgia: Memory in the Age of Fast Capitalism*. New York: Columbia University Press, 2015.

Cross, Gary, and John Walton. *The Playful Crowd: Pleasure Places in the Twentieth Century*. New York: Columbia University Press, 2005.

Cupper, Dan. *The 75th Farm Show: A History of Pennsylvania's Agricultural Exposition*. Harrisburg: Pennsylvania Historical and Museum Commission, 1991.

Curry, Nancy E. "The Reality of Make-Believe." In *"Mister Rogers' Neighborhood": Children, Television, and Fred Rogers*, edited by Mark Collins and Margaret May Kimmel, 51–66. Pittsburgh: University of Pittsburgh Press, 1996.

Danbom, David. *Born in the Country: A History of Rural America*. Baltimore: Johns Hopkins University Press, 1995.

D'Antonio, Michael. *Hershey: Milton S. Hershey's Extraordinary Life of Wealth, Empire, and Utopian Dreams*. New York: Simon and Schuster, 2006.

Davidoff Houts, Mary, and Pamela Cassidy Whitenack. *Images of America: Hershey*. Charleston, SC: Arcadia, 2000.

Davis, Fred. *Yearning for Yesterday: A Sociology of Nostalgia*. New York: Free Press, 1979.

Dekle, Natalie Mykyta. *Building a New Life: The Italian Community in Hershey*. Hershey, PA: Hershey Italian Lodge, 1990.

Dublin, Thomas, and Walter Licht. *The Face of Decline: The Pennsylvania Anthracite Region in the Twentieth Century*. Ithaca, NY: Cornell University Press, 2005.

Dubofsky, Melvyn. *Industrialism and the American Worker, 1865–1920*. Wheeling, IL: Harlan Davidson, 1996.

Dunne, John J. "Father Flanagan of Boys Town." *Irish Monthly* 76, no. 902 (August 1948): 373–75.

Durant, Mary. *The American Heritage Guide to Antiques*. New York: American Heritage Press, 1970.

Durnbaugh, Donald F. "Pennsylvania's Crazy Quilt of German Religious Groups." *Pennsylvania History* 68, no. 1 (Winter 200): 8–30.

Ensminger, Robert. *The Pennsylvania Barn: Its Origin, Evolution, and Distribution in North America*. Baltimore: Johns Hopkins University Press, 1992.

Fasick, Erik. *Three Mile Island*. Charleston, SC: Arcadia, 2018.

Fernandez, Bob. *The Chocolate Trust: Deception, Indenture and Secrets at the $12 Billion Milton Hershey School*. Philadelphia: Camino Books, 2015.

Foschetti, Peter. "The Nativization of an Immigrant Community: A Case Study of the Italians in Hershey, Pennsylvania." Master's thesis, Penn State Harrisburg, 1974.

Gardner, Bruce. *American Agriculture in the Twentieth Century: How It Flourished and What It Cost*. Cambridge, MA: Harvard University Press, 2002.

Gilbert, Russell. *A Picture of the Pennsylvania Germans*. Gettysburg: Pennsylvania Historical Association, 1962.

Gitelson, Joshua. "Populox: The Suburban Cuisine of the 1950s." *Journal of American Culture* 15, no. 3 (Fall 1992): 73–78.

Glass, Joseph W. *The Pennsylvania Culture Region: A View from the Barn*. Ann Arbor, MI: UMI Research Press, 1986.

Green, Hardy. *The Company Town: The Industrial Edens and Satanic Mills That Shaped the American Economy*. New York: Basic Books, 2010.

Guy, John. *Tudor England*. Oxford: Oxford University Press, 1988.

Harvey, Alexander. *The Model Village and Its Cottages: Bournville*. New York: Charles Scribner's Sons, 1906.

Hench, John. *Designing Disney: Imagineering and the Art of the Show*. New York: Disney Editions, 2003.

Herdt, Gilbert. "Transitional Objects in Sambia Initiation." *Ethos* 15, no. 1 (March 1987): 40–57.

Hightower, Jim. *Hard Tomatoes, Hard Times: A Report of the Agribusiness Accountability Project on the Failure of America's Land Grant College Complex*. Cambridge, MA: Schenkman, 1973.

Hill, Barry. *Imagineering an American Dreamscape: Genesis, Evolution, and Redemption of the Regional Theme Park*. Rivershore Press, 2020.

Hostetler, John. *Amish Society*. Rev. ed. Baltimore: Johns Hopkins University Press, 1968.

———. *Amish Society*. 3rd ed. Baltimore: Johns Hopkins University Press, 1980.

Hotchkiss, George, and Richard Franken. *The Leadership of Advertised Brands: A Study of 100 Representative Commodities Showing the Names and Brands That Are Most Familiar to the Public*. New York: Doubleday, Page, 1923.

Jacques, Charles J., Jr. *Hersheypark: The Sweetness of Success*. Jefferson, OH: Amusement Park Journal, 1997.

Kasson, John. *Amusing the Million: Coney Island at the Turn of the Century*. New York: Hill and Wang, 1978.

Kawash, Samira. *Candy: A Century of Pleasure*. New York: Faber and Faber, 2013.

King, Margaret J. "Disneyland and Walt Disney World: Traditional Values in Futuristic Form." *Journal of Popular Culture* 15, no. 1 (Summer 1981): 116–40.

King, Margaret J., and J. G. O'Boyle. "The Theme Park: The Art of Time and Space." In *Disneyland and Culture: Essays on the Parks and Their Influence*, edited by Kathy Merlock Jackson and Mark I. West, 5–18. Jefferson, NC: McFarland, 2011.

Kitch, Carolyn. *Pennsylvania in Public Memory: Reclaiming the Industrial Past.* University Park: Penn State University Press, 2012.

Klapp, Orrin. *Collective Search for Identity.* New York: Holt, Rinehart and Winston, 1969.

Klein, Philip, and Ari Hoogenboom. *A History of Pennsylvania.* University Park: Penn State University Press, 1980.

Koehn, Nancy F., and Erica Helms. "Candy Land: The Utopian Vision of Milton Hershey." Harvard Business School Case 805-066, April 2005.

Kompare, Derek. *Rerun Nation: How Repeats Invented American Television.* London: Taylor and Francis, 2004.

Kraybill, Donald. *The Riddle of Amish Culture.* Baltimore: Johns Hopkins University Press, 2001.

Kurie, Peter. *In Chocolate We Trust: The Hershey Company Town Unwrapped.* Philadelphia: University of Pennsylvania Press, 2018.

Kurtti, Jeff, and Vanessa Hunt. *The Disney Monorail: Imagineering a Highway in the Sky.* Los Angeles: Disney Editions, 2020.

Lamme, Meg, and Lisa Mullikin Parcell. "Promoting Hershey: The Chocolate Bar, the Chocolate Town, the Chocolate King." *Journalism History* 38, no. 4 (Winter 2013): 198–208.

Lang, C. Max. *The Impossible Dream: The Founding of The Milton S. Hershey Medical Center of the Pennsylvania State University.* Bloomington, IN: AuthorHouse, 2010.

Levenstein, Harvey. *Paradox of Plenty: A Social History of Eating in Modern America.* Berkeley: University of California Press, 2003.

Lewis, Tom. *Divided Highways: Building the Interstate Highway, Transforming American Life.* Ithaca, NY: Cornell University Press, 2013.

Lindsay, David. *Madness in the Making: The Triumphant Rise and Untimely Fall of America's Show Inventors.* Lincoln, NE: iUniverse, 2005.

Louden, Mark. *Pennsylvania Dutch: The Story of an American Language.* Baltimore: Johns Hopkins University Press, 2016.

Maher, Neil. *Apollo in the Age of Aquarius.* Cambridge, MA: Harvard University Press, 2017.

Margo, Robert A. "Employment and Unemployment in the 1930s." *Journal of Economic Perspectives* 7, no. 2 (Spring 1993): 41–59.

Marling, Karal Ann, ed. *Designing Disney's Theme Parks: The Architecture of Reassurance.* New York: Flammarion, 1997.

———. "Disneyland, 1955: Just Take the Santa Ana Freeway to the American Dream." *American Art* 5, no. 1–2 (Winter–Spring 1991): 168–207.

Marquis, Alice Goldfarb. *Art Lessons: Learning from the Rise and Fall of Public Arts Funding.* New York: Basic Books, 1995.

McMahon, James D., Jr. *Milton Hershey School.* Charleston, SC: Arcadia, 2007.

———. "Milton Hershey's World: Architecture and Identity in a Model Community and a Modern Cultural Landscape." *Pennsylvania History* 88, no. 4 (Autumn 2021): 548–85.

Mechling, Elizabeth Walker, and Jay Mechling. "The Atom According to Disney." *Quarterly Journal of Speech* 81, no. 4 (1995): 436–53.

Miller, Douglas T., and Marion Nowak. *The Fifties: The Way We Really Were.* New York: Doubleday, 1977.

Murphy, Andrew R. *William Penn: A Life.* New York: Oxford University Press, 2019.

Nye, David. *The American Technological Sublime.* Cambridge, MA: MIT Press, 1994.

Ohmann, Richard. *Selling Culture: Magazines, Markets and Class at the Turn of the Century.* New York: Verso Books, 1996.

Pells, Richard H. *The Liberal Mind in a Conservative Age: American Intellectuals in the 1940s and 1950s.* 2nd ed. Hanover, NH: Wesleyan University Press, 1989.

Pottker, Jan. *Crisis in Candyland: Melting the Chocolate Shell of the Mars Family Empire.* Bethesda, MD: National Press Books, 1995.

Presnell, Don, and Marty McGee. *A Critical History of Television's "The Twilight Zone," 1959–1964.* Jefferson, NC: McFarland, 1998.

Price, Harrison. *Walt's Revolution! By the Numbers.* Orlando, FL: Ripley Entertainments, 2004.

Reinehr, Robert, and Jon Swartz. *The A to Z of Old Time Radio.* Lanham, MD: Scarecrow Press, 2010.

Sampson, Curt. *Hogan.* Nashville: Rutledge Hill Press, 1996.

Samuelson, Dale. *The American Amusement Park.* St. Paul, MN: MBI, 2001.

Schickel, Richard. *The Disney Version: The Life, Times, Art, and Commerce of Walt Disney.* Chicago: Elephant Paperback, 1997.

Schneirov, Richard. "'To the Ragged Edge of Anarchy': The 1894 Pullman Boycott." *OAH Magazine of History* 13, no. 3 (Spring 1999): 26–30.

Schwartz, Marvin, and Betsy Wade. *The "New York Times" Book of Antiques.* New York: Quadrangle Books, 1972.

Skrabec, Quentin. *The Fall of an American Rome: De-Industrialization of the American Dream.* New York: Algora, 2014.

Snavely, Joseph Richard. *The Hershey Story.* Hershey, PA: Sowers Printing, 1950.

Snow, Richard. *Disney's Land: Walt Disney and the Invention of the Amusement Park That Changed the World.* New York: Scribner, 2019.

Sorkin, Michael. "See You in Disneyland." *Design Quarterly*, no. 154 (Winter 1992): 5–13.

Stein, Judith. *Running Steel, Running America: Race, Economic Policy, and the Decline of Liberalism.* Chapel Hill: University of North Carolina Press, 1998.

Steiner, Michael. "Frontierland as Tomorrowland: Walt Disney and the Architectural Packaging of the Mythic West." *Montana: The Magazine of Western History* 48, no. 1 (Spring 1998): 2–17.

Straight, Michael. *Nancy Hanks: An Intimate Portrait.* Durham, NC: Duke University Press, 1988.

Tiffany, Paul A. "The Roots of Decline: Business-Government Relations in the American Steel Industry, 1945–1960." *Journal of Economic History* 44, no. 2 (June 1984): 407–19.

Turner, Frederick Jackson. "The Significance of the Frontier in American History." In *Frederick Jackson Turner: Wisconsin's Historian of the Frontier*, edited by Martin Ridge, 26–47. Madison: State Historical Society of Wisconsin, 1986.

Updike, John. *Of the Farm.* New York: Alfred A. Knopf, 1965.

Virgintino, Michael. *Freedomland U.S.A.: The Definitive History.* N.p.: Theme Park Press, 2018.

Walbert, David. *Garden Spot: Lancaster County, the Old Order Amish, and the Selling of Rural America.* New York: Oxford University Press, 2002.

Watts, Steven. *The Magic Kingdom: Walt Disney and the American Way of Life.* Columbia: University of Missouri Press, 1997.

Weir, Robert E. "Dark Chocolate: Lessons from the 1937 Hershey Sit-Down Strike." *Labor History* 56, no. 1 (2015): 40–57.

Whitenack, Pamela Cassidy. *Hersheypark.* Charleston, SC: Arcadia, 2006.

Wilson, Steven. *Six Flags Great America.* Charleston, SC: Arcadia, 2017.

Winnicott, D. W. *Playing and Reality.* New York: Basic Books, 1971.

Winpenny, Thomas. "Milton S. Hershey Ventures into Cuban Sugar." *Pennsylvania History* 62, no. 4 (Fall 1995): 491–502.

Yoder, Don, and Thomas Graves. *Hex Signs: Pennsylvania Dutch Barn Symbols and Their Meaning.* 2nd ed. Mechanicsburg, PA: Stackpole Books, 2000.

Younger, David. *Theme Park Design and the Art of Themed Entertainment.* Inklingwood Press, 2016.

Zaretsky, Natasha. *Radiation Nation: Three Mile Island and the Political Transformation of the 1970s.* New York: Columbia University Press, 2018.

index

Figures are indicated by italic page numbers. Endnotes are indicated by "n" followed by the endnote number.